MW01277137

ANALYSING THE LATEST REFORMS IN THE LEGAL FRAMEWORK WITH RESPECT TO THE HEALTH SECTOR OF INDIA –A STUDY FROM THE PERSPECTIVE OF WOMEN'S ISSUES

KIRANDEEP KAUR

ACKNOWLEDGEMENT

गुरु गोविंद दोऊ खड़े, काके लागूं पांय, बलिहारी गुरु आपकी, गोविंद दियो बताय
(Guru Govind dono khade kake lagu paye Balihari Guru aapne Govind diyo bataye)

-Sant Kabir Das

I will begin by thanking my Guru, my supervisor and guide Prof. Dr. O.V. Nandimath, without whose guidance, support and constant cooperation this research work would not have been envisioned and achieved. Sir has always been very generous with his time, support and advice. He inspired me and guided me to help me bring out the best that I could put into this work, for which I will be forever thankful. This thesis would not have been a reality had it not been for Prof. Dr. O.V. Nandimath.

Justice Rajendra Babu, with whom I had the opportunity to work for a good one year four months, imbibed within me the zeal for reading, for questioning propositions and for not taking anything for granted. He imbibed in me the spirit of inquiry and research. Long discussions with him over my research work, helped me broaden my perspective. I was lucky and blessed to have got this golden opportunity. Prof. Dr. Venkata Rao has always guided his students and scholars to persevere beyond ones estimated limits. Sir's hard work and boundless commitment towards his duties lead me to believe that time place and opportunity are just constructs, hard work is beyond them and that's what I need to put in to reach the goal. Prof. Dr. Subba Rao's research methodology lectures showed us direction and gave perspective to the questions we were asking in our research by leading us towards the right methods of inquiry. Prof. Dr. Sarasu Esther Thomas has also always inspired me to work hard and give my best. She has been an inspiration for me since the time I have known her and she continues to be so. A big thank you goes to all of them for being such important inspirations in my life as a student and researcher of law.

This PhD thesis began with an impetus from my father, my hero. He wants his daughter to reach all goals that there are. Blessed are daughters who have fathers like him. He has taught me the importance of hard work, sincerity, dedication and honesty by being an example of the same himself. I had to never ask for help from him, he has been there by my side and come to my rescue whenever I have faltered, wavered or lost hope. My success is his happiness. My mother has always stood by me, rock solid, being there for me through rough patches and difficult terrains. She is the reason for my happiness, my insistence towards perseverance and for everything good that ever happens to me. Her selfless love keeps me going in life. A big thank you to my parents for being the world's best Maa Papa.

This thesis owes its successful completion to the heartfelt prayers and cooperation of one more mother of mine, my mother-in-law. From praying for me, to facilitating my contribution of time towards my thesis, I owe it all to her to her. I love her and would like to thank her for being there for me always. My other father, my father-in-law has always taken active interest in my work and inspired me to not lose hope or track. I imbibed the spirit to go on come whatever may, from him. A big thank you to this Mummy and Papa too, for being there for me always. I am also very thankful to Daadi Mumma who believed in me throughout this journey and in whose prayers my welfare always finds place.

Puneetish, Gaganjyot, Chaman and Purvi helped me in not losing faith in my ability to reach my target. Puneetish made sure that I did not lose perspective and that I was motivated all along. "You can do it, bhabhi", is what she always says. Gaganjyot has always been my brutally honest critic. If I want to know the hard reality without sugar coating of kinds, he is the one person to go to. Every time my research tended to become complacent, my brother, Gaganjyot grounded me to reality and helped me realize the drawbacks and overcome them. Thank you to all of them.

The most special thank you of all goes to my husband, Ish Puneet Singh. I am blessed because I have got a life partner like him. All the nights that were spent by me writing this thesis, he was awake with me, there by my side, to ensure that my zeal to go on did not waver. He has throughout taken very active interest in my research. Right from the stage when this thesis was in its nascent state to its present form, Ish Puneet has patiently read and reviewed the work word for word. He has been the pivotal support throughout this journey as it progressed, making me thrive for perfection. Without his love, care, affection and enormous cooperation, I would be nowhere near my goal.

A big thank you to my friends and PhD course mates Sangeetha, Saumya, Neha, Anita and Jeff who formed a protective group where one and all stood by one and all during the ups and downs of each other's PhD pursuits. Right from last moment inquiries to concerns over lulls in the research journey were all made less difficult because of these amazing friends.

A special thank you also goes to Prof. Dr. Rajinder Kaur who has been very generous with her time and guidance. She helped me fight my inhibitions and instilled within me the confidence to do well in my research pursuit. She is an inspiration for every student and researcher of law.

Prof. Dr. M.K. Ghoshal and Dr. Badamath helped me get in touch with psychiatrists and other medical professionals in the psychiatric fraternity and helped me get insight into the medical and practical perspective of my research work. I am very thankful to them and to all the other psychiatrists and NGO personnel who gave me their precious time and aided me with insight into this research. I am thankful to everyone who took out time to respond to my surveys and answer my questions.

The Examination Department and the library team at the National Law School of India University, Bangalore has cooperated and helped me in this research pursuit at every step. A special thank you goes to Padma Ma'am for her kind cooperation. She always responded to every query regarding the technicalities and requirements with such patience and a smile. Thank you to the staff and administration of the Army Institute of Law, Mohali, where I presently work and my dear students for their inspiration and support.

The dearest of all thankyous goes to Almighty God for giving me the strength and bestowing me with the blessings to complete this pursuit. WaheGuru has blessed me with such amazing persons in my life who love me and care for me and have stood by me throughout the ups and downs of this research pursuit.

This thesis is dedicated to Wadi Mummy whom we lost in March, 2017. She was my maternal grand mumma, my first teacher, the lady who taught me how to write my first alphabets, who taught me the tenets of a good life and who always prayed for my success and happiness. I miss you every day Wadi Mummy. Whatever I am today is a reflection of you and your teachings.

Many people come in our lives who hold importance and significance in small, big and bigger ways. One tends to miss out on names and details when one is overwhelmed, that's what happened when one sits to thank persons who have stood there through this journey. Even if I've missed out on mentioning you here, your contribution and support is heart fully acknowledged.

I am thankful to one and all, for being able to have proudly completed my research pursuit and for producing the kind of work I have always wanted to.

TABLE OF CONTENTS:

7.	Relevant Portions of the Report by NCW and NIMHANS 2016 on "Addressing Concerns of Women Admitted to Psychiatric Institutions In India: An In-Depth Analysis"
8.	Questionnaires

A. List of Abbreviations:

AIR	All India Reporter
ASHA	Accredited Social Health Activist
CBR	Community Based Rehabilitation
CEDAW	Convention on the Elimination of All Forms of Discrimination Against Women
CRC	Convention on Rights of the Child
CRL	Criminal
DB	Division Bench
ECHR	European Convention on Human Rights
ECRC	Emergency Care and Recovery Centre
GDP	Gross Domestic Product
GHMC	Government Mental Health Centre
HC	High Court
HP	Himachal Pradesh
IBHBAS	Institute of Human Behaviour and Allied Sciences
ICCPR	International Covenant on Civil and Political Rights
ICD	International Classification of Disease
ICESCR	International Covenant on Economic, Social and Cultural Rights

IMHH	Institute of Mental Health and Hospital
IPHP	Institute of Psychiatry and Human Behaviour
IQ	Intelligence Quotient
MLJ	Madras Law Journal
MSE	Mental Status Examination
NCW	National Commission for Women
NGO	Non-Governmental Organization
NHRC	National Human Rights Commission
NIMHANS	National Institute of Mental Health and Neurosciences
OPD	Out Patient Department
PAD	Psychiatric Advance Directive
PIL	Public Interest Litigation
PPD	Postpartum Depression
PTI	Press Trust of India
RINPAS	Ranchi Institute of Neuro-Psychiatry and Allied Sciences
RMH	Regional Mental Hospital
SC	Supreme Court
SCC	Supreme Court Cases

SCR	Supreme Court Reports
SCW	Supreme Court Weekly
SSD	Somatic Symptom Disorder
TN	Tamil Nadu
UDHR	Universal Declaration of Human Rights
UK	United Kingdom
UN	United Nations
UNCRPD	United Nations Convention on Rights of Persons with Disabilities
UOI	Union of India
UP	Uttar Pradesh
USA	United States of America
W.P.	Writ Petition
WB	West Bengal
WFMH	World Federation of Mental Health
WHO	World Health Organization
WPA	World Psychiatric Association

B. LIST OF TERMINOLOGIES USED:

1987 Act	The Mental Health Act, 1987
2014 Policy	The National Mental Health Policy of India, 2014
2017 Act	The Mental Healthcare Act, 2017
2018 Rules	The Mental Healthcare (Rights of Persons with Mental Illness) Rules, 2018
Draft 2017 Rules	The Draft Mental Healthcare Rules, 2017
HRW Report (2014)	Human Rights Watch, Report published in 2014, titled *"Treated Worse than Animals- Abuses against Women and Girls with Psychological and Intellectual Disabilities in Institutions in India"*
JJ Act, 1986	Juvenile Justice Act, 1986
NCW and NIMHANS Report (2016)	National Commission for Women and National Institute of Mental Health and Neurosciences, Report published in 2016, titled *"Addressing concerns of women admitted to psychiatric institutions in India: An in-depth analysis"*

C. LIST OF TABLES:

D. LIST OF CASES:

- Aman Hingorani v. Union of India and others, AIR 1995 SC 215

- Apparel Export Promotion Council v. A.K. Chopra (1999) 1 SCC 759

- Bandhua Mukti Morcha v. Union of India, AIR 1984 SC 802

- Binoo Sen v. State of West Bengal through the Principal Secretary, Department of Social Welfare and others, 1999(2) Cal. H.C.N. 268

- C. Masilamani Mudaliar v. Idol of Sri Swaminathaswami Mudaliar Thirukoil (1996) 8 SCC 525

- CESC Ltd. v. Subhash Chandra Bose, (1992) 1 SCC 441

- Chandan Kumar Banik v. State of W.B., 1995(Sup4) SCC 505

- Chandigarh Administration v. Nemo, 2009(3) R.C.R.(Civil) 766 (P&H) (DB)

- Chitta Ranjan Bhattacharjee v. State of Tripura, 2010(2) GauLT 514 (Gauhati) (Agartala Bench)

- Common Cause (A Regd. Society) v. Union of India and Another, Writ Petition (CIVIL) NO. 215 OF 2005

- Consumer Education and Research Centre v. Union of India, (1995) 3 SCC 42

- Court on its own motion v. Principal Secretary (Social Justice & Empowerment), 2015(3) R.C.R.(Civil) 684 (HP) (DB)

- D.C. Saxena (Dr.) v. Honourable Chief Justice of India, (1996) 5 SCC 216

- Kubic Darusz v. Union of India, (1990) 1 SCC 568

- Lata Singh v. State of Uttar Pradesh, AIR 2006 SC 2522

- LIC of India v. Consumer Education Research Centre (1995) 5 SCC 482

- Madhu Kishwar v. State of Bihar, (1996) 5 SCC 125

- Maneka Gandhi v. Union of India, 1978 SCR (2) 621

- Nathalie Vandenbyvanghe v. The State Of Tamil Nadu, Habeas Corpus Petition No.1041 of 2008 (Madras)

- O'Connor v. Donaldson , 422 US 563 (1975)

- Parmanand Katara v. Union of India, (1989) 4 SCC 286

- Paschim Banga Khet Mazdoor Samity & ors v. State of West Bengal & ors., (1996) 4 SCC 37

- Peoples Union for Democratic Rights v. Union of India, 1983 SCR (1) 456

- PUCL v. Union of India, (1997) 1 SCC 301

- Rakesh Chand Narain v. State of Bihar, AIR 1989 SC 348

- Rakesh Chandra Narayan v. State of Bihar, 1986(2) Scale 739

- Rakesh Chandra Narayan v. State of Bihar, 1994(3) Scale 1034

- Ravinder v. Government of NCT of Delhi and Ors., W.P. (CRL) 3317/2017

- Ravinder v. Government of NCT & Ors.' W.P. (CRL.) 3317/2017

- Re : Death of 25 Chained Inmates In Asylum Fire In Tamil Nadu, AIR 2002 SC 3693

- Re : Death of 25 Chained Inmates v. Union of India, AIR 2002 SC 979

- Re : Illegal Detention of Macha Llalung, 2007(9) Scale 435

- Re Death Of 25 Mental Asylum Patients v. Union Of India, 2002(3) SCC 36

- Regional Director, ESI Corpn. v. Francis Decosta, 1993 Supp (94) SCC 100

- Robert Heijkamp v. Bal Anand World Children Welfare Trust, 2008(1) BCR 719 (Bombay)

- S. Hariprakash v. Hon'ble Chief Justice, Madras High Court2014(4) MLJ (Criminal) 534

- Shakti Vahini v. Union of India and Ors. W.P. Civil No. 231 of 2010 (Supreme Court of India)

- Shakti Vahini v. Union of India and Ors. W.P. Civil No. 231 of 2010 (Supreme Court of India)

- Sheela Barse v. Union of India, 1986(2) Scale 1

- Sheela Barse v. Union of India, 1993(4) SCC 204

- Sheela Barse v. Union of India, 1995(5) SCC 654

- State of Gujarat v. Kanaiyalal Manilal, 1997(1) GujLH 560 (Gujarat)

- State of Punjab v. Ram Labhaya Bagha, AIR 1998 SC 1703

E. INDEX OF AUTHORITIES:

- Mental Health Atlas 2011, Department of Mental Health and Substance Abuse, World Health Organization

- NCW and NIMHANS, Addressing concerns of women admitted to psychiatric institutions in India: An in-depth analysis (2016)

- Notification No.: S.O.07(E), Ministry of Health and Family Welfare, Government of India (2nd January, 2018)

- Report of the National Commission on Macroeconomics and Health, Ministry of Health and Family Welfare, Government of India (2005)

- The Caracas Declaration of Latin America (1990)

- The Constitution of India

- The Constitution of the Republic of South Africa

- The Constitution of the World Health Organization

- The Draft Mental Healthcare Rules, 2017

- The European Mental Health Action Plan 2013-2020

- The Federal Patient Self-Determination Act, 1991

- The Health and Disability Commissioner (Code of Health and Disability Services Consumers' Rights) Regulations 1996 (New Zealand)

- The Mental Health (Compulsory Assessment and Treatment) Act, 1992 (New Zealand)

- The Mental Health Act, 1983 (United Kingdom)

- The Mental Health Act, 1987

- The Mental Health Act, 2007 (New South Wales, Australia)

- The Mental Health Act, 2007 (UK)

- The Mental Health Care Act, 2002 (Republic of South Africa)

- The Mental Health Law of 2014 (Indonesia)

- The Mental Health Ordinance 2001 (Pakistan)

- The Mental Healthcare Act, 2017

- The National Health Policy of India, 2017

- The National Mental Health Policy of India, 2014

- The New Zealand Bill of Rights Act, 1990

- The Privacy Act, 1993 (Brazil)

- The Privacy Act, 1993 (New Zealand)

- The UN Convention on Rights of Persons with Disabilities and Optional Protocol

- The WHO Resource Book on Mental Health, Human Rights and Legislation (2005)

- UN, Standard Rules on the Equalization of Opportunities for Persons with Disabilities (1993)

- UN, Standard Rules on the Equalization of Opportunities for Persons with Disabilities (1993)

- United Nations Convention on Rights of Persons with Disabilities

- United Nations Declaration on the Rights of Disabled Persons, Proclaimed by General Assembly resolution 3447 (XXX) of 9 December 1975

- United Nations Principles for the Protection of Persons with Mental Illness and for the Improvement of Mental Health Care (1991)

- United Nations, Standard Rules on the Equalization of Opportunities for Persons with Disabilities (1993)

- United Nations, The Protection of Persons with Mental Illness and the Improvement of Mental Health Care (A/RES/46/119)

- Universal Declaration of Human Rights

- WHO Checklist on Mental Health Legislation, Annexure 1 of the WHO Resource Book on Mental Health, Human Rights and Legislation (2005)

- WHO Mental Health Action Plan (2013-2020)

- WHO, Mental Health Care Law: Ten Basic Principles (1996)

- WHO, Mental Health Gap Action Programme (2008)

- WHO, The ICD-10 Classification of Mental and Behavioral Disorders – Clinical Descriptions and Diagnostic Guidelines

- WHO-AIMS Report on Mental Health System in Brazil

- World Health Organization Mental Health Atlas (2011)

- World Health Organization, Mental Health Gap Action Programme (2008)

- World Health Organization, Resolution WHA 65.4

- World Health Organization, Resolution WHA 65.4, The global burden of mental disorders and the need for a comprehensive, coordinated response from health and social sectors at the country level (2012)

- World Health Organization, World Report on Disability (2011)

- World Health Organization, World Report on Disability (2011)

- World Psychiatric Association, The Declaration of Hawaii

Table of Contents -Detailed

Chapter I

I.   INTRODUCTION

1. BACKGROUND

In a predominantly patriarchal society like ours, the position of a woman is vulnerable, particularly if she suffers from mental illness. The dichotomous opinions pertaining to the decision making power of a person with mental illness have been aired time and again in the legal and medical circles. However, the health rights and autonomy of women with mental illness find very little presence in the above discourse.

The Mental Healthcare Bill, 2013 was introduced in the Rajya Sabha in August, 2013. After multiple considerations and changes, it was passed by both the houses of the Parliament and received the President's assent in April, 2017 to become the Mental Healthcare Act, 2017. The 2017 Act came into force very recently, that is, from 29th May, 2018[1] on which date the Mental Health Act, 1987 stood repealed. The Preamble to the 2017 Act voices the aim of the Act[2] to be as follows:

> *"To provide for mental health care and services for persons with mental illness and to protect, promote and fulfill the rights of such persons during delivery of mental health care and services and for matters connected therewith or incidental thereto."*

Chapter III of the 2017 Act introduces the concept of psychiatric advance directives and Chapter IV comprises provisions pertaining to the nominated representative of the person with mental illness. The Act states that any person, not being a minor, has the right to make an advance directive in writing specifying, the way the person wishes to be cared for and treated for a mental

---

[1] Notification No.: S.O. 2173(E), Ministry of Health and Family Welfare, Government of India (29th May, 2018)

[2] The Mental Health Care Act, 2017 was introduced as the Mental Healthcare Bill, 2013, to bring the legal framework pertaining to mental health care in India in consonance with the provisions of UN Convention on Rights of Persons with Disabilities (UNCRPD), signed and ratified by India in October, 2007.

7

illness; and the individual or individuals, in order of precedence, he wants to appoint as his/her nominated representative.

There have been both legal and medical discourses about the moral authority of an advance directive and the real stance of advance directives vis-à-vis autonomy of the patient with mental illness who has issued the directive.[3] However, issues relating to advance directives from the perspective of the autonomy of a female patient with mental illness have not gathered much attention.

Chapter V of the 2017 Act enumerates the rights of persons with mental illness; one of the rights being the right to protection from cruel, inhuman and degrading treatment in any mental health establishment which includes *inter alia* the right to proper clothing so as to protect such person from exposure of his/her body to maintain his/her dignity; and the right to be protected from all forms of physical, verbal, emotional and sexual abuse.

In the background of the above discussion, it is pertinent to note some of the following facts:

- According to WHO, many of the negative experiences leading to mental health risks and responsible for the prevalence of psychological disorders among women predominately *"involve serious violations of their rights as human beings including their sexual and reproductive rights."*[4]
- According to a Report submitted by Disabled People's International (India), *"Almost 80% of women with disabilities are victims of violence*

---

[3]*See* Guy Widdershoven and Ron Berghmans, *Advance Directives in Psychiatric Care: A Narrative Approach,* Journal of Medical Ethics 92-97 (2001)
[4] WHO, Gender Disparities in Mental Health, Available at
http://www.who.int/mental_health/media/en/242.pdf?ua=1 (Last visited on May 10, 2018)

and they are four times more likely than other women to suffer sexual violence."[5]

- According to a Report titled *"Violence against Women with Disabilities"* submitted to the UN Special Rapporteur,[6] *"Patients are covertly discouraged to keep themselves clean and attractive on grounds that they could sexually provoke members of the male ward."*

It is thereby submitted that there is an urgent need to analyse the provisions of the 2017 Act from the perspective of autonomy and rights of women with mental illness, in the background of the ground reality.

2. AIMS AND OBJECTIVES:

The primary aim of the research is to analyse the Mental Healthcare Act, 2017 and its plausible implications on women with mental illness in India.

In the pursuit of the research, also analysed in detail are various relevant issues significant for the mental healthcare discourse. The discussion is from the women's rights perspective. The aim is to generate the *"woman question"*[7] and analyse the legal framework on the existent issue from the perspective of women with mental illness. Concepts like the psychiatric advance directives and their implications are analysed. Critical analysis of the National Mental Health Policy of India and the decisions of various Indian Courts on mental healthcare are juxtaposed to various International instruments and standards and the laws of six other countries. The aim is also to gauge the perspective of personnel involved in mental healthcare, namely psychiatrists and various social workers involved in mental healthcare and rehabilitation.

---

[5]*See also* Ashwaq Masoodi, *Sexual Rights of Disabled Women,* LIVE MINT (December 3, 2014), Available at http://www.livemint.com/Politics/FDPpol4lJ0pX037spUU1kL/Sexual-rights-of-disabled-women.html (Last visited on May 5, 2018)
[6]*Id.*
[7] Katherine T. Barlett, *Feminist Legal Methods,* 103 (4) Harvard Law Review 829 (1990)

3. SCOPE AND LIMITATIONS:

(a) Scope:

This research is strictly a study from the **women's rights issue**. Due to paucity of time and resources, this research is limited to analysing **the latest legal reform** in the health sector that is:

- **The Mental Health Care Act, 2017.**

The Mental Healthcare Act, 2017 came into force very recently, that is, from 29th May, 2018[8] on which date the Mental Health Act, 1987 stood repealed.

In this research, the Mental Health Care Act, 2017 is read with the Mental Health Act, 1987 which it repeals. The 2017 Act is juxtaposed with the provisions of UNCRPD[9] which this Act incorporates and various other International instruments. Also analysed are the National Mental Health Policy of India, 2014[10] and the Mental Healthcare (Rights of Persons with Mental Illness) Rules, 2018[11]. Following are the relevant areas covered in this research work:

- Definition of mental illness;
- Significance of discussing mental healthcare from women's rights perspective;
- Critical analysis of the Report by NCW and NIMHANS, India published in 2016, titled: *"Addressing concerns of women*

---

[8] Notification No.: S.O. 2173(E), Ministry of Health and Family Welfare, Government of India (29th May, 2018)

[9] Available at http://www.un.org/disabilities/documents/convention/convoptprot-e.pdf (Last visited on October 10, 2017)

[10] The National Mental Health Policy of India (2014), Available at https://www.nhp.gov.in/sites/default/files/pdf/national%20mental%20health%20policy%20of%20india%202014.pdf (Last visited on April 5, 2018)

[11] Notification No.: G.S.R. 509(E), Ministry of Health and Family Welfare, Department of Health and Family Welfare, Government of India (29th May, 2018)

admitted to psychiatric institutions in India: An in-depth analysis";[12]

o Human rights of women with mental illness;
o Impact of introducing psychiatric advance directives in the country;
o Comparison of some of the relevant provisions of the Mental Healthcare Act, 2017 with the Mental Health Act, 1987;
o Analysis of the decisions of the Indian Courts on matters pertaining to mental healthcare;
o National Mental Health Policy of India, 2014 and its impact on the Mental Healthcare Act, 2017;
o Analysis of the United Nations Convention on Rights of Persons with Disabilities and other relevant international instruments pertaining to mental healthcare; and
o Analysis of the mental healthcare laws in six other countries.

In the pursuance of this research, empirical research work has also been undertaken.

(b) Limitations:

The researcher had initially ventured into analysing multiple latest reforms in the legal framework pertaining to health, namely: The Transplantation of Human Organs (Amendment) Act, 2011; Draft Assisted Reproductive Technology (Regulation) Bill, 2010; Rights of Persons with Disabilities Bill, 2014; and the Mental Healthcare Bill, 2013, from the women's rights perspective.

- Over time, the Mental Healthcare Bill, 2013 was soon **the Mental Healthcare Act, 2017**, being the latest reform in the health sector as on

---

[12] NCW and NIMHANS Report (2016), Available at
http://ncw.nic.in/pdfreports/addressing_concerns_of_women_admitted_to_psychiatric_institution s_in_india_an_in-depth_analysis.pdf (Last visited on October 10, 2017)

date. It is to be noted that the Mental Healthcare Act, 2017 came into force very recently, that is, from 29th May, 2018[13] on which date the Mental Health Act, 1987 stood repealed. In the pursuance of the research, analysing all the aforementioned legal reforms was found beyond the scope of time, means and access. Therefore, this research was confined to only a thorough analysis of the latest reform in the health sector that is the 2017 Act from the women's rights perspective.

- The analysis is done only from the perspective of **women with mental illness.**
- Mental healthcare issues are multi-pronged and widespread. Whereas this research analyses the implications of the 2017 Act on women with mental illness, it is pertinent to note that the present research **does not** delve into the specific issues of:
  - o Mental disorder and behavioral disorders due to psychoactive substance use and
  - o mental health issues in Indian prisons.

4. SUMMARY OF LITERATURE REVIEW

Paucity of literature with respect to the situation in India:
  - o Literature from medical perspective, human rights perspective and legal perspective is sparse;
  - o Feminist writings on rights of female patients with mental illness in India are very limited;
  - o Paucity of literature analyzing the implications of the Mental Healthcare Act, 2017 on rights of women with mental illness;

---

[13] Notification No.: S.O. 2173(E), Ministry of Health and Family Welfare, Government of India (29th May, 2018)

- Viability of Psychiatric advance directives on rights of women with mental illness in India has not been delved into in any research work;
- Very little written about rights, body autonomy and body politics issues pertaining to women with mental illness in the country;
- No literature comparing the legal framework pertaining to mental healthcare in India with the legal framework in other countries.

Pointers in the available literature:

- Women with mental illness are the vulnerable sections of the society;
- The Mental Healthcare Act, 2017 has found very little discussion in the legal circles;
- Viability of psychiatric advance directives on rights of women with mental illness has not been delved into in any research work;
- Writings linking medical perspective, human rights perspective and legal perspective of position of women in need of mental healthcare in India are very limited in number.

5. HYPOTHESIS

The Mental Healthcare Act, 2017 adequately protects the rights of women with mental illness.

6. RESEARCH QUESTIONS

1. What is mental illness?
2. Are women with mental illness vulnerable?
3. What will be the implications of psychiatric advance directives on the autonomy of women with mental illness?
4. Are the rights of women with mental illness adequately protected under the Mental Healthcare Act, 2017?
5. Are the provisions of the Mental Healthcare Act, 2017 in consonance with the standards laid down in various international mental healthcare standards?

7. SOURCES OF DATA

Primary Sources:

- Bills and Acts
- National Policies
- Laws of other countries
- International Instruments
- Data collected through interviews
- Answers collected through Questionnaires
- Other Data Collected through Empirical Research
- International Health Standards
- Relevant Judgements of the Courts in India

Secondary Sources:

- Books
- Articles (available online and other legal journals available in law libraries)
- Law Commission Reports
- Reports by NCW
- Reports by NGOs
- Newspaper articles
- Studies undertaken by various National and International Organizations along with the work of various NGOs working for women's health issues will also be taken help of in the pursuit of this research.
- Statistics and numbers from surveys conducted by far
- Other data available online or otherwise

8. RESEARCH METHODOLOGY

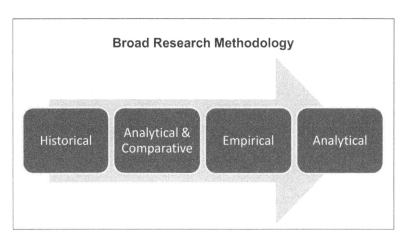

Table (1): BROAD RESEARCH METHODOLOGY

1. **Historical:** Law develops in consonance with time, and its existence is intertwined in the society in which it exists. The background of the study, the very reason why the research was undertaken is delved into. This part of the research work, predominantly analyses the general understanding of the concept of *"mental illness",* and then addresses the reasons that make the analysis of mental healthcare laws from women's rights perspective relevant and important.

2. **Analytical and Comparative:** In this part of the research work, the provisions of the 2017 Act are analysed in detail. In pursuance of the same, the research work also delves into:
   - A comparison of the provisions of the Mental Healthcare Act, 2017 with the provisions of the Mental Health Act, 1987, that it repeals;

- The concept of *"psychiatric advance directives"* and its viability in India. A comparison is drawn with the concept of *advance directives/ living wills.*
- Relevant Judgements of the Courts in India in matters relating to mental health care.
- Various International Human Rights Instruments, including:
  - UDHR
  - ICCPR
  - ICESCR
  - CRC
  - CEDAW
- Legal instruments by United Nations and World Health Organizations pertaining to mental healthcare, and various International Declarations including, *inter alia:*
  - Declaration on the Rights of Disabled Persons, 1975
  - United Nations Principles for the Protection of Persons with Mental Illness and for the Improvement of Mental Health Care, 1991
  - WHO, Mental Health Care Law: Ten Basic Principles
  - United Nations Convention on Rights of Persons with Disability, 2006 and Optional Protocol
  - WHO, Mental Health Action Plan 2013-2020
  - The WHO Mental Health Gap Action Program
  - The Hawaii Declaration
  - Madrid Declaration on Ethical Standards for Psychiatric Practice
  - Caracas Declaration
  - Mental Health Declaration for Europe
  - The World Federation of Mental Health
- Legal framework and situation in other countries to draw a comparative analysis and arrive at conclusions about what, if any, lessons the Indian legal framework can draw from these laws. The laws of the following countries are analysed in this pursuit:
  - United Kingdom
  - South Africa
  - Bangladesh

- o Indonesia
- o New Zealand
- o Brazil

3. **Empirical:** In this part of the research, the research tools which have been put into use are interviews, questionnaires and surveys (both online and offline). Also delved into in detail and analysed are the Report by NCW and NIMHANS, India on *"Addressing the concerns of women admitted to psychiatric institutions in India: an in-depth analysis"* published in 2016; and the Report by HRW on *"Treated Worse than Animals: Abuses against Women and Girls with Psychological or Intellectual Disabilities in Institutions in India"* published in 2014.

This part of the research work can be categorized into the following five sub-parts:

a. Psychiatrists (Interviews): Focused interview method was adopted. 5 psychiatrists were interviewed

b. NGOs (Interviews and visits): Officials and staff at 3 NGOs working with women with mental illness were interviewed, namely: Anjali (Kolkata), Paripurnita (Kolkata) and the Banyan (Chennai).

c. Online Survey: Online survey was conducted which received 110 responses. The survey was conducted through a structured questionnaire. Twelve questions were asked, out of which six were close-ended questions and six were open-ended questions.

d. Offline Survey: Offline survey was conducted which received 75 responses. The survey was conducted through a structured questionnaire. The questionnaire comprised nine questions, out of which five questions were both close-ended and open-ended and four questions were open-ended only.

e. Also delved into in detail and analysed are:

  - Report by NCW and NIMHANS, India on *"Addressing the concerns of women admitted to psychiatric institutions in India: an in-depth analysis"* published in 2016; and

18

- Report by HRW on *"Treated Worse than Animals: Abuses against Women and Girls with Psychological or Intellectual Disabilities in Institutions in India"* published in 2014.

4. **Analytical:** This is the final part of the research work. This phase of the research work categorically discusses the findings of each compartment of the research by juxtaposing the findings next to each other. Research questions are answered based on the research that has been undertaken, hypothesis is tested and suggestions are made.

II. Scoping the Definition of Mental Illness for the Purpose of the Law relating to Mental Healthcare

Mental health is an integral part of a human's wellbeing which may be disturbed by illnesses which range for a span of time, for a crisis in life or for lifetime itself. This Chapter aims to understand the concept of mental illness; differentiate between mental illness and mental retardation; and analyse the various causes and implications of mental illness. A detailed analysis of the term as defined and discussed in countries across the globe is undertaken. The definition has also travelled with time in India and found a more exhaustive detailing in the Mental Healthcare Act, 2017 as compared to the definition in the Mental Health Act, 1987. The Chapter thereby deeply delves into the definition of the term "mental illness" as defined in the 2017 Act. The various factors and implications of mental illness are also discussed at length, a glimpse of the Indian society's take on mental healthcare also finds place in the discussion. The Chapter concludes by appraising the 2017 Act as a welcome change towards a better understanding of mental illness and therefore better treatment meted out to mental healthcare in India subject to its implementation in its letter and spirit.

1. INTRODUCTION

"Health is a state of complete physical, mental and social well-being and not merely the absence of disease or infirmity."

-Constitution of the World Health Organization[14]

Mental health is an integral part of a human's wellbeing. The same may be disturbed by illnesses which range for a span of time, for a crisis in life or for lifetime itself.

The Mental Healthcare Act, 2017 came into force very recently, that is, from 29th May, 2018[15] on which date the Mental Health Act, 1987 stood repealed. The journey from 1987 to 2017 has witnessed changes in the society and advancement in mental healthcare research and practices. People over time have become more vocal about their mental health and well-being. Celebrities have come out and spoken about their experiences with depression, bipolar disorders, obsessive compulsive disorders, etc. Rehabilitation of the mentally ill persons into the society and protection of their human rights both during and after mental healthcare has also acquired significance.

The Mental Health Act, 1987 functioned with the purpose to *"consolidate and amend the law relating to the treatment and care of mentally ill persons, to make better provision with respect to their property and affairs and for matters connected therewith or incidental thereto."*[16]The 2017 Act aims to not only provide for the services pertaining to mental healthcare but also to protect and promote the rights of persons suffering from mental illness during delivery of mental healthcare services.

---

[14] Available at http://www.who.int/governance/eb/who_constitution_en.pdf (Last visited on January 10, 2017)

[15] Notification No.: S.O. 2173(E), Ministry of Health and Family Welfare, Government of India (29th May, 2018)

[16] The Mental Health Act, 1987, Preamble

The definition of the term *'mental illness'* has evolved and widened over time. The causes and implications of mental illness can be better understood by gaining knowledge about the concept of mental illness. The common understanding of the terminology is sometimes faltered and mislead by the beliefs of the society and the culture that one lives in. This Chapter therefore holds significance because it throws light on the concept of mental illness and attempts at clearing the cobwebs of misconceptions and doubts pertaining to mental illness.

2. THE IMPORTANCE OF DEFINING MENTAL ILLNESS FOR THE PURPOSES OF MENTAL HEALTHCARE

Mental illness is a form of illness which is generally discussed in the wraps of anonymity and pretexts of stigma in the country. Mental healthcare is not accessed by many mentally ill persons in India for fear of negative branding by the society. Many have been unable to discern the fact that, just like physical illness, mental illness too needs treatment and care from a healthcare professional. Resort is taken in superstitious pathways where dargahs, deras and babas claim to cure illnesses of the mind. This is so because mental illness is many a time associated by the society with witchcraft, ghosts, evil spirits, sins and repentance.

"Folk mental health traditions, based in religious lifeways and etiologies of supernatural affliction, are overwhelmingly sought by Indians in times of mental ill-health."[17]

---

[17]Anubha Sood, *The Global Mental Health movement and its impact on traditional healing in India: A case study of the Balaji temple in Rajasthan,* Mc Gill Transcultural Psychiatry, Vol. 53 (2016), Available at
http://journals.sagepub.com/doi/abs/10.1177/1363461516679352?journalCode=tpse (Last visited on November 3, 2017); See also Julie Schoonover, Et. al., Perceptions of Traditional Healing for Mental Illness in Rural Gujarat, 80 Annals of Global Health (2014), Available athttp://www.sciencedirect.com/science/article/pii/S2214999614000514 (Last visited on November 5, 2017)

The Supreme Court has time and again given directions to the Government to undertake comprehensive awareness campaigns to educate people about mental healthcare and to ensure that mentally ill persons are sent to doctors and not to religious places such as dargahs or temples.[18] Article 17 of the United Nations Convention of Rights of Persons with Disabilities, 2007[19] states that every person with disabilities, has a right to be respected and to get physical and mental integrity at par with others; and an important step towards that would be, giving them proper healthcare.

It is to be noted that the determination of the mental illness of a person does not in itself imply and cannot be a reason alone to consider such a person to be of unsound mind for the purposes of law, unless he/she is so declared by a competent court.[20]

Defining mental illness and identifying the components that qualify a person to be considered mentally ill and therefore eligible for and in need of mental healthcare is very important. One of the major steps in diminishing the treatment gap is by understanding the concept of mental illness and the importance of mental healthcare therein.

3. MENTAL RETARDATION/ INTELLECTUAL DISABILITY

"Mental illness" and *"mental retardation"* are two such terminologies which are often confused and inter-changed. The definitions of mental illness across most nations exclude mental retardation; therefore, making it important to understand the meaning of the term. To get a considerable understanding of the concept of mental illness it is important to understand what mental retardation is.

---

[18] Re Death Of 25 Mental Asylum Patients v. Union Of India, 2002(3) SCC 36; *See* also Sheela Barse v. Union of India and Another, AIR 1993 SCW 2908
[19] Available at http://www.un.org/disabilities/documents/convention/convoptprot-e.pdf (Last visited on November 1, 2017)
[20] The 2017 Act, Section 3(5)

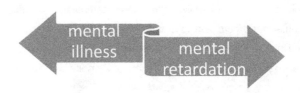

Mental retardation affects a person's intelligence and cognitive abilities[21], and is often referred to as intellectual disability. Mental retardation is a neurodevelopment disorder characterized by the person having a below average intelligence which limits his/her normal life with an IQ^{22} of less than 70-75 as compared to the normal average of 100,[23] thereby resulting in sub-average intellectual functioning.[24] Mental retardation is present at birth but becomes evident with the onset of development and entails lack of skills necessary for normal and independent existence of the person;[25] for example disability pertaining to judgement, thinking planning, learning, solving and action. Mental retardation is generally life-long and cannot be completely treated.[26] It develops and becomes evident during the growing years of the person. Fanconi anemia, down syndrome, hydrocephalus and cerebral palsy are some of the examples of mental retardation.

It is important to note that mental illness is different from mental retardation and so are its causes, symptoms and implications. A person with mental illness may

---

[21] *See* http://www.wisegeekhealth.com/what-is-the-difference-between-mental-retardation-and-mental-illness.htm (Last visited on November 1, 2017)

[22] Intelligence Quotient

[23] *See* http://www.humanillnesses.com/original/Men-Os/Mental-Retardation.html (Last visited on November 1, 2017)

[24] *See* http://lucasdd.info/wp/wp-content/uploads/2015/12/Mental-Retardation-and-Mental-Illness_201405161349276399.pdf (Last visited on November 1, 2017)

[25] *See* https://www.psychologytoday.com/conditions/intellectual-disability-intellectual-developmental-disorder (Last visited on November 1, 2017)

[26] *Id.*

be completely socially sound;[27] and unlike mental retardation, mental illnesses can affect persons of any age and from any background.[28] Also, mental illness if diagnosed is treatable and curable.

4. UNDERSTANDING WHAT CONSTITUTES MENTAL ILLNESS

The 2017 Act defines mental illness in the following words[29]:

> *"'mental illness' means a substantial disorder of thinking, mood, perception, orientation or memory that grossly impairs judgment, behavior, capacity to recognize reality or ability to meet the ordinary demands of life, mental conditions associated with the abuse of alcohol and drugs, but does not include mental retardation which is a condition of arrested or incomplete development of mind of a person, specially characterized by sub-normality of intelligence."*

The definition of *"mental illness"* in the 2017 Act, can be broken down into two stages of eventualities, namely: *'cause'* and *'effect'*.

Mental illness means (cause) a substantial disorder of:	Mental illness results in (effect) gross impairment of:
<ul><li>Thinking,</li><li>Mood,</li><li>Perception,</li><li>Orientation, or</li><li>Memory.</li></ul>	<ul><li>Judgement,</li><li>Behavior,</li><li>Capacity to recognize reality, or</li><li>Ability to meet the ordinary demands of life.</li></ul>

---

[27] *See* http://lucasdd.info/wp/wp-content/uploads/2015/12/Mental-Retardation-and-Mental-Illness_201405161349276399.pdf (Last visited on November 1, 2017)

[28] *Id.*

[29] The 2017 Act, Section 2(s)

Section 2(l) of the Mental Health Act, 1987[30] stated that a mentally ill person means *"a person who is in need of treatment by reason of any mental disorder other than mental retardation."* The Mental Health Act, 1987 did not enumerate any of the above factors and effects of mental illness that find place in the definition of the Act of 2017[31]The 1987 faltered because of lack of clarity about what constituted mental disorder, other than exclusion of mental retardation. The definition given under the 2017 Act fixed this anomaly and laid down a very detailed definition of mental illness. The various traits of mental illness coupled with the resultant effects, throw light towards better understanding of mental illness from the legal perspective.

The terms *'thinking', 'mood', 'perception', 'orientation'* or *'memory'* as used in the definition of *"mental illness"* under the 2017 Act, are however, subject to various interpretations with respect to their content and extent. At the same time, this fact cannot be obviated that unlike physical illness where the degree of harm or effect on the body can be gauged or quantified (example recording the temperature of the body, blood sugar level, blood pressure); disorders in thinking, mood, perception, orientation and memory cannot be compartmentalized into normal and not normal. Psychiatry has laid down tests to examine the disorder and the pertinent ones relate to the actions and lifestyle of the person in question; that is when such a substantial disorder leads to gross impairment of judgement, behavior, capacity to recognize reality or ability to meet the ordinary demands of life, the person is considered to have mental illness. When do the thoughts, emotions, etc. become abnormal is based on facts and circumstances of each case and each person. These mental conditions could be caused because it runs in the family, or because of the circumstances or lifestyle of the person or simply because of alcohol or drug abuse. Determining factors leading to the disorders in thought,

---

[30] Available at http://ncw.nic.in/acts/THEMENTALHEALTHACT1987.pdf (Last visited on October 25, 2017)
[31] The Mental Health Act, 1987, Section 2(i)

27

mood, perception, orientation or memory, are many, and the list is not exhaustive. Mental disorders comprise various symptoms evident in the form of combination/combinations of *"abnormal thoughts, emotions, behavior and relationships with others."*[32] They are detectable and treatable with a co-ordinate administering of medication and counselling.

Section 3 of the 2017 Act lays down various parameters to be borne in mind to determine mental illness. It is stated that mental illness should be determined according to such nationally and internationally[33] accepted medical standards as the Central Government notifies from time to time.[34] A person should not be classified as a person with mental illness except for the purpose of treatment of mental illness only. The 2017 Act lays down factors that are not to form the basis of determination of the mental illness of a person:

- Any factor not directly relevant to the mental health status of the person (like economic, political or social status in the society or membership of a religious, cultural or racial group, etc.);[35]
- Not adhering to certain moral, social, work, political or cultural values;[36]
- Religious beliefs of a person's community;[37]
- Past treatment or hospitalization in a mental health establishment. Even though the same is relevant but it cannot be the justification offered for the determination of mental illness of the person.[38]

It is to be noted that the determination of mental illness for the purposes of the 2017 Act shall not in itself imply that such a person is of unsound mind, unless

---

[32] *See* http://www.who.int/mediacentre/factsheets/fs396/en/ (Last visited on November 5, 2017)
[33] *See* WHO, The ICD-10 Classification of Mental and Behavioral Disorders –Clinical Descriptions and Diagnostic Guidelines, Available at http://www.who.int/classifications/icd/en/bluebook.pdf (Last visited on November 1, 2017)
[34] The 2017 Act, Section 3(1)
[35] The 2017 Act, Section 3(3)
[36] *Id.*
[37] *Id.*
[38] The 2017 Act, Section 3(4)

the same is declared by a competent court.[39]Section 3 of the Act therefore, makes it very clear that social, cultural, religious and other similar factors not related to the mental illness of a person cannot be considered as factors to determine the mental illness of a person. An express clarification of the same by the 2017 Act very explicitly is a welcome change and a necessary check to any such malpractice.

5. CATEGORIES OF MENTAL ILLNESS

There are a lot of mental illnesses recognized and existent in today's time. All the types comprise one or the other impairment in thinking, mood, perception and memory which affects the person's thoughts, behavior, personality or capacity to meet the daily needs of a normal life.[40]

The World Health Organization in its document tilted *"The ICD-10 Classification of Mental and Behavioral Disorders –Clinical Descriptions and Diagnostic Guidelines"*[41]lays down various categories and sub-categories into which mental disorders can be classified. The document was compiled from Chapter V of the Tenth Revision of the International Statistical Classification of Diseases and Related Health Problems (ICD-10).[42] Herein below is a precise version of the categories enumerated in the document:[43]

- **Organic, including symptomatic, mental disorders**, which are further categorized into:
  - Dementia in Alzheimer's disease
  - Vascular dementia

---

[39] The 2017 Act, Section 3(5)
[40] *See* BRENDA HALE, MENTAL HEALTH LAW (2010)
[41] WHO, The ICD-10 Classification of Mental and Behavioral Disorders –Clinical Descriptions and Diagnostic Guidelines, Available at http://www.who.int/classifications/icd/en/bluebook.pdf (Last visited on November 1, 2017)
[42] *See* http://apps.who.int/iris/handle/10665/37958 (Last visited on November 1, 2017)
[43] WHO, The ICD-10 Classification of Mental and Behavioral Disorders –Clinical Descriptions and Diagnostic Guidelines, Available at http://www.who.int/classifications/icd/en/bluebook.pdf (Last visited on November 1, 2017)

- Dementia in other diseases classified elsewhere like Pick's disease, parkinson's disease, Huntington's disease, etc.
- Unspecified dementia
- Organic amnesic syndrome, not induced by alcohol and other substances
- Other mental disorders due to brain damage and dysfunction and to physical disease
- Personality and behavioral disorder due to brain disease, damage and dysfunction
- Unspecified organic or symptomatic mental disorder.[44]

- **Mental disorder and behavioral disorders due to psychoactive substance use**, which are further categorized into mental and behavioral disorders due to use of alcohol, opioids, cannabinoids, sedatives or hypnotics, cocaine and other stimulants, including caffeine. It also includes mental and behavioral disorders due to use of hallucinations, tobacco, volatile solvents and multiple drug use and use of other psychoactive substances.[45]

- **Schizophrenia, schizotypal and delusional disorders**, which are further categorized into:
  - Schizophrenia- Types of Schizophrenia are: Paranoid schizophrenia, Hebephrenic schizophrenia, Catatonic schizophrenia, Undifferentiated schizophrenia, Post-schizophrenic depression, Residual schizophrenia, Simple schizophrenia, Other schizophrenia with varied symptoms
  - Schizotypal disorder
  - Persistent delusional disorders
  - Acute and transient psychotic disorders
  - Induced delusional disorder

---

[44] *Id.*
[45] *Id.*

- Schizoaffective disorders: Types of Schizoaffective disorders are: Schizoaffective disorder manic type, depressive type, mixed type, etc.
- Other nonorganic psychotic disorders.[46]

- **Mood disorders**, which are further categorized into manic episode, bipolar affective disorder, depressive episode, recurrent depressive disorder, persistent mood (affective) disorders and other mood (effective) disorders.[47]

- **Neurotic, stress-related and somatoform disorders**, which are further categorized into phobic anxiety disorders; other anxiety disorders like panic and mixed anxiety disorders; obsessive - compulsive disorder; reaction to severe stress, and adjustment disorders; dissociative (conversion) disorders; somatoform disorders; other neurotic disorders like neurasthenia, depersonalization and other specified neurotic disorders.[48]

- **Behavioral syndromes associated with physiological disturbances and physical factors, further categorized into**: eating disorders; nonorganic sleep disorders; sexual dysfunction, not caused by organic disorder or disease; psychological and behavioral factors associated with disorders or diseases classified elsewhere; abuse of non-dependence-producing substances like steroids, hormones, vitamins, anti-depressants, etc.; mental and behavioral disorders related to puerperium and behavioral syndromes associated with physiological disturbances and physical factors.[49]

- **Disorders of adult personality and behavior**, for example: paranoid personality disorder, schizoid personality disorder, dissocial personality

---

[46] *Id.*
[47] *Id.*
[48] *Id.*
[49] *Id.*

31

disorder, emotionally unstable personality disorder, habit and impulse disorders, etc.

- **Behavioral and emotional disorders** with onset usually occurring in childhood and adolescence and disorders of psychological development.[50]

It is to be noted that these types of mental illnesses are varied and can co-exist in various combinations at the same time, thereby making the defining of mental illness a complex task.

The World Health Organization document on ICD-10 Classification of Mental and Behavioral Disorders –Clinical Descriptions and Diagnostic Guidelines,[51] also includes mental retardation and its various types in the list of mental and behavioral disorders; however, since the definition of mental illness excludes mental retardation, the same does not form part of the classification of the various types of mental illnesses enumerated above.

---

[50] *Id.*

[51] Available at http://www.who.int/classifications/icd/en/bluebook.pdf (Last visited on November 1, 2017)

6. Mental Illness as defined in Laws of other Countries

To get a better understanding of the concept of *"mental illness"* as interpreted worldwide, it is important to delve into the definitions accorded to mental illness in various other jurisdictions of the world.[52] There is a trait of similarity among all the definitions with a hue of minor variations in the understanding of the concept. The definitions of *"mental illness"* in the laws of United Kingdom, South Africa, Pakistan, United States and Australia find place in the discussion hereinafter.[53]

The Mental Health Act[54] of the **United Kingdom** was introduced in 2007. It amended the Mental Health Act 1983, the Domestic Violence, Crime and Victims Act 2004 and the Mental Capacity Act 2005[55] with respect to mentally disordered persons. The 2007 Act defines mental disorder to mean any disorder or disability of the mind. This definition is very simple but subjective, leaving a wider scope of interpretation and resultant confusion.

The **South Africa Mental Health Care Act, 2002**[56] defines mental illness[57] as a *"positive diagnosis of a mental health related illness in terms of accepted diagnostic criteria made by a mental health care practitioner authorized to make such diagnosis."* The Act also uses another terminology that is *"mental health*

---

[52] *See also* WHO, *Mental Health Care Law: Ten Basic Principles* (1996), Available at
http://www.who.int/mental_health/media/en/75.pdf (Last visited on November 1, 2017)
[53] *See also* WHO-AIMS Report on Mental Health System in Bangladesh (2007), Available at
http://www.who.int/mental_health/bangladesh_who_aims_report.pdf (Last visited on November 1, 2017)
[54] The Mental Health Act, 2007, Available at
http://www.legislation.gov.uk/ukpga/2007/12/pdfs/ukpga_20070012_en.pdf (Last visited on November 1, 2017)
[55] CHRISTOPHER JOHNSON, MEDICAL TREATMENT: DECISIONS AND THE LAW- THE MENTAL CAPACITY ACT IN ACTION (2010)
[56] The Mental Health Care Act, 2002, Available at https://www.gov.za/sites/default/files/a17-02.pdf (Last visited on October 30, 2017)
[57] *Id.*

care user[68] who is a person receiving care, treatment and rehabilitation services or using a health service at a health establishment; and includes a prospective user, the person's next of kin, a person authorized by any other law or court order to act on that persons behalf; an administrator appointed in terms of this Act; and an executor of that deceased person's estate. The definition of mental illness under the South Africa Mental health Care Act, 2002 because of being complemented by the definition of a mental health care user, delivers a better understanding of the concept of mental illness.

The **Pakistan** Mental Health Ordinance[59] came into effect in 2001. It repealed the Lunacy Act of 1912. The Ordinance omits terms used in the Act of 1912 such as *'lunatic', 'asylum', "criminal lunatic"*, etc. The Ordinance of 2001 states that mental disorder means mental illness and includes mental impairment, severe personality disorder, mental impairment and any other disorder or disability of mind. This definition however, does not include disorders which arise because of reason only of promiscuity or other immoral conduct, sexual deviancy or dependence on alcohol or drugs. The 18th amendment to the Constitution of Pakistan bestowed responsibility upon provincial governments to pass health legislations. The lax on the part of the provincial governments to pass such legislations,[60] has led to the mental health picture in the nation to be

---

[58] *Id.*

[59] Available at http://www.pimh.gop.pk/docs/Mental%20Health%20Ordinance.pdf (Last visited on October 30, 2017)

[60] It is noteworthy that till date only the provinces of Sindh and Punjab have a mental health law -*See* Amina Tareen and Khalida Ijaz Tareen, *Mental Health Law in Pakistan,* BJPSYCH INTERNATIONAL Vol. 13 (2016), Available at https://www.rcpsych.ac.uk/pdf/PUBNS_IPv13n3_67.pdf (Last visited on November 5, 2017)

a fragmented and disoriented one.[61] It is noteworthy that till date only the provinces of Sindh and Punjab have a mental health law.[62]

According to the **American Psychiatric Association**, mental illnesses are *"health conditions involving changes in thinking, emotion or behavior (or a combination of these)"* and that mental illnesses lead to distress and difficulty in carrying on with social, work or family activities.[63]

The Mental Health Act, 2007[64] of **New South Wales, Australia** provides for treatment and care of persons with mental illness and mental disorders. Mental illness is very succinctly defined in this Act to mean *"a condition that seriously impairs, either temporarily or permanently, the mental functioning of a person and is characterized by the presence in the person of any one or more of the following symptoms: (a) delusions, (b) hallucinations, (c) serious disorder of thought form, (d) a severe disturbance of mood, (e) sustained or repeated irrational behavior indicating the presence of any one or more of the symptoms referred to in paragraphs (a)–(d)."* This definition is a very detailed definition but suffers from the vice of being too exhaustive. It is not inclusive enough to accommodate more possibilities of different conditions which could amount to mental illness in the medical terms.

It is pertinent to note that there is a stark similarity among the various definitions of *"mental illness"* in all the above countries. There is also a general understanding of the concept of *"mental illness"*.

---

[61] Amina Tareen and Khalida Ijaz Tareen, *Mental Health Law in Pakistan,* BJPSYCH INTERNATIONAL Vol. 13 (2016), Available at
https://www.rcpsych.ac.uk/pdf/PUBNS_IPv13n3_67.pdf (Last visited on November 5, 2017)
[61] *See* https://www.psychiatry.org/patients-families/what-is-mental-illness (Last visited on October 28, 2017)
[62] Amina Tareen and Khalida Ijaz Tareen, *Mental Health Law in Pakistan,* BJPSYCH INTERNATIONAL Vol. 13 (2016), Available at
https://www.rcpsych.ac.uk/pdf/PUBNS_IPv13n3_67.pdf (Last visited on November 5, 2017)
[63] *See* https://www.psychiatry.org/patients-families/what-is-mental-illness (Last visited on October 28, 2017)
[64] Mental Health Act, 2007, Available at https://www.legislation.nsw.gov.au/acts/2007-8.pdf(Last visited on October 25, 2017)

In order to understand the viability of any law it is important to weight the same vis-à-vis the corresponding laws in other countries of the world. Having discussed the definitions of mental illness in some other countries, it becomes quite evident that the definition[65] of mental illness as provided in the Indian Mental Healthcare Act of 2017 stands apt and viable on the anvil of comparison. The definition given in 2017 lays down the list of substantial disorders and the gross impairment caused by the same. The terms used in the definition (like thinking, mood, perception, behavior, judgment, ordinary demands of life, etc.) are subjective thereby making the definition inclusive enough to accommodate possibilities beyond those listed in the definition.

7. Concluding

This Chapter appraised the definition of mental illness as laid down in the 2017 Act of India and the fact that this Act of 2017 brings the Mental Healthcare legal framework in consonance with the mandates of UNCRPD. Mental illness is different from mental retardation but the two terms are often confused with each other and inter-changed. Therefore, the necessity to explain and discuss the latter was felt and addressed. Mental illness being a broad concept, there are various classifications into which mental illness can be categorized, cue for which should be taken from the WHO document on ICD-10 Classification of Mental and Behavioral Disorders –Clinical Descriptions and Diagnostic Guidelines.[66]Having discussed the concept of mental illness at length, this Chapter then drew light on the definitions of mental illness in some other

---

[65] The 2017 Act, Section 2(s) - mental illness means *"a substantial disorder of thinking, mood, perception, orientation or memory that grossly impairs judgment, behavior, capacity to recognize reality or ability to meet the ordinary demands of life, mental conditions associated with the abuse of alcohol and drugs, but does not include mental retardation which is a condition of arrested or incomplete development of mind of a person, specially characterised by subnormality of intelligence."*

[66] Available at http://www.who.int/classifications/icd/en/bluebook.pdf (Last visited on November 1, 2017)

countries, and tested the definition of mental illness in the 2017 Act of India in the anvil of comparison.

Having indulged in the above discourse it can therefore be concluded that the 2017 Act is a welcome change towards a better understanding of mental illness. If the 2017 Act is implemented and followed in letter and spirit it has the potential to mete out better results for mental healthcare in India than the Mental Health Act, 1987 was able to provide.

Chapter III

III. ASKING THE "WOMAN QUESTION"

After having discussed at length about the scope of the term "mental health" in Chapter II, Chapter III elaborates upon the significance of discussing the mental health issues of women in particular. Studies reveal that women, often perceived as the weaker section of the society, are more vulnerable and susceptible to oppression and neglect in case of a mental disorder. Gender disparity plays an influential role in mental health. In furtherance of its purpose, this Chapter draws an analysis of HRW Report (2014) on "'Treated Worse than Animals': Abuses against Women and Girls with Psychosocial or Intellectual Disabilities in Institutions in India," which was instrumental for the decision of NCW and NIMHANS to take cognizance of the issue, which culminated in the Report (2016) by NCW and NIMHANS on "Addressing concerns of women admitted to psychiatric institutions in India: An in-depth analysis"

1. PERCEPTIONS ABOUT WOMEN AND THEIR MENTAL HEALTH

Gender disparity plays an influential role in mental health. Factors that affect the same include the disparity in the control women and men exercise over their lives respectively. Their diverse positions in the societal setup and the difference in treatment meted out to them in the society, thereby results in difference of their susceptibility to various risks associated with mental illness. [67]

Women, often perceived as the weaker section of the society, are more vulnerable and susceptible to oppression and neglect in case of a mental illness.[68] The explanations offered both in the scientific circles and the magic and faith-healers dominated thought process since time immemorial was that a woman is weak, physically and mentally and/or that she is easily influenced by the supernatural and the bad spirits,[69] she is more susceptible to mental instability and emotional breakdowns. [70]

English literature and the annals of sociological history are replete with such accounts from olden times. Women in the nineteenth century were sent to asylums and were made subject to correctional treatments, if their behavior did not fit into the societal set-up. Some of the many grounds cited were over-education[71], refusal to marry, simple ill will towards the woman, suppressed menstruation, depression after a loss or just using of abusive language.[72]

---

[67] WHO, *Gender Disparity and mental health: The Facts,* Gender and Women's Mental Health, Available at http://www.who.int/mental_health/prevention/genderwomen/en/

[68] *See* BRUCE LUBOTSKY LEVIN, ET. AL., WOMEN'S MENTAL HEALTH SERVICES- A PUBLIC HEALTH PERSPECTIVE (1998)

[69]Cecilia Tasca, Et. al., *Women and Hysteria in the History of Mental Health,* Clin Pract Epidemiol Ment Health. 2012; 8: 110–119.Published online 2012 Oct 19. Available at https://www.ncbi.nlm.nih.gov/pmc/articles/PMC3480686/

[70] The History of Women's Mental Illness, Available at http://www.epigee.org/the-history-of-womens-mental-illness.html

[71] SHOWALTER, E. THE FEMALE MALADY: WOMEN, MADNESS, AND ENGLISH CULTURE 1830-1980 (1985)

[72]Pouba, K., and Tianen, A., *Lunacy in the 19th Century: Women's Admission to Asylums in United States of America,* Oshkosh Scholar, Volume I, April 2006. Wisconsin: University of Wisconsin Board of Regents, Available at https://minds.wisconsin.edu/handle/1793/6687,

Genuine cases of mental illness were addressed with general understanding about women and their expected role in the society including their sexuality and expected physical functions. Women were labelled as insane and were locked in madhouses for reasons like depression, post-natal symptoms, menapausal symptoms, alcoholism, dementia, infidelity, etc. In the west, till the 1800s,[73] women who suffered from any kind of mental illness were considered to have a disease of the soul for which there was no remedy, and therefore, the only treatment meted out to them was ostracizing them to asylums for the insane. In these asylums the inmates were often put in cages treated worse than cattle, were given limited food, with lack of proper sanitation and hygiene.

The nineteenth century witnessed growing interests in the medical fraternity pertaining to illnesses of the mind. Since there was sparse existent research on this area, doctors who indulged in such research resorted to experiments of their own.[74] One such experiment was that of the *"rotary chair"* where the patient was made to sit in a chair which was spun at great speed with an attempt to *"reset the brain."*[75]

Mere expression of anger or unhappiness by a woman was equated with madness and any conduct by a woman which fell outside the set notions of the society were perceived as hysteria.[76] The milder forms of treatment included abstaining from socializing, eating of bland food, abstaining from reading/writing

---

Ritgerð, Et. al., *Women and Madness in the 19th Century –the effects of oppression on women's mental health* (2013), Available at https://skemman.is/bitstream/1946/16449/1/BA-ElisabetRakelSigurdar.pdf (Last visited on April 5, 2017)

[73] The History of Women's Mental Illness, Available at http://www.epigee.org/the-history-of-womens-mental-illness.html (Last visited on April 5, 2017)

[74] SHOWALTER, E. THE FEMALE MALADY: WOMEN, MADNESS, AND ENGLISH CULTURE 1830-1980 (1985)

[75] The History of Women's Mental Illness, Available at http://www.epigee.org/the-history-of-womens-mental-illness.html

[76] See CHARLOTTE PERKINS GILLMAN, THE YELLOW WALLPAPER (1892); See also EHRENREICH AND DEIRDE ENGLISH, FOR HER OWN GOOD: TWO CENTURIES OF THE EXPERTS ADVICE TO WOMEN (2005)

and solitary confinement.[77] Sending her to an asylum (public/private) or mad house was considered the ultimate remedy and the treatment meted out to her there was animal-like.[78] By the mid-nineties mental disorders linked to pregnancy and child-birth accounted for over ten percent admissions of women in asylums.[79]The medical fraternity associated a woman's mental setup pertaining to her reproductive cycles of puberty, pregnancy, childbirth and menopause to her nervous condition.[80] The term associated with the same was that of the *"wondering womb"*, which lead to such conditions.[81]

Reasons for mental illness and treatment for mental illness were very different and were backed by completely different reasoning for men and women respectively.[82] Hysteria was linked to intellectual women.[83] Women were made to abstain from socializing, reading and writing and shoved into being limited to the *"passive housewife role."[84]* Anorexia loomed in as an attempt by women to fit into standards of an ideal beauty in the society, a trophy to be exhibited by the husbands. Nymphomania was labeled on women feared to be aggressive. Women who showed strong beliefs, desires or inclinations, were thus put into asylums, to set example for the other women to keep away from toeing their footsteps. Spinsters and lesbians were also generally labelled as insane because such women were considered as a threat to the patriarchal societal

---

[77] GAIL A. HORNSTEIN , AGNES'S JACKET: A PSYCHOLOGIST'S SEARCH FOR THE MEANINGS OF MADNESS (2009)
[78]*See* BRUCE M. Z. COHEN, PSYCHIATRIC HEGEMONY: A MARXIST THEORY OF MENTAL ILLNESS (2016)
[79] Hilary Marland, *Women and Madness,* Available at https://warwick.ac.uk/fac/arts/history/chm/outreach/trade_in_lunacy/research/womenandmadne ss/ (Last visited on January 5, 2017)
[80] The Treatment of Women for Mental Illness 1850-1900, Available at https://gver2013.wordpress.com/ (Last visited on January 5, 2017)
[81] Katie L. Frick, *Women's Issues then and now- A Feminist Overview of the Past two centuries,* Available at http://batstar.net/item/ulrichmi.htm (Last visited on December 10, 2017)
[82] The Treatment of Women for Mental Illness 1850-1900, Available at https://gver2013.wordpress.com/ (Last visited on January 5, 2017)
[83] Katie L. Frick, *Women's Issues then and now- A Feminist Overview of the Past two centuries,* Available at http://batstar.net/item/ulrichmi.htm (Last visited on December 10, 2017)
[84] *Id.*

set-up.[85]Treatment meted out to women in asylums included *"pouring water on the head, compressing the supraorbital nerve, stopping the patient's breathing, slapping the face and neck with wet towels and exercising pressure in some tender area."[86]*

2. WHY TALK ABOUT THE MENTAL HEALTH OF WOMEN?[87]

Asking *"the woman question"[88]* is many a time not encouraged. Objections are often raised pertaining to the same on the ground that men are equally vulnerable and their rights need to be protected too.[89] However, when one observes the socio-political setup of India, there is a hue of disparity in rights, privileges and vulnerabilities of men and women in every sphere and walk of life.[90]

Similarly asked is the question of *"Why talk of women mental health?"[91]*Some psychiatrists object to talking about mental health of women in particular on the ground that when we are not talking about mental health of men, why treat the women differently. The Indian Psychiatric Society which was formed as early as

---

[85] *Id.*

[86] The Treatment of Women for Mental Illness 1850-1900, Available at https://gver2013.wordpress.com/ (Last visited on January 5, 2017)

[87] Indira Sharma and Abhishek Pathak, *Women Mental Health in India,* Indian J Psychiatry57(Suppl 2) S201–S204 (2015), Available at https://www.ncbi.nlm.nih.gov/pmc/articles/PMC4539862/ (Last visited on October 29, 2017); Savita Malhotra and Ruchita Shah, *Women and Mental Health in India: An overview,* Indian J Psychiatry 57(Suppl 2): S205–S211 (2015), Available at https://www.ncbi.nlm.nih.gov/pmc/articles/PMC4539863/ (Last visited on October 29, 2017)

[88]*Women Questions"* can be defined as questions *"designed to identify the gender implications of rules and practices which might otherwise appear to be neutral and objective,"* and would include questions like, *"have the women been left out of consideration? If so, in what way; how might that omission be corrected? What difference would it make to do so?"* -Katherine T. Barlett, *Feminist Legal Methods,* 103 (4) Harvard Law Review 829 (1990)

[89] *See* SHARLENE NAGY HESSE-BIBER, HANDBOOK OF FEMINIST RESEARCH, THEORY AND PRAXIS (2012)

[90] *See* SALLY SHELDON AND MICHAEL THOMSON, FEMINIST PERSPECTIVES ON HEALTH CARE LAW (1998)

[91]Indira Sharma and Abhishek Pathak, *Women Mental Health in India,* Indian J Psychiatry57(Suppl 2) S201–S204 (2015), Available at https://www.ncbi.nlm.nih.gov/pmc/articles/PMC4539862/ (Last visited on October 29, 2017)

in 1947 brought out its first paper with a special focus on women's health only in the year 1969.[92] Critics state that in the wake of gender equality and equal rights of women, considering them more vulnerable is questionable. In reply to this criticism it can be argued that the Constitution of India, despite providing for the right to equality and the right to equal protection of law under Article 15 provides for positive discrimination in the favor of women, wherein a law can make discrimination in the favor of women to protect their interest in the society.

One has to understand the present discourse in the lights of the societal setup of the country. The WHO Checklist on Mental Health Legislation (Annexure 1 to WHO Resource Book on Mental Health, Human Rights and Legislation, 2005)[93] in its checklists for a mental health legislation enumerates women with mental illness as part of the vulnerable section of persons with mental illness.

The World Health Report, 1998 states that *"Women's health is inextricably linked to their status in society. It benefits from equality, and suffers from discrimination."*[94] Despite being financially independent, many a woman in the Indian household is looked down upon and ridiculed. The dowry system in various hues and colours is still prevalent in the nation. Joint family system, preference of the male child, status of the daughter-in-law at her marital home, marriage being sacrosanct and preferably permanent, are among the many factors that are responsible for the scenario. Some of the important roles of an Indian woman are child-bearing, child rearing and taking care of the matrimonial household. Women who are unable to get accustomed to this family setup and find it difficult to cope, become victims of depression and other forms of mental illness over time.

---

[92] D Bhattacharya, J.N. Vyas, *Puerperal psychosis*, Indian J Psychiatry 11:36–9 (1969)
[93] Available at
https://ec.europa.eu/health/sites/health/files/mental_health/docs/who_resource_book_en.pdf
(Last visited on April 5, 2018)
[94] Available at http://www.who.int/whr/1998/en/whr98_en.pdf (Last visited on March 15, 2017)

Crimes against women, including sexual assault, rape, marital rape, domestic violence are on a rise in the nation.[95] Being bereft of their dignity and self-esteem, such women find it difficult to recoup from the trauma and slip into the abyss of post-traumatic stress disorder (PTSD).[96]Common outcomes of violence are not only PTSD, but also suicidal behaviour, depression and anxiety.[97]

The provisions of WHO's Ottawa Charter for Health Promotion (1986)[98] recognizes the multi-dimensional scenario of healthcare in the following words:

> *"To reach a state of complete physical, mental and social well-being, an individual or group must be able to identify and to realize aspirations, to satisfy needs, and to change or cope with the environment. Health is, therefore, seen as a resource for everyday life, not the objective of living. Health is a positive concept*

---

[95]Rashida Manjoo, Report of the Special Rapporteur on violence against women, its causes and consequences, A/HRC/26/38/Add.1 (2014), Available at http://evaw-global-database.unwomen.org/-/media/files/un%20women/vaw/country%20report/asia/india/india%20srvaw.pdf (Last visited on January 5, 2018)

[96] See WHO, *Women's Mental Health: An Evidence Based Review* (2000), Available at http://apps.who.int/iris/bitstream/handle/10665/66539/WHO_MSD_MDP_00.1.pdf;jsessionid=DC96E59F98CE54D041B6BF0E0C04D4D8?sequence=1 (Last visited on January 5, 2018); See ES DeJonghe. Et.al., *Women survivors of intimate partner violence and post-traumatic stress disorder: Prediction and prevention*, J Postgrad Med October Vol 54 Issue 4 (2008), Available at http://www.bioline.org.br/pdf?jp08102 (Last visited on January 5, 2018); See Su-Ying Chung, Et.al., *Emotional Memory and Posttraumatic Stress Disorder: A Preliminary Neuropsychological Study in Female Victims of Domestic Violence,* J Psychiatry 17:6 (2014), Available at https://www.omicsonline.org/open-access/emotional_memory_and_posttraumatic_stress_disorder_a_preliminary_148.php?aid=32408 (Last visited on January 5, 2018)

[97] See WHO, *Women's Mental Health: An Evidence Based Review* (2000), Available at http://apps.who.int/iris/bitstream/handle/10665/66539/WHO_MSD_MDP_00.1.pdf;jsessionid=DC96E59F98CE54D041B6BF0E0C04D4D8?sequence=1 (Last visited on January 5, 2018)

[98] WHO's Ottawa Charter for Health Promotion (1986), Available at http://www.who.int/healthpromotion/conferences/previous/ottawa/en/ (Last visited on January 25, 2018)

emphasizing social and personal resources, as well as physical capacities."[99]

Common mental disorders like depression, anxiety and somatic symptom disorder (SSD)[100] are found more prevalent among women than in men in India. Authors have linked this scenario to the social set-up, including status of women in Indian families, patriarchy, self-esteem issues of women, gender roles of women, discrimination at workplace and violence meted out to women at various set-ups.[101]

Generally, whenever mental health of women is brought up, many of us relate it to the mental health issues that women face because of their reproductive role. Postpartum depression (PPD)[102] is a major form of mental illness among middle-aged women, but the discourse of mental health issues of women cannot be merely limited to only that. The relation between reproductive functions of women and their mental health has been receiving more attention, while the other areas, aspects and perspectives of mental healthcare of women remain comparatively ignored.[103]

---

[99] *Id.*

[100] Somatic symptom disorder (SSD) involves a person feeling extreme levels of anxiety about some physical symptoms like pain, fatigue, etc. The person has disturbing thoughts, behaviors and feelings related to the pain, fatigue, etc. which negatively affects his/her normal daily life. Available at https://medlineplus.gov/ency/article/000955.htm (Last visited on January 5, 2018)

[101] *See* WHO, *Women's Mental Health: An Evidence Based Review* (2000), Available at http://apps.who.int/iris/bitstream/handle/10665/66539/WHO_MSD_MDP_00.1.pdf;jsessionid=D C96E59F98CE54D041B6BF0E0C04D4D8?sequence=1 (Last visited on January 5, 2018)

[102] Postpartum depression (PPD) is a mental illness associated with mood disorders related to childbirth and include symptoms ranging from extreme sadness, low energy, anxiety, sleep disorder to eating disorder, etc. PPD generally sets in such women between one week and one month of childbirth.

[103] WHO, Department of Mental Health and Substance Abuse, *Gender Disparities in Mental Health,* Available at http://www.who.int/mental_health/media/en/242.pdf?ua=1 (Last visited on April 4, 2018)

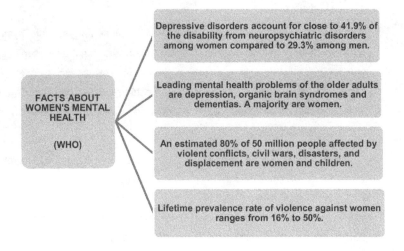

FACTS ABOUT WOMEN'S MENTAL HEALTH

(WHO)

Depressive disorders account for close to 41.9% of the disability from neuropsychiatric disorders among women compared to 29.3% among men.

Leading mental health problems of the older adults are depression, organic brain syndromes and dementias. A majority are women.

An estimated 80% of 50 million people affected by violent conflicts, civil wars, disasters, and displacement are women and children.

Lifetime prevalence rate of violence against women ranges from 16% to 50%.

Table (2): WHO, Facts about Women's Mental Health[104]

---

[104] WHO, Gender and Women's Mental Health, Available at
http://www.who.int/mental_health/prevention/genderwomen/en/ (Last visited on March 5, 2018)

3. HUMAN RIGHTS WATCH REPORT (2014)[105] –DRAWING A PICTURE OF VIOLENCE AGAINST AND ABUSE OF WOMEN IN MENTAL HOSPITALS AND OTHER INSTITUTIONS

Published in 2014, the Report by Human Rights Watch, titled, *"'Treated Worse than Animals': Abuses against Women and Girls with Psychosocial or Intellectual Disabilities in Institutions in India,"[106]* is very vital and relevant to understand why there is a need to delve into mental healthcare from the perspective of women with mental illness. This report highlighted the ugly side of mental healthcare for women in India, the side which was replete with examples of human rights violations, abuse, exploitation and the absence of informed consent.

From 2012 to 2014 HRW team visited twenty-four mental hospitals (public and private) and state facilities for residential care. Around two hundred persons were interviewed, including fifty-two women/girls were interviewed who had *"psychological or intellectual disabilities"* who were or had been in mental healthcare institutions. Also interviewed were families of some of these women, professionals of mental healthcare, service providers, police officers and some government officials. This Report focused on issues, including involuntary/forced admissions to mental health establishments; overcrowding in such institutions, leading to lack of access to general healthcare, inadequate hygiene, improper sanitation and inappropriate clothing facilities, etc.; forced treatment which included electro-convulsive therapy; abuse and violence, both physical and sexual. The Report also threw light on the inability of women to get proper access to justice, legal redressal mechanisms, government services and support.

---

[105] HRW, *Treated Worse than Animals- Abuses against Women and Girls with Psychological and Intellectual Disabilities in Institutions in India* (2014), Available at
https://www.hrw.org/report/2014/12/03/treated-worse-animals/abuses-against-women-and-girls-psychosocial-or-intellectual (Last visited on April 5, 2018)
[106] *Id.*

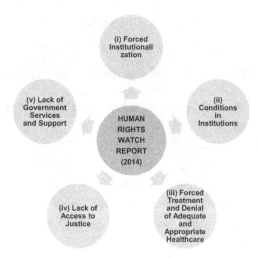

Table (3): Factors discussed in HRW Report (2014)[107]

Drawing a causal relation to the above factors, HRW Report (2014) observed that the stigma surrounding mental illness, shortage of community services, and lack of proper awareness among the family members of the patients were the main causes leading towards forced institutionalization of women with mental illness. According to the HRW Report, the common notion in the society pertaining to persons with mental illness, especially women is that such women lack the capacity to comprehend and are therefore not capable of taking any logical and reasoned decision for their own welfare.

Twenty-five cases were found where the family members of the women with mental illness had either hidden or abandoned them in mental hospitals or residential facilities; the reason for the same mainly being, stigma surrounding mental illness and the lack of support and understanding from the society pertaining to the situation.

---

[107] *Id.*

HRW Report (2014) summarizes some of the following deplorable conditions meted out to the women in some of the mental health establishments visited by its team:

- Prolonged detention;
- Involuntary treatment;
- Sexual abuse;
- Physical abuse;

- Over-crowding;
- Lack of proper sanitation;
- Lack of privacy;
- Forceful treatment without choice, etc.

HRW Team also reported usage of derogatory language for women with mental illness in such institutions including terms like *"pagal"* (Hindi for *'mad'*) or *"mentally retarded"* for them. This was proof enough of the reinforcement of the stigma and derogation towards such women in the Indian society.

In the background of the above report, it becomes quite pertinent that *"asking the woman question"* pertaining to mental healthcare is the need of the hour, especially in the wake of the passing of the 2017 Act. HRW Report (2014) was instrumental in NCW and NIMHANS, India to take cognizance of the issue, which culminated in the Report (2016) by them on *"Addressing concerns of women admitted to psychiatric institutions in India: An in-depth analysis"*[108] which is analysed in the forthcoming Chapter.

---

[108] NCW and NIMHANS Report (2016)

IV. CRITICAL ANALYSIS OF THE REPORT BY NCW AND NIMHANS 2016 ON "ADDRESSING CONCERNS OF WOMEN ADMITTED TO PSYCHIATRIC INSTITUTIONS IN INDIA: AN IN-DEPTH ANALYSIS"

After having addressed the question of "Why ask the Women Question?" in Chapter III which inter-alia also discussed the facts about women's mental health published by WHO and analysed HRW Report (2014), this Chapter continues in the same light. This Chapter analyses the Report by the National Commission for Women, India and the National Institute of Mental Health and Neurosciences, India published in 2016, titled: "Addressing concerns of women admitted to psychiatric institutions in India: An in-depth analysis". In the process of analysis, a summary of the vital findings in the report is also drawn.

1. SCOPE OF THE REPORT

NCW and NIMHANS treaded the path of research on women admitted in psychiatric institutions in India by visiting ten psychiatric institutions in the country and published a Report in 2016 with respect to the same.[109] The research involved visit by the NIMHANS and NCW teams to ten mental hospitals, chosen on the basis of higher number of long-stay patients, namely:

- Regional Mental Hospital (RMH), Yerwada, Pune
- Government Mental Health Centre (GHMC), Kozhikode, Kerala
- Regional Mental Hospital (RMH), Thane, Maharashtra
- Institute of Psychiatry and Human Behaviour, Bambolim, Goa
- Calcutta Pavlov Hospital
- Behrampore Mental Hospital, Murshidabad
- Ranchi Institute of Neuro-Psychiatry and Allied Sciences (RINPAS), Jharkhand
- Institute of Mental Health and Hospital (IMHH), Agra
- Mental Hospital, Bareilly
- Institute of Mental Health (Government Mental Hospital), Amritsar, Punjab

This study was initiated in the background of the HRW Report (2014) which only focused on abuses meted out to women in mental hospitals and women's homes. The NIMHANS and NCW Teams wanted to find out the other side of the story too, the side of the caretakers and health care providers along with women with mental illness in such institutions and thereby analyse the generalization portrayed by HRW Report (2014). The research was women-centric and limited to their status in the institutions.

Mrs. Lalitha Kumarmangalam, the erstwhile Chairperson of NCW in the foreword to the Report published in 2016 states that:

---

[109]NCW and NIMHANS, *Addressing concerns of women admitted to psychiatric institutions in India: An in-depth analysis* (2016) Available at http://ncw.nic.in/pdfreports/addressing_concerns_of_women_admitted_to_psychiatric_institution s_in_india_an_in-depth_analysis.pdf (Last visited on October 10, 2017)

"Mentally ill women, experience social and economic marginalization which is exacerbated not only due to gender inequity and inequality but also stigma and insensitivity surrounding mental illness in India."

This Chapter analyses the NCW and NIMHANS Report (2016). In the process of analysis, a summary of the vital findings in the report is also drawn. The Report analyses the following factors that affect or are likely to affect women with mental illness in the psychiatric institutions, namely:

- Clinical factors;
- Social factors;
- Cultural factors;
- Familial factors;
- Economic factors; and
- Legal factors.

2. ANALYSIS OF THE DATA COLLECTED IN THE TEN HOSPITALS BY THE NCW AND NIMHANS TEAMS

The visiting teams from NCW and NIMHANS to the ten psychiatric institutions, collected data pertaining to **female patients** in each of these institutions with respect to the following matters in particular:

- Facilities like food, clothing, environment, personal care, etc;
- Circumstances of admissions to the institutions;
- Issues pertaining to treatment;
- Consent to treatment;
- Participation and involvement in treatment;
- Involvement of family care givers;
- Addressing of the concerns and needs specific to women;
- Rehabilitation; and
- Rights within the community.

The data was collected by a coordinate combination of the following three methods, that are:

- Observations by the NCW/NIMHANS teams that visited each institution respectively;
- Interviews with the following group of persons in each of these institutions, namely:
  - o Women patients;
  - o Family care-givers;
  - o Service providers and
  - o Administrators
- Questionnaire based self-reports from these institutions

i. Regional Mental Hospital (RMH), Yerwada, Pune

RMH, Pune celebrated the centenary of its foundation in 2005. It was established in Colaba in 1907 and was later shifted to Yerwada, Pune in 1915. The bed strength of this hospital presently is 2540.The NCW and NIMHANS team reported multiple deficiencies in mental and physical healthcare in RMH, Pune.

Some of the important observations by the NCW and NIMHANS team that visited RMH, Pune are enumerated herein below:

- Shortage of staff and not sufficient training of staff;
- Lack of enough financial resources;
- Scarcity of rehabilitation facilities and options;
- Presence of insects and mosquitoes in the living areas;
- Lack of emergency healthcare, both physical and mental;
- Lack of privacy, when the patients conversed with family members or commuted through letters, the same were heard and read;
- Almost two-third patients had not given informed consent for treatment and were not apprised of their rights pertaining to healthcare;
- Closed wards with inadequate lighting and ventilation;

- Overcrowding of wards and shortage of mattresses and beds;
- Water for bathing and washing clothes was inadequate and no hot water facilities were provided for the same;
- Patients were compulsorily made to wear uniforms of the hospital, some of those uniforms being torn and dirty;
- Lack of privacy during bathing;
- Patients were provided with sanitary napkins during their periods but many of them did not know how to use them;
- Medical rounds were not very frequent;
- Sufficient space for spiritual and religious purposes was given to the patients;
- Rehabilitation rates were very low;
- Wrong addresses had been provided by family members of some patients, thereby resulting in many patients being long term patients with a future of perpetual stay at the hospital.

The hospital team requested for prompt action by the government to address their needs and requirements. They were in favour of facilitating autonomy of the patients in healthcare decision making to ensure welfare in healthcare.

ii. Government Mental Health Centre (GHMC), Kozhikode, Kerala

GHMC, Kerala was established in Kozhikode in 1872, originally with nine beds as a lunatic asylum. Presently GHMC houses 700 beds. The Hospital was reviewed by the Director General of Health Services in the year 2004, which had recommended renovation or change of hospital buildings, increasing of staff and working towards a more effective rehabilitation process. The NHRC Report of 2008 on GHMC, reported a slight enhancement in the budget of the hospital resulting in new constructions, including an open ward, a new canteen, new medical record section, etc. However, over-crowding still continued to be a concern in GHMC.[110]

Some of the pertinent observations by the NCW and NIMHANS team that visited GHMC are enumerated herein below:

- Over-crowding in wards;
- Few women were found in lock-ups and some were found moving about naked;
- Unwanted visitors from schools just for tour were a common practice;
- Poor hygiene in toilets, bathing areas and dining space;
- Some bathroom doors were partially broken, therefore affecting privacy of the patients during bathing and changing of clothes;
- Bedbugs and mosquitoes in wards and sometimes pillows were not given to some patients;
- Healthcare needs of bedridden patients were not properly addressed;
- Funds to the Hospital arrive from the State budget, and regular delay in arriving of funds, leads to delay in payment of electricity and water bills, resulting in administrative hitches;
- Two patients reported sexual advances by the male members of the staff;
- Instead of sanitary napkins, cloth was given during periods;
- Open female ward, was where patients were admitted with a family member, and this ward witnessed regular discharge of the patients post treatment;
- Support from families of the patients admitted for long-term was almost absent;

---

[110] *See* NHRC, CARE AND TREATMENT IN MENTAL HEALTH INSTITUTIONS- SOME GLIMPSES IN THE RECENT PERIOD (2012), Available at
http://nhrc.nic.in/Documents/Publications/Care_and_Mental_Health_2012.pdf (Last visited on May 30, 2017)

- Most of the patients were admitted to the hospital through reception orders and their family members were not traceable, thereby leaving very little scope for rehabilitation and reconciliation with their families;
- No access to newspapers or magazines;
- Majority patients, however, reported being treated with respect and dignity;
- Paucity of female attenders, female care givers and female security staff is another vital concern in GHMC.

One of the most important recommendations of the visiting NCW and NIMHANS team was that the hospital should work towards better non-psychiatric medical care of its patients; and rehabilitating them into the society. Positive work of the hospital staff and authorities along with increase in beds in proportion to the patient intake were also recommended as vital for the betterment of the conditions in GHMC.

iii.   Regional Mental Hospital (RMH), Thane, Maharashtra

RMH, Thane was established in the year 1901. It was the hospital with the largest bed strength of 1880 in the year 1998. Presently the hospital houses around 750 female patients divided into separate clinic units. There are separate wards for the following, respectively:

- Acutely ill female patients;
- Female patients who have stabilized a bit;
- Women with intellectual disabilities and epilepsy; and
- Long-stay female patients.

The NCW and NIMHANS team reported one of the major concerns at RMH being that of insufficient financial resources and shortage of human resources. Patients were either dumped in the hospitals or were picked from the streets in a chronically ill state wherein the mental illness had long set in.

Some of the important observations by the NCW and NIMHANS team are enumerated herein below:

- Female wards were old with leaking ceilings and poor ventilation;
- Over-crowding in the wards, with around 60 patients in a small ward;
- One toilet each is shared by 50 female patients;
- Gross inadequacy in hygiene facilities is a major concern;
- Chronic wards are in better condition, with proper lighting and ventilation;
- Kitchens were clean and some patients had been identified as *helpers* in the kitchens;
- As a result of limited water supply, the female patients had no privacy while bathing, using the toilet or changing clothes;
- The government has provided petticot-kurta as the uniform for the female patients, which were not only found to be uncomfortable by some patients, but were also not available in all sizes, thereby causing discomfort to the patients;
- Only less than half the number of female patients were provided with footwear, the rest moved about bare feet;
- Most of the patients were not permitted to keep personal possessions or have access to telephones;
- There is a sick room for women with physical illness, with basic facilities for healthcare including oxygen facilities;
- Electro-compulsive therapy is available with a full time anesthetist in the hospital.

It was observed by the NCW and NIMHANS team that the dilapidated and unhygienic conditions in the Hospital had made it a breeding ground for multiple illnesses. Leakage during rainfall, makes most of the wards damp and therefore, inhabitable during the rainy season. Neptune[111] and Tarasha[112] are

---

[111] Neptune Foundation, Available at http://www.neptunefoundation.in/ (Last visited on May 5, 2017)

[112] Tarasha, Available at http://www.tiss.edu/view/11/projects/all-projects/tarasha/ (Last visited on May 5, 2017)

two NGOs that have been working in active coordination with RMH, Thane, and have helped in reuniting some female patients to their family members. Tarasha, a TISS project, aided in providing vocational training to the patients and have helped them in getting jobs.

iv.   Institute of Psychiatry and Human Behaviour (IPHP), Bambolim, Goa

The Institute of Psychiatry and Human Behaviour (IPHP) is a relatively smaller hospital with 300 beds set up in 2001 under the Goa Medical College.

Some of the important observations by the NCW and NIMHANS team are enumerated herein below:

- Existence of separate children's ward, peri-natal ward and de-addiction ward;
- Disorganized inpatient wards without separate areas for dining, recreational activity or exercise;
- Forensic ward of both males and females is located inside the female closed ward which causes discomfort to the patients because of regular presence of police escorts, male prison patients, etc;
- The out-patient department is over-crowded;
- There is a small occupational therapy unit accessible to only some inpatients;
- Two-third of the patients interviewed complained of violation of confidentiality and not being provided with information relating to their treatment.

The NCW and NIMHANS team observed that there was a need to fill up vacant posts at IPHP for the proper administration of the institution. The team also recommended the improvement in the open ward facilities, taking of steps to ensure the setting up of community rehabilitation facilities and long-stay facilities for the patient.

v.   Calcutta Pavlov Hospital, Kolkata, West Bengal

The Calcutta Pavlov Hospital was set up in the year 1966. It is managed by the Government of West Bengal and has the active involvement of the National Medical Hospital. There are a total of 270 female patients who are kept in a three-storeyed living with some space around it. The building is locked.

Some of the important observations by the NCW and NIMHANS team are enumerated herein below:

- Existence of proportionately large number of out-of-state patients from Uttar Pradesh and Bihar and from remote villages of West Bengal;
- Most of the admissions to the hospital were involuntary;
- Mosquitoes and pests because of poor drainage system;
- No dining space;
- Hair of inmates is cut short for convenience, but their consent is obtained for the same, a barber visits every weeks to cut their hair short;
- Existence of bed bugs was reported by some patients;
- Sanitary napkins provided were inadequate and patients reported that they had to share undergarments with other female patients;
- Involvement of clinical psychologists, but there were no psychiatric social workers;
- Increased focus on medical management, however, staff-patient ratio is low making intensive management difficult;
- ECT is rarely used on patients;
- Lack of lockers to keep personal belongings, and no place to wash and dry clothes, thereby making personal hygiene a major concern;
- Some patients reported being threatened, beaten up and being verbally abused by the staff members;

The NCW and NIMHANS team observed that most of the female patients in the Hospital were chronic and were very less likely to be taken back into the families, thereby making discharge a concern. The team praised the active involvement of two NGOs, namely, Anjali[113] and Paripurnita[114] for facilitating involvement of the female patients into productive work.

vi.   Behrampore Mental Hospital, Murshidabad, West Bengal

The Behrampore Mental Hospital is the only hospital in India with more beds for female patients than male patients.[115] The Hospital was initially a jail and was later converted into a mental hospital in the year 1980. The NHRC Report of 1999 had observed that the conditions in this hospital were deplorable and poor and the 2008 Report noted that there had been very less improvement in the conditions and facilities since 1999.

The NCW and NIMHANS team found that the admissions in the Behrampore Mental Hospital were predominantly involuntary. Some of the important observations by the NCW and NIMHANS team are enumerated herein below:

- Community bathing for patients being a blatant violation of the right to privacy, most patients were bathed together in the corridor in front of the taps;
- Patients were not provided with undergarments;
- There is irregular supply of sanitary napkins and no instructions are given to the patients regarding the disposal of the napkins (used sanitary napkins were found randomly lying on the corridor floors);
- There is very little opportunity for the patients to interact with the treating team, the doctors were seen to mainly rely on the nurses' report for treating the patients;
- Most of the mental health faculty members were found to be involved in private practice outside the hospital;
- There have been incidents of patient abuse by the members of the staff;

---

[113] *See* more at http://www.anjalimentalhealth.org/ (Last visited on January 2, 2018)
[114] The researcher had the opportunity to visit both Anjali and Paripurnita in Kolkata; details of the interview and the data collected is enumerated in Chapter XII of the research.
[115] 116 beds for female patients and 114 beds for male patients.

- Medication and treatment facilities are adequate and up to date;
- There is a small rehabilitation unit, which however, does not suffice the purpose of rehabilitation for all the patients;
- Inadequate number of toilets, some patients even defecate in the corridors which are not very regularly cleaned;
- Linen is not cleaned regularly and there is no locker facilities to keep personal belongings;
- Sleeping space is inadequate and patients are huddled close to each other on the floor to sleep;
- The space surrounding the building housing the female ward is unclean, thereby raising the possibility of health risks to the women patients;
- Window panes are broken and kitchen space is dirty and not at all well kept;
- Verbal abuse of patients have been reported and also instances of physical fights among patients;

In one of its observations in the report, the NCW and NIMHANS team states that *"the overall condition of the mental hospital is terrible…and continues to have gross inadequacies and gross violation of human rights."* The team reported the involvement of the NGO Anjali which engaged 20 women from the female ward, in certain social and recreational activities. The NGO has been allotted two rooms in the OPD of the Hospital for the purpose. The team strongly recommended the imminent need for the hospital to cater to issues pertaining to cleanliness, disposal of sewage and sanitation; and that the hospital kitchen should be relocated to a cleaner place. It is to be noted that privacy of female patients emerges as one of the primary areas of concern in this institution.

vii. Ranchi Institute of Neuro-Psychiatry and Allied Sciences (RINPAS), Jharkhand

The Ranchi Institute of Neuro-Psychiatry and Allied Sciences (RINPAS), Jharkhand has a bed strength of 600 out of which 200 beds are for female patients with mental illness. Almost 60% of the female patients are long stay patients who have been in the hospital for around 10 years. There is a full-fledged half-way home built in the hospital with a strength of 100 beds (50 for male patients and 50 for female patients) but the same was not found functional because of lack of sufficient human resources.

Some of the important observations by the NCW and NIMHANS team are enumerated herein below:

- 85% of the long-stay female patients were admitted into the hospital by reception orders and only 15% had been admitted to the hospital by their relatives;
- Shortage of staff, last recruitment having made in the year 2004;
- The psychiatrist-bed ratio is 1:100, and the nurse-bed ratio is 1:80;
- The buildings are very old, dating to over 80 years ago and the building structure is very jail-like;
- Majority of the patients rated the following facilities in the hospital as good:
  - Food and dining facilities;
  - Personal hygiene;
  - Comfort;
  - Sleeping facilities;
  - Resting facilities;
  - Medication facilities; and
  - Treatment facilities.
- Patients are bathed in groups;
- Toilets are located in the outside, the patients complain of difficulty in going out in the night;

- Patients did not report incidents of abuse at the hospital;
- Most patients were not in contact with the members of their families.

Despite the human resources crunch, the team was of the opinion that the hospital staff was dedicated and was providing quality care to the best of their abilities. The NCW and NIMHANS team recommended collaboration with NGOs for rehabilitation of patients by encouraging the NGOs to set up sheltered workshops, homes and day care centers in the community for female patients with mental illness so that they can gradually be reintegrated into the society. The report emphasized upon the need to track the family members of the patients with the help of the police in order to reunite them with their family.

viii.   Institute of Mental Health and Hospital (IMHH), Agra

The hospital was started as an asylum way back in the year 1859. In 1995 it was declared autonomous and a State-owned hospital. It renamed the Institute of Mental Health and Hospital (IMHH), Agra in the year 2001.The hospital is spread across a vast area of 170 acres. There are a total of 10 wards with each ward having 30 patients. Some patients are also admitted in the family wards where family members accompany the patient during the treatment and take them back home on improvement.

The admissions in the hospital are mostly involuntary in nature. Admissions in the hospital are through one of the following ways:

- Through reception orders by the Chief Judicial Magistrate;
- Through Protection Homes for Women in the State of UP;
- Through family members;
- Local residents, social workers and NGOs also bring patients for admission in the hospital.

Some of the important observations by the NCW and NIMHANS team are enumerated herein below:

- Poor privacy while bathing, 2-3 patients bathe together at a time;

- Staff members arrange group activities and cultural events for the patients on a regular basis;
- Majority of the patients rated the following facilities in the hospital as good:
  - Food and dining facilities;
  - Personal hygiene;
  - Comfort;
  - Sleeping facilities;
  - Resting facilities;
  - Medication facilities; and
  - Treatment facilities.
- Patients did not report physical, verbal or sexual abuse;
- Hospital uniforms are compulsory;
- Social and religious requirements are reasonably catered to;

The major concern of the female patients was the desire to return home. The NCW and NIMHANS team recommended in its report the need to involve NGOs and setting up of half-way homes so that the cured patients could be reintegrated into the society.

ix.   Mental Hospital, Bareilly

The Mental Hospital of Bareily was established as an asylum in the year 1862. The architecture of the Hospital is jail-like. It was rated very poorly by the NHRC Report of 1999. However, there have been considerable improvements since then.

Some of the important observations by the NCW and NIMHANS team are enumerated herein below:

- Majority of the patients rated the treatment and other facilities in the hospital as satisfactory;
- Patients expressed concern about the cleanliness of the drinking water;

- Patients have to wear hospital uniforms, but are not provided undergarments;
- Some patients complained of being verbally abused by the staff and 16% reported of having been beaten;
- Patients' hair are cut short without their consent;
- Lack of human resources;
- Doctors do not see the patients on a regular basis.

The hospital had a small recreational center. However, activities in the recreational center were very rare. Patients also reported that they were forced to work in wards and were verbally abused by the staff on refusing to do work.

x. Institute of Mental Health (Government Mental Hospital), Amritsar, Punjab

Government Mental Hospital, Amritsar was set up in the year 1948. It was later renamed as the Institute of Mental Health, Amritsar. In 2001, the administrative control of the hospital was given to the Punjab Health Systems Corporation. A new building with 450 beds was set up in 2003. The hospital spans over an area of 60 acres and is the only hospital that caters to the mental healthcare needs of the people of Punjab, Haryana and Chandigarh.

Some of the important observations by the NCW and NIMHANS team are enumerated herein below:

- The Hospital receives out-of-state patients also;
- There is shortage of staff;
- 90% of the patients in the hospital had been admitted through reception orders[116];
- All the patients were of the opinion that the basic facilities in the hospital were good;

---

[116] On being brought through reception orders, patients are initially admitted for a period of 89 days and are discharged on the 90th day. However, they then re-apply for reception orders.

- Cleanliness was a very positive feature of this hospital. Not only were the wards, kitchen and corridors clean, the floor and the beds of the patients were neat and tidy too;
- The patients were not satisfied with the physical, outdoor and cultural activities in the hospital;
- Family members do not want to take back the patients and want the hospital to take care of the patients for life;
- There are power-cuts for 8-10 hours continuously, therefore making the need for 24 hours supply of electricity a matter of immediate concern.

There are no half-way homes, long stay homes or NGOs working on this area in the city of Amritsar. There are *Nari Niketans* meant for juvenile offenders, where some women with mental illness find shelter, but the Niketans are not well-equipped to cater to the needs of the mentally ill women. The Hospital however, has close co-operation from the Pingalwaras. Pingalwaras is an NGO having around 3000 beds spread across the state of Punjab, gives shelter and care to orphans, destitute, old, poor, homeless, differently abled, abandoned persons, including persons with mental retardation and mental illness among others.[117]The mentally ill persons among them in Pingalwara are brought to the Hospital for mental healthcare and treatment.

---

[117]*See* more at http://pingalwara.org/ (Last visited on February 23, 2018)

3. SUMMARIZING THE FINDINGS OF THE REPORT:

This Report by NCW and NIMHANS holds great significance to the present study. It is the latest and most important secondary data on the situation of women with mental illness in Mental Hospitals/ Psychiatric Institutions in the country researched by two premiere institutions of the country. The Report acknowledges the vulnerability of women with mental illness in the country and concludes with very vital suggestions pivotal to remedying the existent situation. The ten hospitals visited by the NCW and NIMHANS team draw light on the practicalities and detailed conditions and situations in these hospitals. Treatment meted out to women is elaborately observed and succinctly summarized by the Report. Being a report, the research and study for which was spread over a span of a long time, and having been published as recently as in 2016, it was considered pivotal to authenticate the propositions of the present research.

V. HUMAN RIGHTS UNDER THE MENTAL HEALTH CARE ACT, 2017 —ANALYSING THE IMPLICATIONS ON RIGHTS OF WOMEN WITH MENTAL ILLNESS IN INDIA

The Mental Healthcare Act, 2017 aims to provide for mental health care and services for persons with mental illness in India and to protect, promote and fulfill the rights of such persons during delivery of mental health care and services. Chapter V of the Act enumerates the rights of persons with mental illness, including the right to equality, right to confidentiality, the right to protection from cruel, inhuman and degrading treatment in any mental health establishment (which includes the right to proper clothing so as to protect such person from exposure of his/her body to maintain his/her dignity, and the right to be protected from all forms of physical, verbal, emotional and sexual abuse), right to community living, etc. After having discussed the NCW and NIMHANS Report (2016) in Chapter IV, this Chapter treads towards the path of analysing the provisions of the Act from the perspective of rights of women with mental illness in need of mental health care. A comparison is also drawn with the relevant provisions of the United Nation Convention of Rights of Persons with Disabilities.

1. INTRODUCTION

The mention of women with mental illness is rarely made in the legal discussions pertaining to human rights. "Rights of women" and "rights of differently abled persons including persons with mental illness" are discussed time and again in the academic, legal and medical sector, but separately and in segregated contexts. There needs to be a confluence in these two arenas of discussions to address the predicament of the overtly marginalized sector in these two categories, that is, the women with mental illness.

In the Indian society which has a strong hue of patriarchy, women are a marginalized section. Women's rights activists are struggling to work for equal rights of women in various spheres of life. In this background, it is pertinent to note that the plight of women with mental illness is overtly vulnerable and much worse. Being unable to be fit mentally all the time, such women are more likely to be exploited, violated and deprived of their rights.

Sections 18 to 28 in Chapter V of the 2017 Act enumerate the various rights of persons with mental illness. These rights are a progressive and welcome change in the legal framework and are in adherence to the mandates of UNCRPD.

Being a very recent Act, the academic discourse analyzing its provisions is sparse and its influence and effect on the rights of women with mental illness has hardly found place in any legal discourse. This Chapter aims to analyse these Sections of the Act with respect to women with mental illness and bring out to the forefront the challenges which might come up in the actual enforcement of these rights. The Preamble of the 2017 Act states that the aim of the Act *inter alia* is:

> "to provide for mental health care and services for persons with mental illness and to protect, promote and fulfill the rights of such persons

during delivery of mental health care and services and for matters connected therewith or incidental thereto."

Rights of persons with mental illness during delivery of mental health care and services have found express mention for the first time in any enactment in India.[118] Chapter V of the Act enumerates these rights which are a penumbra of hope, reflected from the ultimate right of health. Following are the categories of rights of persons with mental illness recognized with respect to their mental health care under the Act:

1.	Section 18	Right to access mental healthcare
2.	Section 19	Right to community living
3.	Section 20	Right to protection from cruel, inhuman and degrading treatment
4.	Section 21	Right to equality and non-discrimination
5.	Section 22	Right to information
6.	Section 23	Right to confidentiality
7.	Section 24	Restriction on release of information in respect of mental illness
8.	Section 25	Right to access mental records
9.	Section 26	Right to personal contacts and communications
10	Section 27	Right to legal aid

---

[118] Right to health recognized as a part of the right to life guaranteed under Article 21 of the Constitution of India in Parmanand Katara v. Union of India, (1989) 4 SCC 286; Consumer Education and Research Centre v. Union of India, (1995) 3 SCC 42; Paschim Banga Khet Mazdoor Samity and Ors. v. State of West Bengal, (1996) 4 SCC37; Bandhua Mukti Morcha v. Union of India, AIR 1984 SC 802

11	Section 28	Right to make complaints about deficiencies in provision of services

2. ACCESS TO MENTAL HEALTHCARE

Union Health and Family Minister, Government of India, Mr. Jagat Prakash Nadda once stated in the Lok Sabha (in the year 2016) that almost 650-700 lakhs people in India are in need of care for various kinds of mental disorder, around 70-80% of whom do not receive adequate care and protection.[119]

Section 18 of the Act gives to every person the right to have access to mental health care and treatment from mental health services run or funded by the Appropriate Government[120]. It is to be noted that access to health care is pivotal for the exercise of all other rights in mental health care treatment. Impediments to access to health care range from multifarious factors like family, society, financial status, location, etc. Lack of awareness about mental health care, and the general tendency to ignore mental aberrations as mere temperamental issues also bar persons suffering from mental illness from getting access to mental health care. The adherence to traditional healing methods for mental illness leads to many persons with mental illness never getting access to mental health care. There is the need to read the provisions of Section 18 of the Act in the background of these existent dynamics in the Indian society.

---

[119] Report of the National Commission on Macroeconomics and Health, Ministry of Health and Family Welfare, Government of India (2005), Available at
http://www.who.int/macrohealth/action/Report%20of%20the%20National%20Commission.pdf
(Last visited on May 23, 2017)

[120] Appropriate Government means- *"(i) in relation to a mental health establishment established, owned or controlled by the Central Government or the Administrator of a Union territory having no legislature, the Central Government; (ii) in relation to a mental health establishment, other than an establishment referred to in sub-clause (i), established, owned or controlled within the territory of— (A) a State, the State Government; (B) a Union territory having legislature, the Government of that Union territory."* (The 2017 Act, Section 2(b))

The *"right to access mental healthcare and treatment"* for the purposes of the Act means *"mental health services"*:

- Available at costs that are affordable;
- Available in the required quantity and of good quality;
- Accessible territorially;

There should not be any discrimination on the basis of gender, sexual orientation, caste, culture, religion, political or social beliefs, disability, class or any other basis for that matter. The services should be available in such a manner that is acceptable and usable by the person with mental illness and the treatment should be such that the family members and care-givers of the person should be ready to acknowledge the same.

If these mandates are fulfilled, it is quite acceptable that access to mental health care treatment will be open and available to one and all. However, the present infrastructure and Government expenditure on this sector of health shows that the implementation process of these requirements has a long way ahead.

According to the Mental Health Atlas 2011 prepared by the Department of Mental Health and Substance Abuse of WHO, there are only forty-three state-run mental hospitals in India and 10,000 beds for psychiatric patients in the general hospitals.[121] Most states have only one or two mental hospitals located in remote areas; and the 72 percent population of India which is in the rural areas has access to only 25 percent of the locations where mental health care facilities are available.[122]

Proper implementation of the right to access mental healthcare can go a long way in enabling the persons with mental illness to a good life. Section 18 states *inter alia* that the *"right to access mental healthcare"* includes the right to have

---

[121] WHO, Department of Mental Health and Substance Abuse, *Mental Health Atlas 2011*, Available at http://www.who.int/mental_health/evidence/atlas/profiles/ind_mh_profile.pdf (Last visited on May 13, 2017)
[122] HRW Report (2014)

access to mental health care treatment without any prejudice of sex or sexual orientation.[123] Section 18 mandates the Appropriate Government to make sufficient provisions as maybe necessary for persons with mental illness, including making of the provisions of acute mental healthcare services, sheltered accommodation, half-way homes, supported accommodation, etc.[124]

Section 18(5) requires the Appropriate Government to integrate mental health services into general healthcare services at all strata of healthcare including secondary, primary and tertiary healthcare and in all health programmes run by it. The WHO Resource Book on Mental Health, Human Rights and Legislation (2005)[125]also recommends the integration of mental health services into primary health care and with other social services. However, one is made to worry if integrating mental healthcare into general health services may further hinder the patients from approaching mental healthcare, who could hesitate because of the stigma of being acknowledged or seen at the mental health section of a general hospital. The healthcare for mental illness is also specialized in its sphere and integrating the same into general health care would require sensitization of the general healthcare service providers.

The district of Thiruvananthapuram in Kerala, India is one such part of India where mental health care has been integrated in primary healthcare and where the doctors and other healthcare staff diagnose and treat mental disorders as a part of their primary healthcare treatment.[126] Iran is the only country which has had nationwide integration of mental health into primary care. Integrating is a process and is not a one-off event.[127]The role of mental health service

---

[123] The 2017 Act, Section 18(2)
[124] The 2017 Act, Sections 18(3) and 18(4)
[125] Available at
https://ec.europa.eu/health/sites/health/files/mental_health/docs/who_resource_book_en.pdf
(Last visited on April 5, 2018)
[126] WHO, *Integrating Mental Healthcare into Primary care- A Global Perspective*, Available at
http://apps.who.int/iris/bitstream/handle/10665/43935/9789241563680_eng.pdf;jsessionid=F53
A3969041545A222796166C952B382?sequence=1 (Last visited on January 5, 2018)
[127]*Id.*

coordinator in the general healthcare units would be vital in this process of integrating which would also incur the need to have more human and financial resources to cater to the process.[128] Ensuring the confidentiality and privacy of the patient is another thing which should be carefully catered to in such a situation.

WHO, in its report titled *"Integrating mental health into primary care –A global perspective"* published in 2008, highlights the importance of training both at the pre-service and/ or in-service level of primary care workers on mental health issues as an essential prerequisite.[129] The integration of mental health services into primary care is essential, but must be accompanied by complementary services having secondary care components to which primary care workers can turn for referrals and supervision.

It is relevant to quote excerpts from the HRW Report (2014) here:

> *"Rachna Bharadwaj, the superintendent of the female wing of Asha Kiran, a residential facility, told us about a girl with an intellectual and psychosocial disability who was sent to a mental hospital for treatment for a month and returned with a broken arm. Although the girl was in pain and could not move her arm, which was hanging limp on her side, staff in the mental hospital had not bothered to take her to a general hospital to treat her injury. In the end, the injury required two surgeries to mend... In another case, one woman came back to the institution after staying in a mental hospital for treatment with an ulcer on her foot that was infected with fat black worms that the mental hospital hadn't bothered to treat."[130]*

In the background of this existent scenario, integrating mental healthcare with general healthcare could be of great advantage; however, proper

---

[128] *Id.*
[129] *Id.*
[130] *Id.*

implementation of this integration process mandates the involvement of handsome funding and human resources.

3. EQUALITY

A study reported by the India Today in July, 2016 stated that one in four women in mental health asylums in India were abandoned by their family members.[131] Most of the family members refused to take them and many had given false addresses at the time of admission of the woman at the asylum.[132] The NCW and NIMHANS Report (2016) when referring to the Regional Mental Hospital (RMH), Yerwada, Pune, Maharashtra (one of the ten institutions visited by the multi-disciplinary team of NCW and NIMHANS) stated that 451 patients in the 1000 bed-capacity facility, were long-stay patients, some of whom said that they had been in RMH for decades together and no one in their family had come to see them during their stay.[133] In Regional Mental Hospital, Thane, Maharashtra, no efforts had been made to reunite the patients with their families after their recovery and many of them are thus, languishing in the Institution. In Calcutta Pavlov Hospital, West Bengal too, there were hardly any efforts made to contact family members of patients who had recovered, leading to many patients to stay in the institution perpetually.[134]

Section 19 of the Act recognizes the right of community living of persons with mental illness. It is stated that every person with mental illness shall:

- have a right to live in, be part of the society and to be not be segregated from it; and

---

[131] PTI, *One in four women in mental asylums abandoned by family,* India Today (July 18, 2016), Available at https://www.google.co.in/amp/m.indiatoday.in/lite/story/one-in-four-women-in-mental-asylums-abandoned-by-family/1/717710.html (Last visited on May 25, 2017)
[132] *Id.*
[133] *Id.*
[134] *Id.*

- not continue to remain in a mental health establishment just because he/she does not have a family or is not accepted by his/her family or is homeless or due to absence of community based facilities.

The Section further states that where it is not possible for a mentally ill person to live with his/her family or relatives, or where a mentally ill person has been abandoned by his/her family or relatives, the Appropriate Government shall provide appropriate support including legal aid and facilitate exercising his/her right to family home and living in the family home. For the same, the Appropriate Government is to support the setting up of less restrictive community based establishments including half-way homes, group homes, etc. for persons who no longer require treatment in restrictive mental health establishments.[135]

Community living is a process of rehabilitation of patients who have recovered from the mental illness, into the society. The same is possible only with close coordination with voluntary groups, NGOs and manpower on the part of Government. Special care needs to be taken to ensure that this process is enabling and reintegrating, and that the patients do not deteriorate at any point of time. Patients are generally at the final convalescent stage and therefore, community living facilities cannot be completely devoid of mental healthcare facilitators.

Section 21(1) states that in all provisions of healthcare, every person with mental illness has to be treated as equal to persons with physical illness irrespective of caste, gender, sex, sexual orientation, religion, etc. Section 21(4) states that medical insurance for treatment of patients with mental illness has to be made available, by health insurers, in the same manner as is made available for treatment of physical illness. Section 21 thus, helps in ensuring the protection of the right to equality in healthcare, of all persons with mental illness in a concerted manner.

---

[135] *See* D. NAGARAJA AND PRATIMA MURTHY, NHRC, MENTAL HEALTH CARE AND HUMAN RIGHTS (2008)

Section 21 also in particular protects the rights of a woman with mental illness who is mother of a small child. Section 21(2) and (3) state that a child below three years of age shall not ordinarily be separated from his/her mother if the latter is a woman receiving treatment or rehabilitation at a mental health establishment, unless there is a risk to the child from the mother due to her mental illness. However, the woman has a right to continue to have access to the child under the supervision of an establishment staff during the period of separation. The decision to separate the woman from her child has to be reviewed every fifteen days and the separation has to be terminated as soon as the decision is arrived at that the conditions which were posing risk to the child from his/her mother because of the mother's mental illness no longer exist. This is a laudable change in the law as it keeps intact one of the most fundamental right of a woman to be able to nurture her child. The periodic review process also helps in obviating the situation whenever the woman is healed enough to take care of her baby. Principle 11 of the UN Resolution on the Protection of Persons with Mental Illness and the Improvement of Mental Health Care, 1991,[136] states that no treatment, unless otherwise provided in the Resolution,[137] will be given to a patient without his/her informed consent. Similar provisions find place in the 2017 Act of India.[138]

The wombs of girls with mental illness are silenced as soon as they attain puberty.[139] Says the mother of a young girl with cerebral palsy, *"I was told the hysterectomy would help avoid hygiene issues during menstruation,"* and on asking about the side-effects of the operation, she was not even offered any reply.[140] The practice came to fore in 1994 when the incident of hysterectomies

---

[136] UN, The protection of persons with mental illness and the improvement of mental health care (A/RES/46/119), Available at http://www.un.org/documents/ga/res/46/a46r119.htm (Last visited on January 7, 2017)
[137] *See* NEIL C. MANSON AND ONORA O'NEILL, RETHINKING INFORMED CONSENT IN BIOETHICS (2007)
[138] Section 2(i) of the 2017 Act defines "informed consent" for the purposes of the Act.
[139] Divya Sreedharan, *The Silenced Wombs,* THE HINDU (August 4, 2013), Available at http://www.thehindu.com/features/the-yin-thing/the-silenced-wombs/article4985813.ece (Last visited on January 5, 2017)
[140] *Id.*

being conducted on 11 mentally challenged women between the ages of 15-35 (in a Pune Government Hospital) was reported in the national daily newspapers. This practice still continues, with parents quietly going for hysterectomies of their daughters without their consent. In response to the 1994 incident, the Indian Journal of Medical Ethics came out with an article titled *"Hysterectomy in the Mentally Handicapped"*[141]which lashes the logic put up by people endorsing these non-consensual hysterectomies. The discussion herein below summarizes some pertinent points to be noted, with respect to the issue[142]:

- **Hygiene issues and menstruation:** Menstruation is no disease, and an inherent part of a woman's life cycle. A woman without disability would never go for hysterectomy for the sake of convenience and hygiene. Just as excreta from bowel and bladder need attention in the physically and mentally disabled, similar care can be provided for the outpourings of the uterus during menstruation.

- **Health risks associated with hysterectomy:** Hysterectomy is a very major surgery with a mortality rate of I-2 per 1000 operations and an even higher complication rate. If the ovaries are left in, their function often recedes after hysterectomy, lowering the levels of estrogen in the body. This may lead to complications like cardiovascular disease and, osteoporosis. No standard textbook on gynaecology or psychiatry has ever recommended hysterectomy for the disabled.[143]

- **Sexual abuse and rape:** Hysterectomies are mostly carried out for the never-spoken reason: *"so that the girl doesn't become pregnant if abused."*[144]The abusers, generally being, men who meet them on an

---

[141] Paryay, *Hysterectomy in the Mentally Handicapped,* Indian Journal of Medical Ethics, Vol.2, No. 3 (1994), Available at http://ijme.in/index.php/ijme/article/view/1790/3858 (Last visited on January 3, 2015)
[142]*Id.*
[143]*Id.*
[144] Divya Sreedharan, *The Silenced Wombs,* THE HINDU (August 4, 2013), Available at http://www.thehindu.com/features/the-yin-thing/the-silenced-wombs/article4985813.ece (Last visited on January 5, 2017)

everyday basis, hospital staff, peers and own family members.[145] Though, physical and verbal abuse is prevalent in state-run institutions, sexual violence remains hidden as victims, sometimes don't understand what is being done to them, and even if they do, are very less likely to talk about the same.[146] Same applies to women with disability, especially mentally challenged women staying with their family where the abusers are generally the family members and relatives.

It is submitted that there should be an express prohibition in the Act on hysterectomies of women with mental illness undergoing mental healthcare treatment. The same is vital to fully protect the right to equality and non-discrimination of persons with mental illness as guaranteed under Section 21. The reason for removing the uterus of a woman should be purely gynecological.

4. RIGHT TO PROTECTION FROM CRUEL, INHUMAN AND DEGRADING TREATMENT

Section 20 of the Act lays down the right of persons with mental illness to be protected from cruel, inhuman and degrading treatment in mental healthcare establishments. This right includes the right:

- to live in safe and hygienic environment;
- to have adequate sanitary conditions;
- to have reasonable facilities for leisure, recreation, education and religious practices;
- to privacy;
- for proper clothing so as to protect such person from exposure of his body to maintain his dignity;
- to not be forced to undertake work in a mental health establishment and to receive appropriate remuneration for work when undertaken;

---

[145] *Id.*
[146] HRW Report (2014)

- to have adequate provision for preparing for living in the community;
- to have adequate provision for wholesome food, sanitation, space and access to articles of personal hygiene, in particular, women's personal hygiene be adequately addressed by providing access to items that may be required during menstruation;
- to not be subject to compulsory tonsuring (shaving of head hair);
- to wear own personal clothes if so wished and to not be forced to wear uniforms provided by the establishment; and
- to be protected from all forms of physical, verbal, emotional and sexual abuse.

Right to life protected under Article 21 of the Constitution of India, includes within its ambit the right to live with dignity and to be protected from cruel and inhuman treatment. Section 20 of the Act therefore, stands fairly good in the test of the mandates of the right to life and personal liberty as guaranteed by the Indian Constitution and recognized by the Supreme Court of India in various landmark judgements.[147]

It is imperative to analyse the provisions of Section 20 of the Act from the perspective of women with mental illness in the background of the existent mental healthcare scenario in India. In the female ward of the Regional Mental Hospital (RMH), Yerwada, Pune, Maharashtra, one of the ten institutions visited by the multi-disciplinary team of NCW and NIMHANS, lighting was inadequate, and because of inadequate beds and mattresses there was overcrowding; the eating area was full of flies. The patients had to wear compulsory uniforms many of which were torn, and there was lack of privacy during bathing.[148] In the female ward of GHMC, Kozhikode, Kerala, more than two-third members said that they were not provided sanitary napkins regularly and many said they were not taught how to dispose them. In Regional Mental Hospital, Thane,

---

[147] Maneka Gandhi v. Union of India, 1978 SCR (2) 621; Francis Coralie v. Union Territory of Delhi, 1981 SCR (2) 516; Bandhua Mukti Morcha v. Union of India, AIR 1984 SC 802; Peoples Union for Democratic Rights v. Union of India, 1983 SCR (1) 456
[148] NCW and NIMHANS Report (2016)

Maharashtra, the female wards were reported to be *"old leaking and dilapidated,"* there are no mosquito meshes and there is only one toilet per fifty female patients.[149] During rains there is leakage and the wards become damp making it very difficult to maintain proper hygiene and cleanliness, failure of which leads to malaria and other water-borne diseases.[150] Here too there was no privacy while bathing or changing clothes, some of the toilets did not even have doors. Sanitary napkins are not provided in this institution and patients are given innerwear only during their menstruation days. In Calcutta Pavlov Hospital, West Bengal, there are 270 women with mental illness living in a three-storey building with a locked gate, where the patients complained of lack of space and proper hygiene.[151] In Behrampore Mental Hospital, Murshidabad, West Bengal, 188 women lived on two floors and each woman does not have a separate bed of her own.[152] Most women patients were bathed together in open taps in the corridor, very few patients have undergarments, and they were provided with sanitary napkins only on demand, most of whom disposed them off by throwing them out of the window.[153]

The above accounts are a few examples of degrading treatment meted out to women with mental illness in these institutions. Enforcing these rights guaranteed under Section 20 to the female patients with mental illness is therefore, the most important, imminent and urgent need of the day.

---

[149] *Id.*
[150] *Id.*
[151] *Id.*
[152] *Id.*
[153] *Id.*

5. OTHER IMPORTANT POSITIVE RIGHTS GUARANTEED UNDER THE ACT

Sections 22 to 28 of the Act enumerate certain important positive rights of patients with mental illness in mental healthcare which hold significance in the present scenario. The rights are:

- **Right to information (Section 22):** Right of the person with mental illness and his/her nominated representative to information regarding admission to a mental healthcare institution and to his/her treatment therein.

- **Right to confidentiality (Sections 23 and 24):** Right of the person with mental illness to confidentiality with respect to his/her mental health, mental healthcare, treatment, and physical healthcare. No photograph or any other information relating to a person with mental illness who is undergoing treatment at a mental health establishment shall be released to the media without the consent of the person with mental illness. It is to be noted that the right to confidentiality of person with mental illness extends to all information stored in electronic or digital format in real or virtual space.

- **Right to access medical records (Section 25):** Right of the person with mental illness to access to his/her basic medical records.

- **Right to personal contacts and communication (Section 26):** Right of the person with mental illness admitted to a mental health establishment to refuse or receive visitors and to refuse and make telephone and mobile calls at reasonable times and to send and receive emails, etc.

- **Right to legal aid (Section 27):** Right of the person with mental illness to receive free legal services to exercise the rights guaranteed under the Act.

- **Right to make complaints regarding deficiencies of services at the mental healthcare institution (Section 28):** Right of the person with mental illness and his/her nominated representative to complain regarding deficiencies in provision of treatment, care and services in a mental health establishment. The complaint can be made before the medical officer or mental health professional in charge of the establishment and if not satisfied with the response; the concerned Board and if not satisfied with the response; the State Authority.

These positive rights if properly implemented will help in fulfilling the other rights guaranteed under the Act, that is the right to access to mental healthcare, right to equality and protection from cruelty in mental healthcare and protection of the dignity of women with mental illness receiving mental healthcare.

6. THINKING ALOUD

Article 3 of the UNCRPD lays down eight general principles on which the Convention is based, that are:

- Respect for inherent dignity, individual autonomy including the freedom to make one's own choices, and independence of persons;
- Non-discrimination;
- Full and effective participation and inclusion in society;
- Respect for difference and acceptance of persons with disabilities as part of human diversity and humanity;
- Equality of opportunity;
- Accessibility;
- Equality between men and women;
- Respect for the evolving capacities of children with disabilities and respect for the right of children with disabilities to preserve their identities.

The Preamble of UNCRPD recognizes the fact that women and girls with disabilities are often at greater risk *"of violence, injury or abuse, neglect or negligent treatment, maltreatment or exploitation."* Article 6 of the UNCRPD requires State parties to take measures to ensure the full and equal enjoyment by them of all human rights and fundamental freedoms set out in the Convention.

It is submitted that the 2017 Act has adhered to the mandates of UNCRPD by providing for protection of rights of persons with mental illness undergoing or requiring mental healthcare. When it comes to the rights of women with mental illness and bringing them at par with the other sections of the society, the terrain is rocky and is full of obstacles. For these impediments to be overcome, concerted efforts of all the stake holders and authorities involved in mental healthcare is required. Applying the principle of *"best interest"* of the person with mental illness and the principle of *"medical necessity"* by the person taking mental healthcare decisions for himself/herself or by anyone taking the decision on his/her behalf, keeping in mind that the *"least restrictive"* methods of treatment for mental healthcare should be incorporated.[154] A coordinate combination of these three principles dependant on the situation of each woman with mental illness respectively is the way ahead to ensure the adherence to the principles and human rights envisaged in the 2017 Act.

---

[154] *See* Ravinder v. Government of NCT of Delhi and Ors., W.P. (CRL) 3317/2017

VI. UNDERSTANDING PSYCHIATRIC ADVANCE DIRECTIVES AND THEIR PLAUSIBLE IMPLICATIONS ON WOMEN WITH MENTAL ILLNESS IN INDIA

Chapter III of the Mental Healthcare Act, 2017 introduces the concept of psychiatric advance directives and Chapter IV comprises provisions pertaining to the nominated representative of the person with mental illness. The Act states that any person, not being a minor, has the right to make an advance directive in writing specifying, the way the person wishes to be cared for and treated for a mental illness; the individual or individuals, in order of precedence, he wants to appoint as nominated representative. There have been both legal and medical discourses about the moral authority of an advance directive and the real stance of advance directives vis-à-vis autonomy of the patient with mental illness who has issued the directive. This Chapter analyses the issues relating to advance directives from the perspective of the autonomy of women with mental illness in India.

1. Understanding the Concept of "Psychiatric Advance Directives"

Advance planning of treatment for a situation of mental illness in the future, by way of written advance directives has been debated among the contemporary mental health care professionals and academicians.[155]

The concept of psychiatric advance directives is often explained in common parlance as the concept of *living will*, wherein the person states in a competent state of mind, how he/she wishes to be treated during the state of incompetency. Advance directives are meant to establish a person's preferences for treatment if the person becomes incompetent in the future or is unable to communicate those preferences.[156]

Psychiatric advance directives, as stated by some academicians, owe their origin to the concept of a Ulysses contract or a self-binding contract. A Ulysses contract/pact[157] is a contract entered voluntarily in the present with consequences which are binding on the person entering into the contract in the future, when he/she is incompetent to take a decision.

Psychiatric advance directives, also referred to as *"mental health advance directives"* are considered by some as an ideal mechanism for persons with mental health issues to express their treatment preferences in the future.[158] Advance directives are particularly vital with respect to mental illness which is

---

[155] Guy Widdershoven, *Advance directives in psychiatric care: a narrative approach,* Journal of Medical Ethics, Vol. 27 No. 2 92-97 (2001)

[156] Debra S. Srebnik, et. al., *Advance Directives for Mental Health Treatment,* Psychiatric Services, Vol 50 No. 7 (1999)

[157] The term *"Ulysses contract/pact"* owes its origin to the story of the pact that Ulysses had entered to with his men when they were approaching the Sirens. Ulysses desired to listen to the Siren's song, knowing fully well that doing the same would render him incapable of exercising rational thought. He directed his men to tie him to the mast so that he could listen to the song, and ordered his men to not change the course of the ship under any circumstances, and to keep their swords pointed at him; and thereby restraining him from breaking free from the bonds. His men were asked to put wax in their ears so that they did not have to listen to the Siren's song.

[158] Paul S. Appelbaum, *Commentary: Psychiatric Advance Directives at Crossroads- When Can PADs be Overriden?* J Am Acad Psychiatry Law 34: 395-397 (2006)

many a time characterized by alternating periods of competence and incompetence; and these advance directives afford a person with mental illness the opportunity to state their treatment preferences when they are in a competent state.[159] Unlike persons making decisions with respect to end-of-life treatment, psychiatric patients have generally experienced both the disorder and the treatment on previous occasions and therefore, are in a stronger position to make informed choices and meaningful decisions.[160]

2.   TYPES OF "PSYCHIATRIC ADVANCE DIRECTIVES"

Psychiatric advance directive (also referred to as mental health advance directive) is a written document, wherein a person who has the legal capacity in the present, states how he/she wants to be treated in the future when, because of any mental illness, he/she is incapable of taking decisions with respect to his/her health and treatment. The two broad categories of psychiatric advance directives are: *instructional directive* and *proxy directive.* An advance directive may also have both the elements of an instructional directive and a proxy directive.

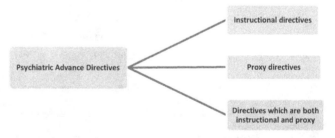

Table (4): Types of Psychiatric Advance Directives

---

[159] Debra S. Srebnik, et. al., *Advance Directives for Mental Health Treatment,* Psychiatric Services, Vol 50 No. 7 (1999)
[160] Paul S. Appelbaum, *Commentary: Psychiatric Advance Directives at Crossroads- When Can PADs be Overriden?* J Am Acad Psychiatry Law 34: 395-397 (2006)

i.   Instructional directives

Instructional directives include instructions by the person with mental illness about his/her treatment preferences and the reasons for those preferences. Instructional directives generally contain detailed instructions given by the person himself/herself directing the treatment providers in advance, what to do in the case of a mental health crisis, when the person becomes incompetent and unable to communicate his/her decisions pertaining to medical treatment.[161] Instructional directives include the treatment directives and may include the reasons for giving such directives. Such directives may be given with respect to the following points[162]:

- *Medication details:* medications to be administered, dosage, method and timing of administration of medication;
- *Medical emergencies:* issues relating to addressing emergency medical situations through restraint, sedition, etc.[163]
- *Preference for particular doctor, hospital, medical clinic, etc.*
- *Specific treatments:* for example: electro-compulsive therapy, group therapy, etc.
- *Identification of persons:* who are permitted for hospital visit; who are to take care of the child, parents, financial care, home of such a person
- *Experimental treatments or research studies:* willingness to be a part of, or to not be a part of experimental treatments
- Other matters relating to medical care.

---

[161] Debra S. Srebnik, et. al., *Advance Directives for Mental Health Treatment,* Psychiatric Services, Vol 50 No. 7 (1999)

[162]*See* Debra S. Srebnik, et. al., *Advance Directives for Mental Health Treatment,* Psychiatric Services, Vol 50 No. 7 (1999); Guy Widdershoven, *Advance directives in psychiatric care: a narrative approach,* Journal of Medical Ethics, Vol. 27 No. 2 92-97 (2001); Janet Heinrich and Virginia P. Tilden, *Policy Perspectives: Advance Directives,* The American Journal of Nursing, Vol. 100 No. 12 49-51(Dec., 2000)

[163] Advance directives are not applicable to emergency treatments under the Mental Health Care Act, 2017.

Drawing an exhaustive list of what can form a part of an instructional psychiatric advance directive is difficult, keeping in mind the facts, circumstances and sensitivity of each person respectively.[164]

ii.   Proxy psychiatric advance directive:

Proxy advance directive enables the person to designate someone else as a health-care proxy to take medical decisions on behalf of such person when he/she becomes incapable to take such decisions because of mental illness.[165] A proxy psychiatric advance directives authorizes the proxy to legally take decisions pertaining to mental health care of the person during the time of the person's incompetency. The proxy acts at such a time of incompetency of the person making the directive, by using substituted judgement standard, that is act on behalf of the person and in the same way as the person would have acted had he/she been competent to take the decisions on his/her own. Best-judgement is therefore exercised by the proxy keeping in mind the gravity of the situation and the wishes of the person; which is also the major reason why proxy directives are used more frequently than sheer instructional directives.

iii.   Psychiatric advance directives which are both instructional and proxy:

A directive which has both the elements of an instructional directive and a proxy directive specifies both the instructions as to the way the person wishes to be treated during incompetency and also nominates a proxy who will act on behalf of the person to execute those directions. In common day parlance, psychiatric advance directives are a combination of both instructional and proxy. The person gives certain instructions in his/her advance directives, pertaining to his/her mental health care for if and when the situation of incompetency arises; and authorizes a proxy to execute those instructions and to take decisions

---

[164] Janet Heinrich and Virginia P. Tilden, *Policy Perspectives: Advance Directives,* The American Journal of Nursing, Vol. 100 No. 12 49-51(Dec., 2000)
[165] Debra S. Srebnik, et. al., *Advance Directives for Mental Health Treatment,* Psychiatric Services, Vol 50 No. 7 (1999)

pertaining to any other issues that may crop up during the person's mental illness.

3. CAPACITY TO MAKE DECISIONS PERTAINING TO MENTAL HEALTHCARE AND TREATMENT

Section 4 of the 2017 Act states that it shall be deemed that every person, including a person who has mental illness has the capacity to make decisions regarding his/her mental healthcare if such a person has the capability to:

- Understand the information provided;
- Understand the reasonably foreseeable consequences;
- Communicate his/her decision.[166]

If a decision made by a person with mental illness under this Section is perceived by others to be a wrong decision, the same would not entail questioning the decision making capacity of such a person under the Act as long as the other provisions of Section 4 are fulfilled.

This right of a person under Section 4 is a precursor to the right to make decisions in advance about one's mental healthcare and therefore, reinforces the capacity of a person to make an advance directive pertaining to his/her mental healthcare in the future.

4. PSYCHIATRIC ADVANCE DIRECTIVES UNDER THE MENTAL HEALTH CARE ACT, 2017

Chapter III of the 2017 Act provides for advance directives; and Chapter IV of the 2017 Act lays down provisions pertaining to nominated representative.[167] Both the chapters work in tandem with each other.

---

[166] The 2017 Act, Section 4

Section 5 states that every person, who is not a minor, shall have a right to make an advance directive in writing, specifying any or all of the following:

- the way the person wishes to be cared for and treated for a mental illness;
- the way the person wishes not to be cared for and treated for a mental illness;
- the individual or individuals, in order of precedence, he/she wants to appoint as his nominated representative as provided under Section 14.

An advance directive can be made by a person irrespective of his/her past mental illness or treatment for the same.[168] According to the Act, it can be invoked only when such person ceases to have capacity to make mental health care or treatment decisions and shall remain effective until such person regains capacity to make those decisions.[169] Any decision made by a person while he has the capacity to make mental health care and treatment decisions shall over-ride any previously written advance directive by such person; and an advance directive contrary to any law for the time being in force is considered void ab initio.[170] An advance directive can be revoked, amended or cancelled any time by the person making the same.[171] Section 6 of the Act discusses about the manner of making an advance directive. It is to be noted that advance directives are not applicable to emergency treatments under the Mental Health Care Act, 2017.[172]

Enforceability of an advance directive under the Act: It is the duty of every medical officer in charge of a mental health establishment and the

---

[167] *See* also Jeffrey Swanson, et. al., *Psychiatric Advance Directives Among Public Health Consumers in Five US Cities: Prevelance, Demand and Correlates,* 34J Am Acad Psychiatry 3443–57 (2006)
[168] The 2017 Act, Section 5
[169] *Id.*
[170] *Id.*
[171] The 2017 Act, Section 8
[172] The 2017 Act, Section 9

psychiatrist in charge of a person's mental healthcare, to provide treatment and mental healthcare to the person with mental illness, in accordance with the person's valid advance directive.[173] Following a valid advance directive bears no adverse consequences for a medical practitioner or a mental health professional in case of unforeseen circumstances.[174] However, the medical practitioner or mental health professional is not liable for not following an invalid advance directive, if the copy of a valid directive was not provided to him/her.[175] The person writing the advance directive and his nominated representative have the duty to ensure that the medical officer in charge of a mental health establishment or a medical practitioner or a mental health professional, as the case may be, has access to the advance directive when the situation arises.[176]

When a mental health professional or a relative or a care-giver of a person desires not to follow an advance directive: While treating a person with mental illness, if the mental health professional or the relative or care-giver of the person, wishes not to follow an advance directive, an application to the concerned Board has to be made to review, alter, modify or cancel the advance directive.[177]Upon receipt of such an application, the Board has the power to review, alter or modify or cancel the advance directive in question. The opportunity of hearing to all concerned parties (including the person whose advance directive is in question) should be given by the Board. Before arriving at a decision, the Board should take into consideration, the following factors: [178]

- whether the person making the advance directive had the capacity to make decisions relating to his/her mental healthcare or treatment when such advanced directive was made; or
- whether the advance directive was made by the person out of his own free will and was well-informed before making the decision;

---

[173] The 2017 Act, Section 10
[174] The 2017 Act, Section 13(1)
[175] The 2017 Act, Section 13(2)
[176] The 2017 Act, Section 11(3)
[177] The 2017 Act, Section 11
[178]Id.

- whether the person intended the advance directive to apply to the existing circumstances, which may be different from those anticipated; or
- whether the content of the advance directive is contrary to the other laws of India.[179]

Nominated representative: Chapter IV of the Mental Health Care Act, 2017 lays down provisions pertaining to nominated representative. Every person, who is not a minor, has the right to appoint a nominated representative for the purposes of this Act.[180] Where no nominated representative is appointed by a person, the following persons, in the order of precedence shall be deemed to be the nominated representative of a person with mental illness for the purposes of this Act, namely:

- the person appointed as the nominated representative in the advance directive;
- a relative;
- a care-giver;
- a suitable person appointed by the concerned board
- if no such person is available to be appointed as a nominated representative, the Board shall appoint the Director, Department of Social Welfare, or his designated representative, as the nominated representative of the person with mental illness. Any person representing an organization registered under the Societies Registration Act, 1860 or any other law for the time being in force, working for persons with mental illness, may temporarily be engaged by the mental health professional to discharge the duties of a nominated representative pending appointment of a nominated representative by the concerned Board.

All persons with mental illness have the capacity to make mental healthcare or treatment decisions; however, each of them may require varying levels of

---

[179] *Id.*
[180] The 2017 Act, Section 14

support from their nominated representative to make decisions.[181] While fulfilling his duties under this Act, the nominated representative is required to[182]:

- consider the current and past wishes, the life history, values, cultural background and the best interests of the person with mental illness;
- give particular importance to the views of the person with mental illness to the extent that the person understands the nature of the decisions under consideration;
- provide support to the person with mental illness in making treatment decisions;
- have right to seek information on diagnosis and treatment to provide adequate
- support to the person with mental illness;
- have access to the family or home based rehabilitation services on behalf of and for the benefit of the person with mental illness;
- be involved in discharge planning;
- be informed about every instance of restraint[183] within a period of twenty-four hours;
- apply to the mental health establishment for admission;
- apply to the concerned Board against violation of rights of the person with mental illness in a mental health establishment;
- have the right to give or withhold consent for research, etc.

---

[181] *Id.*
[182] The 2017 Act, Section 17
[183] The 2017 Act, Section 97

5.   Psychiatric Advance Directive & Women with Mental Illness

Persons with mental illness form a part of the marginalized sections of society because of their incapacity to exercise their rights in times of their mental illness. The situation gets gravely difficult particularly when it is the case of a woman with mental illness.[184] In a society with a strong hue of patriarchy, women with mental illness qualify as one of the most marginalized sections.[185]

Self-determination is vital for any person's well-being and existence. The right to decide about once future health care needs is considered an indispensable part of one's autonomy.[186] However, the exercise of this autonomy by persons with mental illness receives limited recognition and the facility to be implemented in very rare cases. The introduction of psychiatric advance directives under the 2017 Act can therefore, be considered a significant development.

6.   Addressing the Apprehensions Pertaining to Psychiatric Advance Directives:

Some mental illnesses are periodic in nature, example being, schizophrenia, obsessive compulsive disorder, bipolar disorder, etc. Psychiatric advance directives are vital in these situations. Even if a person with mental illness complies with the mandates of medication, a future manic condition cannot always be obviated.[187] A person who has lived the experience of his/her mental

---

[184]Bhargavi Davar And T.K. Sundari Ravindran, Gendering Mental Health (2015)
[185]Id.
[186] Sheila A. M. McLean, Autonomy, Consent and the Law (2010)
[187] Guy Widdershoven and Ron Berghmans, *Advance Directives in Psychiatric Care: A Narrative Approach,* Journal of Medical Ethics 92-97 (2001)

illness, therefore, is in the best position to determine how he/she wishes to be treated in the case of a future bout of mental illness.[188]

Appointing of a nominated representative under the Act is in the nature of a proxy psychiatric advance directive. Appointing a nominated representative through an advance directive in whom the patient has confidence entitles the patient to ensure that his/her rights will be protected and the medical care will be properly taken care of.

Corollaries with respect to the advance directives provisions in the Mental Health Care Act, 2017, can be drawn to similar provisions in statutes recognizing advance directives in the legal systems of other countries in the world. The Federal Patient Self-Determination Act, 1991 in the US introduced the government requirements to implement advance-directive policies at health care facilities receiving funding through Medicaid and Medicare.[189] The Mental Capacity Act, 2005 of UK which lays down similar provisions about advance care planning, categorizing the same into three categories, namely: advance statements, advance decision to refuse treatment and lasting power of attorney.

As part of the research, the researcher had the opportunity to interview five psychiatrists with multiple years of experience. All the interviews were focused interviews and the questions asked were open-ended.[190] All the doctors were of the opinion that the Mental Healthcare Act, 2017 as a whole was a welcome change; however, the concept of advance directives was received with apprehension and skepticism. One of these Doctors was of the view that in the Indian societal setup, majority of patients with mental illness are brought for medical treatment by a family member; and an advance directive may bring the

---

[188] The Mental Health Legal Centre Inc., Advance Directives Project –Information for Clinicians, Available at
http://www.communitylaw.org.au/mentalhealth/cb_pages/images/AD_Clinicians_Info_Feb09.pdf
(Last visited on April 10, 2017)
[189] See also Jeffrey Swanson, et. al., Psychiatric Advance Directives Among Public Health Consumers in Five US Cities: Prevalence, Demand and Correlates, 34J Am Acad Psychiatry 3443–57 (2006)
[190] See Chapter XII, Interview with Psychiatrists

patient at crossroads with the very family which wishes the patient's welfare.[191] This view is subject to contradiction because of the fact that an invalid advance directive can be amended and repealed under the Mental Healthcare Act, 2017 at any point of time.

The apprehensions of one of the Doctors, whom the researcher interviewed was that advance directives under the Act will lead to unnecessary informalities. This criticism can be put to rest by ensuring that the mandates and requirements of a valid advance directive are adhered to at the very beginning when the advance directive is written. The provision for amendment or cancellation of one's advance directives under the Act gives these directives flexibility and validates to the patient's wishes by giving him/her the opportunity to change his/her directions with time and with his/her changing situations.

A corollary can be drawn to advance directive with respect to passive euthanasia, from the decision of the Supreme Court of India in *Common Cause (A Regd. Society) v. Union of India and Another*[192] wherein the Supreme Court upheld the constitutionality of passive euthanasia and laid down guidelines for advance directive relating to the same. The advance directive which the Supreme Court discusses in this case can be only executed by an adult who is of sound mind and is in a position to communicate. The advance directive becomes operative subject to various checks and conditions, only when the executor of the directive becomes terminally ill, has been through and is also presently going through prolonged medical treatment with *"no hope for recovery and cure of the ailment"*. Though the ethos of the advance directive pertaining to passive euthanasia and the advance directive pertaining to mental healthcare is predominantly different, the common factors between the two are that both are given by the executor in a fit state of mind and are made with respect to treatment when the person will not be in the state of mind to take decision.

---

[191] *See* also Chapter XII, Compiling the Results of the Close-Ended Questions of the Online and Offline Survey
[192] W.P. (CIVIL) NO. 215 OF 2005

Having upheld the constitutionality of advance directives pertaining to passive euthanasia in *Common Cause (A Regd. Society) v. Union of India and Another*[193], the Supreme Court has upheld the concept of advance directive in general as well, which can be considered as an indirect affirmation of the legality and constitutionality of psychiatric advance directives envisaged in the 2017 Act.

7. IMPLICATIONS:

People with mental illness very easily lose their right to participate in decision making in the present societal setup.[194]In this background, the concept of psychiatric advance directives play an enabling role for the person with mental illness to be an active part in at least the decision making of his/her own health care. One of the mandates of a valid advance directive under the Mental Healthcare Act, 2017 is that an advance directive can only be made by the person in the state when he is able to understand the meaning and implications of his directions.

Women with mental illness in India find a lesser role in the societal and family setup when it comes to their decision making power, and are sometimes even abstained from their right to a family, food, shelter, etc. In situations like these, and also in situations where the female patient is in a better status and is being able to exercise her rights, psychiatric advance directives is a big tool of entitlement for such women. The entitlement is towards autonomy, towards the fulfillment of the right to decide how/where/when/by whom she wishes to be treated if and when she is not be competent to take decisions in the future because of her mental illness. Psychiatric advance directives as recognized under the Act have the potential to ensure that female patients get the full

---

[193] *Id.*

[194] The Mental Health Legal Centre Inc., Maximising Consumers autonomy, dignity and control, Available at http://www.communitylaw.org.au/mentalhealth/cb_pages/living_wills.php (Last visited on April 12, 2017)

opportunity to have a say in and influence the treatment they receive, and that their preference is respected and fulfilled in all possible situations.

The Draft Central Regulations, 2017[195]lay down the regulations pertaining to the manner of making an advance directive. It is stated that an advance directive for the purposes of the 2017 Act should be made according to Form CR-A of the Draft Central Regulations, 2017. A nominated representative who is named in the advance directive should sign in the advance directive thereby consenting to the same.[196] He/she may withdraw his/her consent at any time from the same by writing an application to that effect to the Mental Health Review Board and handing over a copy of the application to the person who made the advance directive.[197] All advance directives are to be countersigned by two witnesses stating that the advance directive was signed by the person making the same in their presence.[198] A person making the advance directive is required to keep a copy with himself/herself and give a copy to his/her nominated representative.[199] Release of a copy of the advance directive to the media or any unauthorized person is not permitted.[200] All advance directives are to be registered with the concerned Mental Health Review Board free of cost.[201] An advance directive should be made online by the Board within 14 days of receiving the same.[202] A person can change his/her advance directives any number of times, there are no restrictions on the number.[203] Each change in an advance directive is required to undergo the same process and regulations as

---

[195] Draft Central Regulations, 2017 made by the Central Government in exercise of the powers conferred under Section 122 of the 2017 Act on behalf of the Central Mental Health Authority subject to modification by the Central Mental Authority on its constitution. Draft Central Regulations, 2017, Available at https://mohfw.gov.in/sites/default/files/Final%20Draft%20Rules%20MHC%20Act%2C%202017%20%281%29.pdf (Last visited on April 27, 2018)
[196] Draft Central Regulations, 2017
[197] Id.
[198] Id.
[199] Id.
[200] Id.
[201] Id.
[202] Id.
[203] Id.

an advance directive to be considered valid.[204] Every time a new advance directive is made, the person making the advance directive and/or his/her nominated representative must inform the treating mental health professional about the same.[205]

It is submitted that the checks to the viability of a psychiatric advance directive are sufficiently placed in the provisions of the 2017 Act and proper implementation of the law in its letter and spirit will help in fulfilling the goal with which this concept is being introduced in India. The Draft Central Regulations, 2017 add further regulations and checks to ensure the smooth functioning and proper implementation of psychiatric advance directives. Subject to the implementation of the laws, psychiatric advance directives will have positive implications on the autonomy of women with mental illness and the exercise of their right to choice over the treatment meted out to them. The concept of psychiatric advance directives is a welcome change to entitle the female patients with mental illness to come out of the shackles and consequences of labelled incompetency and existent marginalization. It is a positive step and will enable women in need of mental healthcare to exercise autonomy and their right to independent decision making with respect to their mental healthcare requirements and choices. However, it is important to note that independence, free consent and autonomy of the woman making an advance directive should be particularly facilitated and ensured at all stages of the process, so that the psychiatric advance directive is her own decision taken by her for her best interest.

---

[204] Id.
[205] Id.

VII. COMPARING THE PROVISIONS OF THE MENTAL HEALTHCARE ACT, 2017 WITH THE RELEVANT PROVISIONS OF THE MENTAL HEALTH ACT, 1987

The Mental Healthcare Act, 2017 replaces the Mental Health Act, 1987. In order to address the present and future, it is important to analyse and draw a link with what was the situation in the past. This Chapter compares two major aspects of the 2017 Act and the 1987 Act, namely: (i) the procedures pertaining to admission, treatment and discharge under the two Acts; (ii) various Authorities under the two Acts. This Chapter holds significance because one cannot ignore the fact the 2017 Act has not been introduced in a vacuum but is replacing a 31 year old legislation. Therefore, it becomes important to understand the major administrative changes in the law enforcement mechanism that will be brought about by the virtue of the new law.

1. ADMISSION, TREATMENT AND DISCHARGE – A COMPARISON OF THE 1987 ACT AND THE 2017 ACT

i.   Admission and discharge of a *'voluntary'* patient under the 1987 Act; and an *'independent'* patient in a mental health establishment under the 2017 Act

Mental Health Act, 1987   **Mental Healthcare Act, 2017**

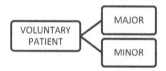
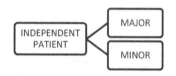

A corollary can be drawn between admission of a person with mental illness on a voluntary basis under the 1987 Act[206] with the admission of a person with mental illness as an independent patient in a mental health establishment under the 2017 Act[207]. The 2017 Act is more circumspect with respect to admissions in mental healthcare institutions and lays down more elaborate criteria to confirm admission in such a institution. Voluntary admission is further categorized both under 1987 Act and the 2017 Act into voluntary admission of an adult and a minor respectively.

---

[206] The 1987 Act, Sections 15 to 18.
[207] The 2017 Act, Sections 85 to 88.

Admission:

- ADULT:

The 1987 Act states that any person who is of the opinion that he/she is mentally ill can approach a psychiatric hospital or psychiatric nursing home for treatment and request for being admitted as a *"voluntary patient."* The medical officer concerned shall conduct an inquiry, within a period of 24 hours, on being satisfied that the person needs treatment as an inpatient, and has to thereby admit the person as a voluntary patient.

The 2017 Act, defines an *"independent patient or an independent admission"* for the purposes of the Act as admission of a person with mental illness to a mental health establishment who has the capacity to make mental healthcare and treatment decisions or requires minimal or negligible support in arriving at such decisions. Any person who is of the opinion that he/she is mentally ill can approach a psychiatric hospital or psychiatric nursing home for treatment and request for being admitted as an independent patient.

The 2017 Act encourages all admissions to a mental health establishment to be independent admissions unless the conditions are such that supported admission becomes inevitable. The medical officer or the mental health professional in charge of the establishment has to be satisfied that the applicant has a mental illness of such severity that he/she requires admission to a mental health establishment, and is likely to benefit from such an admission. The medical officer should also ensure that the person has understood the nature and implications of such an admission, and is acting with free and informed consent.

The 1987 Act, however, did not lay down any of the express aforementioned criteria enumerated in the 2017 Act. The 2017 Act further adds that an independent person has to be admitted on his own request and the presence of a nominated representative or a care-giver at the time of admission is not required. The 2017 Act also states that an independent patient will not be made subject to any treatment without his informed consent.

- **MINOR:**

The 1987 Act[208] states that if the guardian of the minor is of the opinion that he/she is mentally ill, he/she can approach a psychiatric hospital or psychiatric nursing home for treatment and request for the minor to be admitted as a voluntary patient. The medical officer concerned shall conduct an inquiry, within a period of 24 hours, on being satisfied that the minor needs treatment as an inpatient, has to thereby admit the minor as a voluntary patient.[209]

Under the 2017 Act,[210] the nominated representative of the minor can apply to the medical officer of a mental health establishment for the admission of the minor in the mental health establishment. The minor may be admitted to the establishment, provided that two psychiatrists[211] have independently examined the minor on the day of admission or seven days preceding thereto, and both of them, based on their independent examination, independently conclude that the minor has a mental illness of such severity that he/she requires admission to a mental health establishment, it is in his/her best interest and that he/she is likely to benefit from such an admission and that it would not be possible to fulfil the mental healthcare requirements of the minor without the admission. Best interest of the minor includes best interest of the minor with regard to his/her health, safety and well-being. As far as possible, the wishes of the minor should be taken into account. Before arriving at the decision to admit the minor, it also needs to be ascertained that all community oriented and community based alternatives to admission have failed or are unsuitable for the situation, condition and needs of the minor. With respect to the treatment of the minor in

---

[208] The 1987 Act, Section 16
[209] *See* R.N. SAXENA, THE MENTAL HEALTH ACT, 1987 (2000)
[210] The 2017 Act, Section 87
[211] Or one psychiatrist and one mental health professional or one psychiatrist and one medical practitioner

the mental health establishment, the 2017 Act lays down some important conditions to be fulfilled by the establishment, the same are enumerated herein below:

- the accommodation of the minor shall be separate from the adults in the establishment;
- the accommodation of the minor should be of the same quality that is provided to other minors admitted to hospitals for other treatments;
- the accommodation should cater to the needs of the minor, taking into account his/her needs, requirements and development; and
- the nominated representative should at all times be permitted to stay with the minor in the mental health establishment; and in case of a minor girl, if the nominated representative is a male, a female attendant has to be appointed by the nominated representative for the same.

In order to ensure that the minor is not forced into an admission into the mental health establishment, each time a minor is admitted to a mental health establishment, the concerned Board has to be apprised of the same within 72 hours. The Board reserves the right to visit the minor, interview him/her and review and analyse his/her medical records. If a minor has been in the mental health establishment for a month, on the completion of thirty days, the Board should be informed about the same. The Board shall review the admission and treatment of all minors admitted for thirty days and on completion of every thirty days period, within seven days of being informed about the same.

Discharge:

Under the **Mental Health Act, 1987,** a voluntary patient shall be discharged from the establishment within 24 hours of an application by him to be so discharged. However, the discharge may not be issued if the same is not in the interest of the person. Within 72 hours of such an application the medical officer shall constitute a Board comprising two medical officers to examine whether the person needs further treatment in the mental health establishment, and shall act according to the findings of the board.

An independent patient, under the **Mental Healthcare Act, 2017,**[212] shall be immediately discharged on a request so made by the person. However, a mental health professional may prevent such a discharge for a period of up to 24 hours and proceed with necessary assessment within those 24 hours to ascertain whether the independent patient will require admission as a patient with support needs, if the former has reason to believe that such patient:

- is unable to decipher the purpose, nature and significance of his/her decisions, which requires him/her to get substantial or high support from his/her nominated representative; or
- has recently been threatening to cause bodily harm to himself/herself or has attempted or attempting to cause bodily harm to himself/herself; or
- has recently been acting violently towards any other person; or
- shows signs of inability to take basic care for himself/herself which places him in a position of individual risk of harm to himself.

If any of the above criteria is fulfilled, the voluntary patient shall, within a period of 24 hours of his/her request to be discharged as an independent patient, be admitted as supported patient under Section 89 of the 2017 Act. If any of the above criteria is not fulfilled, the independent patient shall be discharged within a period of 24 hours of his/her request to be discharged.

If a minor who is admitted in a mental health establishment, attains the age of 18 years while he/she is still in the establishment, he/she shall be classified as an independent patient by the medical officer at the establishment, and the provisions of the Act shall apply to him/her accordingly.

Section 98 of the 2017 Act lays down the provision pertaining to discharge planning which apply to all discharges from mental health establishments

---

[212] The 2017 Act, Section 88

governed by this Act. Discharge planning is incumbent whenever the person undergoing the treatment for mental illness in a mental health establishment:

- Is to be discharged into the community; or
- Is to be discharged into a different mental health establishment; or
- A new psychiatrist is to undertake the care and treatment of the person.

Discharge planning would involve the participation of the psychiatrist, who was till date responsible for the person's care and treatment, in consultation with the person with mental illness, his/her nominated representative and/or family member/care-giver and the psychiatrist who will be responsible for the care and treatment of the person in the near future, in the planning pertaining to what treatment or services would be apt for the person and also drawing of a detailed plan for the treatment and care.

ii.   Admission under *"special circumstances"* under the 1987 Act;
Admission and treatment in mental health establishments of persons with
mental illness who have *"high support needs"* under 2017 Act

Mental Health Act, 1987	Mental Healthcare Act, 2017

```
┌─────────────────────┐      ┌────────────────────┐        ┌──────────────────┐
│  Admission under    │      │ Persons  with high │        │  up to 30 days   │
│ special circumstances│      │ support needs      │───────┤                  │
└─────────────────────┘      │ (supported         │        └──────────────────┘
                             │ admission)         │
                             │                    │        ┌──────────────────┐
                             └────────────────────┘───────┤  beyond 30 days  │
                                                           └──────────────────┘
```

Admission under special circumstances under the Mental Health Act, 1987:

Mentally ill persons may be admitted under certain special circumstances[213]
under the 1987 Act. Any mentally ill person who is not willing to express his/her
willingness to be admitted as a voluntary patient or is unable to express
willingness to be admitted as a voluntary patient in a psychiatric hospital or
psychiatric nursing home, can be admitted if an application with respect to the
same is made by his/her relative or friend, and the medical officer in charge is
satisfied that it is in the interest of the person to admit him/her in the psychiatric
hospital or psychiatric nursing home, as the case may be.

Involuntary admission under special circumstances is only viable when the
patient is mentally ill and the medical professionals have reached a satisfaction
to that effect. Admission under special circumstances for the mere observation

---

[213] The 1987 Act, Section 19

of the patient amounts to a violation of the right to life, liberty and dignity of the person so admitted.[214]

No person so admitted as an inpatient shall be kept in the psychiatric hospital or psychiatric nursing home as an inpatient for a period exceeding ninety days except in accordance with the other provisions of this Act.

The application should be accompanied by the certificates of two medical practitioners, minimum one of them being a medical practitioner in a Government service. The certificates should certify *inter alia* that the mentally ill person is in such a condition, that he/she should be kept as an inpatient in a psychiatric hospital or psychiatric nursing home. The medical officer, in charge of the concerned hospital or nursing home as the case maybe, however, may get the medically ill person examined by two medical practitioners working in the hospital rather than requiring certificates. A mentally ill person so admitted or any other person on his/her behalf may apply to the Magistrate for his/her discharge from the hospital or nursing home. The Magistrate may, after making such necessary inquiry, as he/she may deem fit, allow the application and discharge the mentally ill person, or may dismiss the application. A person admitted as an inpatient under special circumstances cannot be so kept for more than 90 days, subject to the other provisions of the 1987 Act.

Supported admission under the Mental Healthcare Act, 2017

Supported admission under the Mental Healthcare Act, 2017 is subject to various time bound brackets to ensure that no person with mental illness languishes in a mental health establishment beyond the necessary time. Examining the patient to ensure that the situation demands a supported admission is mandated by various requirements under the 2017 Act, thereby minimizing the scope of calculated and manipulated admissions of persons with mental illness.

---

[214] Dr. Sangamitra Acharya & Anr. v. State (NCT of Delhi) & Ors., W.P. (CRL.) 1804/2017 & CM No. 9963/2017

- **Up to 30 days**

A person with mental illness may be admitted to a mental health establishment through supported admission for a period of 30 days,[215] if the medical officer of the concerned mental health establishment receives an application from the nominated representative in this regard. Following are the pre-requisites for such an admission to take place:

- The person with mental illness should be examined on the day of admission or within 7 days preceding the date of the admission independently by one psychiatrist and a mental health professional/medical practitioner that the concerned person has a mental illness of such a nature that:

  - He/she has attempted or threatened to cause harm to himself/herself or his/her body; or
  - He/she has been behaving violently towards others or has threatened to cause harm to others; or
  - He/she is showing incapability to take care of himself/herself thereby putting himself/herself at the brink of harm.

- The mental health professional/medical practitioner should certify, after taking into account any psychiatric advance directive, that in the circumstances, admission to the mental health establishment is the least restrictive care option possible;

- The person is unable to take decisions or decipher them and therefore, it is not possible to admit him/her independently.

For supported admission, the informed consent of the person or his nominated representative (if he/she is unable to understand the implications of his/her decisions for the time being) should be obtained and any advance directive of the person should also be considered. If an admission of this nature takes place, the medical officer/ mental health professional has to report to the

---

[215] The 2017 Act, Section 89

concerned Board about such admission within 3 days of the admission, in case of a woman or a minor; and within 7 days of the admission in any other case. The provisions of the Act are considerate towards the sensitivity and the plausibility of misuse of such a provision, in the case of a minor and a woman and therefore require the reporting to the concerned Board to be made as soon as possible. Application can be made to the Board for reviewing the decision of such an admission of the person with mental illness by the person with mental illness, or his/her nominated representative or a representative from a registered non-governmental organization. The Board should review the application within 7 days of receiving an application for review.

The conditions and progress of the person admitted with support shall be timely reviewed, and if the person is better and the requisite criteria are no longer being fulfilled because of his/her improvement, he/she shall be discharged or be admitted as an independent patient. If the person is discharged, such a person is not eligible for re-admission as a supported patient till 7 days have elapsed from the date of his/her discharge.

After the expiry of 30 days from the date of admission, if the patient does not fulfill the afore-discussed criteria any more, he/she shall no longer remain in the establishment. However, if any of the afore-mentioned situations continue the patient may be continue to remain in the mental health establishment for more than 30 days on the fulfillment of the below-mentioned criteria.

- **Beyond 30 days**

If a person with mental illness admitted to a mental health establishment through supported admission requires continuous admission and treatment beyond 30 days,[216] or requires a re-admission within 7 days of discharge, he may be admitted on the fulfillment of certain conditions. Following are the pre-requisites for such an admission to take place:

---

[216] The 2017 Act, Section 90

- The person with mental illness should be examined on the day of admission or within 7 days preceding the date of the admission independently by one psychiatrist and a mental health professional/medical practitioner that the concerned person has a mental illness of such a nature that:
  - He/she has attempted or threatened to cause harm to himself/herself or his/her body; or
  - He/she has been behaving violently towards others or has threatened to cause harm to others; or
  - He/she is showing incapability to take care of himself/herself thereby putting himself/herself at the brink of harm.
- The mental health professional/medical practitioner should certify, after taking into account any advance directive, that in the circumstances, admission to the mental health establishment is the least restrictive care option possible;
- The person is unable to take decisions or decipher them and therefore, it is not possible to admit him/her independently.

For supported admission, the informed consent of the person or his nominated representative (if he/she is unable to understand the implications of his/her decisions for the time being) should be obtained and any advance directive of the person should also be considered. If an admission of this nature takes place, the medical officer/ mental health professional has to report to the concerned Board about such admission within 7 days of the admission. The Board may within 21 days of such an intimation either permit the re-admission or may order for discharge of the patient. While taking the decision, the Board shall examine whether there is a need for the institutional care of such person and whether an environment less restrictive than a mental health establishment can be provided in the community. The Board may also require the medical officer or psychiatrist in charge to come up with a plan for community based treatment and the progress that can be made by following the plan. Mere absence or paucity of community based services in a place of treatment cannot be the reason for re-admission beyond the period of 30 days.

The conditions and progress of the person admitted with support shall be timely reviewed, and if the person is better and the requisite criteria are no longer being fulfilled because of his/her improvement, he/she shall be discharged or be admitted as an independent patient. If a person with mental illness admitted to a mental health establishment through supported admission is permitted continuous admission and treatment beyond 30 days, further extension of time may be facilitated, on the fulfillment of the afore-discussed conditions, but subject to the following time limits wherein the review process has to be repeated.

  a. Time period extension in the first instance → up to 90 days
  b. Time period extension in the second instance → up to 120 days
  c. Time period extension from the third instance onwards → up to 180 days each time

iii. Reception orders under the Mental Health Act, 1987 and Orders by Magistrate under the Mental Healthcare Act, 2017

A. Reception Orders under the Mental Health Act, 1987

A reception order is an order issued by the Magistrate, under this Act, for the admission and detention of a mentally ill person in a psychiatric nursing home or hospital.[217]

On Application: An application for a reception order can be made by the medical officer in charge of the psychiatric hospital or psychiatric nursing home or by the husband/wife or any other relative of the person with mental illness to the Magistrate in whose local jurisdiction the psychiatric hospital or nursing

---

[217] The 1987 Act, Section 2(s)

home is situated. If the Magistrate is satisfied that it is in the interest of the health and safety of the person with mental illness, the Magistrate may pass a reception order.[218]

On production before the Magistrate:

Under the 1987 Act every officer in charge of a police station, may take into protection, a person found wandering about who seems to be mentally ill and unable to take care of himself/herself and/or maybe dangerous to the society because of his/her mental illness.[219]Every person who is detained or taken into protection and detained has to be produced before the nearest Magistrate within a period of twenty-four hours and shall not be detained beyond twenty-four hours without the permission of the Magistrate. If the Magistrate is satisfied that it is in the interest of the health and safety of the person with mental illness to be admitted in a psychiatric hospital or nursing home, the Magistrate may pass a reception order.[220]

B. Orders by Magistrate under the Mental Healthcare Act, 2017

It is the duty of the officer in-charge of a police station, if he has sufficient reason to believe that there is a person residing within the police station's local limits and he/she is being ill-treated or neglected, the former shall report the same before the Magistrate.[221] It is also the duty of any person who has reason to believe that a person has mental illness and is being ill-treated or neglected, to report the same before the officer-in-charge of the local police station. The Magistrate shall cause such person with mental illness to be produced before him and take necessary action therewith.[222]

---

[218]*See* the 1987 Act, Section 22
[219] The 1987 Act, Section 23
[220] The 1987 Act, Section 24
[221] The 2017 Act, Section 101
[222]*Id.*

Under the 2017 Act when any person is brought before the local Magistrate, and the person is mentally ill or appears to be so, the Magistrate may through an order in writing, convey the person to a public mental health establishment for assessment and/or treatment as the case may be.[223] The Magistrate may also authorize the admission for a period not exceeding ten days of the person with mental illness in a mental health establishment for his/her assessment and necessary treatment, after which the mental health professional in charge of the health establishment has to submit a report to the Magistrate for necessary action.[224]

Role of officer in-charge of the local police station: The 2017 Act also imposes a duty on the officer-in-charge of every police station in the country to take under his/her protection any person found wandering in the local limits of the station if the officer is of the opinion that the person has mental illness and his/her thereby incapable of taking care of himself/herself or because of his/her mental illness could be of risk to himself/herself or to others.[225]Before taking into his/her protection, the police officer concerned shall apprise the person of the grounds for taking him/her under protection. The person taking into protection has to be taken to the nearest public health establishment within twenty-four hours, and under no circumstances be put in a police lock-up or prison.[226] In the public health establishment, the medical officer in-charge has to arrange for the check-up and assessment of the person taking under protection so that proper treatment can be meted out to the latter in consonance with the provisions of the Act. Every officer-in-charge of a police station is also required to report to the Magistrate of any person with mental illness in his/her private residence who is neglected or ill-treated.[227]

---

[223] The 2017 Act, Section 102
[224] *Id.*
[225] The 2017 Act, Section 100
[226] *Id.*
[227] The 2017 Act, Section 101

2. SPECIFIC PROVISIONS PERTAINING TO TREATMENT UNDER THE MENTAL HEALTHCARE ACT, 2017

Informed consent is defined for the first time pertaining to persons with mental illness in India. It becomes vital for the sheer fact that determining factors for informed consent of the person with mental illness are complicated and need to be addressed very sensitively. The 2017 Act defines *"informed consent"*[228]as consent given for a specific intervention and which adheres to the following conditions:

- Consent given without any force/threat/fraud/mistake/misrepresentation/undue influence of any kind;
- Consent in order to be informed, must be obtained after providing sufficient information pertaining to the risks and benefits of the specific treatment and the existent alternatives to it;
- The information so provided should be in a language that the person giving the consent understands and should be made in a manner conducive for him to understand the implications of the same.

The Act also defines a *"least restrictive"* alternative/environment/option as one which aptly addresses the treatment needs of the person and imposes the least possible restrictions on the person's rights.[229] These provisions are important for the protection of patients with mental illness, especially women with mental illness, who are facilitated protection from exploitation and abuse, because of these protective mandates imposed by the law.

The 2017 Act also lays down restrictions pertaining to *"emergency treatment"*[230] of the person with mental illness in certain exceptional situations. It is stated that any medical treatment, including treatment pertaining to mental

---

[228] The 2017 Act, Section 2(i)
[229] The 2017 Act, Section 2(j)
[230] The 2017 Act, Section 94

healthcare can be given to a person with mental illness in the establishment/community (after obtaining the informed consent of the nominated representative, when the latter is available). An emergency treatment is administered where the same is immediately and urgently necessary to prevent:

- death or irreversible harm to the person with mental illness;
- the person with mental illness inflicting serious harm to himself/herself or to others and/or to property belonging to himself/herself or others as the case maybe, where the same is a consequence of the mental illness of the person.

However, the medical officer in-charge or the psychiatrist in-charge is not allowed to administer any medical treatment to the person with mental illness which is not directly related to the emergency treatment; or to administer electro-convulsive therapy. The emergency treatment should not ordinarily continue for a period longer than seventy-two hours or as soon as the person is assessed at a mental health establishment.

The 2017 Act also lays down certain restrictions pertaining to **electro-convulsive therapy** as a form of treatment for persons with mental illness in India.[231] It is stated that electro-convulsive therapy should not be performed on persons without the use of anesthesia or muscle relaxants. Electro-convulsive therapy should not be performed on minors with mental illness. However, if in the opinion of the treating psychiatrist, the therapy is required, informed consent of the guardian of the minor should be obtained before proceeding with the treatment.[232]**Sterilization** should never be done to men/women with mental illness as way of treatment of those persons. Moreover, **chaining** in any manner is also prohibited under the Act.[233]

The 2017 Act also lays down essential conditions to be fulfilled before **psychosurgery** is performed as a treatment for the person with mental

---

[231] The 2017 Act, Section 95
[232] Id.
[233] Id.

illness.[234] It is stated that psychosurgery shall not be performed on a person with mental illness till the informed consent of the person on whom the surgery is being performed is obtained and approval to perform the same has been obtained from the concerned Board.[235]

Treating with dignity is one of the most important principles that should be adhered to in the mental healthcare of persons with mental illness. To be as much in touch with humanity as possible is vital for recovery from any form of mental illness. Therefore, the Act clearly states that nobody shall be subjected to **solitary confinement or seclusion**.[236] The Act also forbids usage of physical restraint on the person with mental illness, except when usage of **physical restraint** is the only way to avert imminent harm to the person with mental illness or to others, and the usage is authorized by the psychiatrist in-charge of person with mental illness in the hospital. The restraint shall not be continued beyond the time that is absolutely necessary in the situation. The reason for the restraint, the manner and duration of the same should be recorded in the medical records of the person with mental illness by the medical officer or the mental health officer in charge of the hospital, and the nominated representative of the person should be informed about the restraint within twenty-four hours of the same. The restraint shall not in any case be administered as a punishment or as a deterrent to any person with mental illness. A mental health establishment is required under the Act to maintain record of instances of restraints and send report of the same to the concerned Board.[237] It is important to note that a mental health professional or medical practitioner is forbidden to perform any function and discharge any duty which he/she is not authorized to perform under the 2017 Act and to recommend any medicine not so authorized in the field of his/her profession.[238]

---

[234] *See* also Draft Central Regulations, 2017, Paragraph 13
[235] The 2017 Act, Section 96
[236] The 2017 Act, Section 97
[237] *See* also Draft Central Regulations, 2017, Paragraph 14
[238] The 2017 Act, Section 106

3. AUTHORITIES UNDER THE MENTAL HEALTHCARE ACT, 2017

The Central Authority for Mental Health Services under the 1987 Act is succeeded by the **Central Mental Health Authority** under the Mental Healthcare Act, 2017. On establishment of the Central Mental Health Authority, all assets and liabilities of the Central Authority for Mental Health Services stand vested and transferred to the former.[239]Some of the important functions of the Central Mental Health Authority under the 2017 Act are discussed herein below[240]:

- Registering mental health establishments under the control of the Central Government, maintaining registers and providing information pertaining to the same;
- Developing norms for quality and service provided by mental health establishments under the Central Government;
- Supervising all mental health establishments under the control of the Central Government;
- Maintaining a national register of clinical psychologists, mental health nurses and psychiatric social workers;
- Training of law enforcement officials, mental health professionals and other health professionals about the provisions of the Act; and
- Advising the Central Government on matters pertaining to mental healthcare, etc.

The State Authority for Mental Health Services under the 1987 Act is succeeded by the State Mental Health Authority under the 2017 Act. All assets and liabilities of the State Authority for Mental Health Services stand vested and transferred to the **State Mental Health Authority**.[241]Some of the important

---

[239] The 2017 Act, Section 42.
[240] The 2017 Act, Section 43.
[241] The 2017 Act, Section 54.

functions of the State Mental Health Authority under the 2017 Act are discussed herein below[242]:

- Registering mental health establishments in the State except those registered with the Central Mental Health Authority[243] and maintaining and publishing a register of the establishments so registered;
- Developing norms for quality and service provided by mental health establishments in the State;
- Supervising all mental health establishments in the State;
- Maintaining a register of clinical psychologists, mental health nurses and psychiatric social workers;
- Training of law enforcement officials, mental health professionals and other health professionals about the provisions of the Act; etc.

The State Mental Health Authority has to constitute the **Mental Health Review Boards** for the purposes of the 2017 Act.[244]The constitution of the Boards by the State Authority for a particular district or group of districts will be such as will be prescribed by the Central Government.[245]

The powers and functions of the Mental Health Review Board, as enumerated in the Act are as follows[246]:

- Register, review, alter or cancel an advance directive of the person with mental illness;
- Appoint a nominated representative of the person with mental illness;
- To receive and decide upon applications pertaining to non-disclosure of information, deficiencies in care and services, etc.;

---

[242] The 2017 Act, Section 55.
[243] Hospitals registered with the Central Mental Health Authority under Section 43 of the 2017 Act.
[244] The 2017 Act, Section 73.
[245]See The 2017 Act, Section 74.
[246] The 2017 Act, Section 82.

- To visit and inspect and thereby keep track of the health services in prisons and jails;
- To conduct inquiry, on receipt of a notice thereby, pertaining to violations of rights of persons with mental illness in a mental health establishment and on non-compliance of the order or direction impose penalty;
- Take steps to protect the rights of persons with mental illness;

Any person aggrieved by the order of the Board may approach the High Court of the State where the Board is located, and prefer an appeal before the same.[247]

It is important to note that any contravention of the provisions of the 2017 Act is punishable at the first instance with a punishment of imprisonment up to six months and fine up to Rs.10,0000/- or both; and for every such contravention made subsequently, imprisonment up to two years and/or with a fine between Rs.50,000/- and Rs.5,00,000/-.[248] The 2017 Act also lays down penalties for establishing or maintaining of mental health establishment in contraventions of the Act.[249]

SUMMARIZING: The Mental Healthcare Act, 2017 came into force very recently, that is, from 29th May, 2018[250] on which date the Mental Health Act, 1987 stood repealed. In order to address the present and future, it is important to analyse and draw a link with what was the situation in the past. This Chapter compared two major aspects of the 2017 Act and the 1987 Act, namely: (i) the procedures pertaining to admission, treatment and discharge under the two Acts; (ii) various Authorities under the two Acts. This Chapter holds significance because one cannot ignore the fact the 2017 Act has not been introduced in a vacuum but is replacing a 31 year old legislation. Therefore, it was important to

---

[247] The 2017 Act, Section 83
[248] The 2017 Act, Section 108
[249] The 2017 Act, Section 107
[250] Notification No.: S.O. 2173(E), Ministry of Health and Family Welfare, Government of India (29th May, 2018)

understand the major administrative changes in the law enforcement mechanism that will be brought about by the virtue of the new law. The 2017 Act which was introduced in the light of UNCRPD aims for just, equitable and holistic mental healthcare in India through its various provisions. It can be concluded by stating that as compared to the 1987 Act, the 2017 Act is a progressive step for mental healthcare in India. The provisions of the 2017 Act are meticulously drafted and cater to minute details pertaining to admission, treatment and care of persons with mental illness in the country.

VIII. ANALAYSING THE DECISIONS OF INDIAN COURTS ON MATTERS RELATING TO MENTAL ILLNESS

The fundamental rights guaranteed under Part III of the Constitution of India vociferously support the rights in healthcare of persons with mental illness. The Courts in India have always come to the rescue of persons with mental illness and have protected their rights. There have been multiple Judgements by the Hon'ble Supreme Court of India and also by the various Hon'ble High Courts of the country pertaining to mental healthcare of persons with mental illness. Chapter VII of this research drew comparison between the working of the Mental Health Act, 1987 and the Mental Healthcare Act, 2017. This Chapter also analyses the era of the Mental Health Act, 1987 and the time before that by delving into the decisions of the Indian Courts pertaining to mental healthcare till date.

The Courts in India have time and again dealt with issues pertaining to rights and healthcare of persons with mental illness. This Chapter aims to bring together all the pertinent judgements on this area to fore and analyse the same from the perspective of women with mental illness wherever relevant. The Mental Healthcare Act, 2017 came into force very recently, that is, from 29th May, 2018[251] on which date the Mental Health Act, 1987 stood repealed. Chapter VII of this research drew comparison between the working of the Mental Health Act, 1987 and the Mental Healthcare Act, 2017. This Chapter also analyses the era of the Mental Health Act, 1987 and the time before that by delving into the decisions of the Indian Courts pertaining to mental healthcare till date.

- **In Re : Death of 25 Chained Inmates In Asylum Fire In Tamil Nadu[252]**

The matter before the Hon'ble Supreme Court of India was pertaining to a gruesome news item published in the leading newspapers of the country, regarding the grave tragedy at a mental asylum in Eravadi, Tamil Nadu where twenty-five inmates were charred to death when a fire had broken out because they were unable to escape, the reason for the same being that they were chained to poles or beds. The Hon'ble Supreme Court asked the respondents for the factual report in the first place.[253] The Court then required every State in the country to file an affidavit requiring *inter alia* the following details:[254]

    ○ When was the State Mental Health Authority set up in the State (If a State does not have a State Mental Health Authority, the reason for the same and a date by when the State Mental Health Authority be established and will become operational);

---

[251] Notification No.: S.O. 2173(E), Ministry of Health and Family Welfare, Government of India (29th May, 2018)

[252] AIR 2002 SC 3693

[253] *See* In Re: Death of 25 Chained Inmates In Asylum Fire In Tamil Nadu v. Union of India & ors., 2001(5) Scale 64

[254] *See* Re : Death of 25 Chained Inmates v. Union of India, AIR 2002 SC 979

o The dates of meetings of the State Mental Health Authority till date and a short summary of the decisions taken by far since the inception of the Authority;

o Undertakings from the State that a meeting of the State Mental Health Authority be conducted at least once in every four months;

o The number of prosecutions undertaken and penalties or other punitive measures imposed by the State under the Mental Health Act, 1987.

The Supreme Court also required every State and Union Territory in the country to conduct an assessment survey and file a report pertaining to the following:[255]

o Average number of mental health resource personnel in the state;

o Bed strength, outpatient facilities and rehabilitation facilities in the public and private sector.

The Chief Secretary of each State was asked to file an affidavit whether any minimum standards had been set up for licensing Mental Health Institutions and whether the registered mental health institutions were adhering to the prescribed minimum standard. The Union of India was directed to file a policy to set up at least one Mental Health Hospital run by the Central Government in each State and to consider the viability of framing uniform rules setting standards of service for Mental Health Institutions. Section 43 of the Mental Health Act, 1987, states that a patient can apply to the Magistrate for discharge. Minimum two members of the Legal Aid Board of every State are required to be appointed to visit the institutions monthly and assist the patients and their family members in applying for discharge from the Institution. The Supreme Court held that it is mandatory for the Judicial Officer concerned, to explain to the patients their rights at the time of admission, and inform them about whom to approach in case any of those rights are violated.[256] The Court also recommended the setting up of rehabilitation schemes for patients who do not have any support in

---

[255] In Re : Death of 25 Chained Inmates In Asylum Fire In Tamil Nadu, AIR 2002 SC 3693
[256] Id.

the community, which would include the setting up of *"Supported Shared Home like Accommodation."*[257]

- **Sheela Barse v. Union of India**[258]

The Supreme Court condemned the admission of non-criminal mentally ill persons in prisons and held that the same was illegal and unconstitutional. The Court directed the Judicial Magistrate to get any such person produced before him/her to be examined by a mental health professional and thereafter, send such a person to the nearest place of treatment and care.

- **Binoo Sen v. State of West Bengal through the Principal Secretary, Department of Social Welfare and others**[259]

In this case the Calcutta High Court directed that, whenever it is brought before the notice of a Court that a person produced before it, suffers from any form mental illness, before remanding such a person to a Home, the Court must send the person for a medical check-up at a hospital which is well-equipped to conduct such a test and provide mental healthcare to him/her.

- **Chandan Kumar Banik v. State of W.B.**[260]

This case came before the Supreme Court in the form of a PIL wherein a letter addressing the court accompanied by a picture of a patient chained in the Mental Hospital located in Hooghly, West Bengal was attached. After getting a reply pertaining to the situation from the Government of West Bengal, the Court also appointed a Committee to investigate into the issue. Taking due note of the condition of administration in the hospital, amenities available to and accessible by patients, the Supreme Court expressed its displeasure about the fact that the administration of the Hospital was under the charge of only a Sub-Divisional

---

[257] *Id.*
[258] AIR 1993 SCW 2908; *See* also Sheela Barse v. Union of India, 1995(5) SCC 654; Sheela Barse v. Union of India, 1993(4) SCC 204 ; Sheela Barse v. Union of India, 1986(2) Scale 1
[259] 1999(2) Cal. H.C.N. 268
[260] 1995(Sup4) SCC 505

Officer. The Court observed that the head of the management at an institution like this should be an official who is able to understand and appreciate the treatment and care of persons with mental illness. As several lapses and flaws in the functioning of the Hospital were enumerated in the Report submitted by the Investigating Committee, the Supreme Court directed that a copy of the Report be sent to the Chief Secretary to the Government of WB and thereafter be placed before the concerned Minister of the WB Government for necessary action in pursuance of the improvement of the conditions in the Hospital.

- **Chandigarh Administration v. Nemo;[261] and**
- **Suchita Srivastava and Another v. Chandigarh Administration[262]**

The Chandigarh Administration had come before the Punjab and Haryana High Court to seek permission to medically terminate the pregnancy of a mentally retarded girl. The High Court Court set up an Expert Body to look into the issue that whether the termination of the pregnancy would be in the best interest of the victim. The girl had been raped by one of the guards of the Nari Niketan. This brought into fore the lurking risk which girls at such institutions face, that of being vulnerable to sexual and physical attacks by the care-givers at the institution. The Punjab and Haryana High Court issued *inter alia* the following directions for the functioning of the Nari Niketan and similar institutions:

> o A Medical Board to visit fortnightly Nari Niketan, Ashreya and other similar institutions. The Medical Board to be notified and to comprise specialists, particularly a gynecologist, skin specialist, counsellor and headed by the Director, Health Services, Chandigarh. The periodical examination to particularly take note of any form of sexual or other abuse of any inmate in such institution;

---

[261] 2009(3) R.C.R.(Civil) 766 (P&H) (DB)
[262] AIR 2010 SC 235

- The Chandigarh Administration to provide the best medical treatment to all the inmates of such Government run or Government aided institutions;
- The description and details of each inmate and their photographs respectively to be displayed in the website of the concerned Department and the said information to be updated on a regular basis;
- Chandigarh Administration to not keep or employ male staff members for the internal working of such institutions if there are any female inmates in the institution.

In furtherance of the matter, the Supreme Court held that the *"woman's right to privacy, dignity and bodily integrity should be respected"* which includes her reproductive choice to continue with the pregnancy.[263]

- **Tulshidas Kanolkar v. State of Goa**[264]

In this case, a woman with mental disability was repeatedly raped. The Supreme Court observed that in such a case, apart from physical violence, there is also *"exploitation of her helplessness"*. Justice Arijit Pasayat, stated it was exigent to prescribe a higher penalty for the rape of a mentally challenged woman whose *"mental age may be less than 12 years"*.

- **Chitta Ranjan Bhattacharjee v. State of Tripura**[265]

In this PIL, the petitioner requested the High Court of Guwahati to issue directions to the State Government to perform its duties with respect to mentally ill persons as mandated by the Mental Health Act, 1987. The Court issued *inter alia* the following directions to the State:

- Create awareness among the general public regarding the functioning of the Act;

---

[263] Suchita Srivastava and Another v. Chandigarh Administration, AIR 2010 SC 235
[264] AIR 2004 SC 978.
[265] 2010(2) GauLT 514 (Gauhati) (Agartala Bench)

- o Ensure existence of necessary facilities for mental healthcare through mental hospitals, psychiatric hospital and other mental healthcare facilities;
- o Issue guidelines in police station laying down pints of awareness about respecting the rights of persons with mental illness; etc.

- **D.K. Basu v. State of WB**[266]

In this case, one of the issues before the Supreme Court was that of custodial violence including deaths in the lock-ups. The Court issued directions pertaining to the same and required the directions to be put in the form of a notice in a conspicuous place in every police station in the country. The Court also took note of the failure by the authorities in the country to properly cater to the requirements of persons with mental illness, who are found loitering on the streets or other places. The Court noted that despite the existence of the Mental Health Act, 1987, because there is no awareness about the provisions of the legislation, the fundamental rights of persons with mental illness are being grossly hampered. The Court therefore issued directions to the State to create awareness about the provisions of the Mental Health Act, 1987 and facilitate the implementation of its provisions by taking necessary action. The Court also required setting up of a Scheme for rehabilitation of persons with mental illness who lack the capacity to take care of themselves, or whose family members are unwilling to take care of them. State authorities were further directed to provide such persons with mental healthcare facilities. Directions were issued to create awareness through the All India Radio and other electronic media regarding the role of the society to protect the rights of persons with mental illness.

---

[266] (1997)1 SCC 416

- **Court on its own motion v. Principal Secretary (Social Justice & Empowerment)[267]**

In this case, the High Court of Himachal Pradesh issued directions to the Government of Himachal Pradesh pertaining to mental healthcare and rehabilitation of persons with mental illness. Enumerated herein below are some of the directions issued by the Hon'ble High Court to various authorities of the State Government of Himachal Pradesh:

   o The Principal Secretary (Health) was directed to fill up the posts of psychiatrists in all district hospitals in Himachal Pradesh;

   o The Principal Secretary (Health) was directed to provide clothing and footwear to the patients at the Himachal Pradesh Hospital for Mental Health and Rehabilitation four times in a year depending on the change of weather;

   o The Director, Women and Child Development, was directed to ensure that mentally ill patients are admitted in the Mental Health and Rehabilitation Centre, Boileauganj, Shimla;

   o The rehabilitation grant for women with mental illness was increased to Rs. 50,000/-;

   o Women with mental illness were not to be admitted to Nari Niketan, Mashobra. Such women to be admitted to the pscychiatric wards of general hospitals or in the Mental Health and Rehabilitation Centre, Boileauganj, Shimla;

   o Steps to be taken to ensure that patients who have been cured can return to their homes;

   o Enough number of posts to be approved, created and filled up within three months to assist and attend to the inmates at the H.H. Mental Health and Rehabilitation Centre, Shimla;

The High Court also directed the Superintendents of Police in the State were directed to comply with the provisions of Section 23 of the Mental Health Act,

---

[267] 2015(3) R.C.R.(Civil) 684 (HP) (DB)

1987 and to produce within 24 hours before the Magistrate, any person taken into protection and/or detained under Section 23.[268]

- **Joseph v. State of Kerala[269]**

In this case, the High Court of Kerala directed the Mental Health Centres under the control of the Government of Kerala to ensure that the provisions of the Mental Health Act, 1987, particularly Sections 15, 16 and 17 are adhered to. A mentally person who lacks the capacity to give consent for mental healthcare treatment, can be admitted in a psychiatric hospital only if an application in furtherance of the same is made by a relative or friend of the person, and the medical officer in-charge at that point at that hospital must be satisfied that admitting the person as an in-patient is the only viable option.

- **State of Gujarat v. Kanaiyalal Manilal[270]**

The High Court of Gujarat held in this case that the treatment and care of mentally ill persons in psychiatric hospitals and nursing homes is the statutory obligation of the State Government in a welfare State like India.

- **In Re: Illegal Detention of Machal Lalung v. ABC[271]**

The present writ petition was filed before the Supreme Court under Article 32 of the Constitution, and was made pertaining to mentally challenged under-trail prisoners languishing in mental hospitals for years. The Supreme Court directed necessary steps to be taken to conclude the trials of these prisoners and/or release them to their family members respectively.[272]

---

[268] *See* also Dr. Upendra Baxi v. State of U.P., 1998(9) SCC 388; and Upendra Baxi v. State of Uttar Pradesh, 1983(2) SCC 308
[269] 2014(5) R.C.R.(Civil) 457 (Kerala)
[270] 1997(1) GujLH 560 (Gujarat)
[271] 2007(9) Scale 432; *See* also In Re :- Illegal Detentionof Machal Lalung, 2007(9) Scale 434; Re : Illegal Detention of Macha Llalung, 2007(9) Scale 435
[272] *See* also Veena Sethi v. State of Bihar, 1982 SCC(Cri) 511; and S. Hariprakash v. Hon'ble Chief Justice, Madras High Court2014(4) MLJ (Criminal) 534

- **Nathalie Vandenbyvanghe v. The State of TN**[273]

A French national came as a tourist to India and lost his passport in India. He did not know English, and was found loitering on the streets, lost. He was brought along with 114 other persons by the Police and reception orders were issued against all the 114 of them including the French national. On contacting the French embassy, the French national's daughter was apprised that her father was at a psychiatric hospital in Chennai. She came to India and filed the instant habeas corpus petition before the High Court of Madras. The facts are that on 9th July, 2008, following persons were surrounded by the Police and declared by a team of doctors to be suffering from bipolar disorder mania and a certificate to that affect had been issued, namely:

- o Inspector of Police at Kottar Police Station brought fifty male persons;
- o Inspector of Police at Nesamony Nagar Police Station brought forty-five male persons as well as twenty female persons.

They were then brought to and admitted at the Institute of Mental Health at Chennai. The Hon'ble High Court of Madras held that:

> "This exposes the psycho-fever of the police to proceed against those who are wandering in the streets to be treated as mentally ill persons disregard of their actual physical and mental condition. We must express our total dissatisfaction over the way by which the entire matter had been handled not only by the police, but also at the level of the doctors and the learned Judicial Magistrate as well."[274]

The Court further held that persons with mental illness are not criminals and the State owes its duty towards the protection of their human rights. The medical officers were not careful enough before certifying a person as mentally ill; and that a person is not entitled to any less attention than others, just because he/she is found wandering about on the streets.

---

[273] Habeas Corpus Petition No.1041 of 2008 (Madras)
[274] Nathalie Vandenbyvanghe v. The State Of Tamil Nadu, Habeas Corpus Petition No.1041 of 2008 (Madras)

- **Rakesh Chand Narain v. State of Bihar**[275]

A letter was addressed to the Chief Justice of India in 1986[276] relating the plight of patients at the Mental Hospital at Kanke near Ranchi. The Supreme Court required the State Government of erstwhile Bihar to file a counter-affidavit and the Chief Judicial Magistrate of Ranchi to issue a report pertaining to the issue.[277] Three years later, in the present case, the Supreme Court observed that the Scheme which had been submitted before the Court had not been implemented properly. The Court held that India, being a welfare State, has a duty towards the health of every citizen including the mental healthcare of persons with mental illness. The Court constituted a Committee of Management for the Mental Hospital at Kanke to work towards the transformation of conditions in the said Hospital. The Court was of the concerted opinion that if the conditions in the Mental Hospital at Kanke could reach the level of mental healthcare at NIMHANS, Bangalore the quality of the Karke Hospital would improve and the patients at the latter would be able to benefit from the modern scientific treatments available in mental healthcare. Later in a Judgement in the year 1994, the Supreme Court directed that the Ranchi Manasik Arogyashala should be made an autonomous institution.[278]

- **Robert Heijkamp v. Bal Anand World Children Welfare Trust**[279]

The question before the Hon'ble Bombay High Court, in this case was whether a child of a mentally ill person be considered as a child in need of care and protection under the Juvenile Justice Act, 1986. The Court was of the opinion that such a child would ordinarily be deemed to be abandoned under the JJ Act, 1986.[280] However, the determination of the mental illness of such a parent cannot be done by an authority under the JJ Act, 1986, and can only be done

---

[275] AIR 1989 SC 348

[276] *See* also Aman Hingorani v. Union of India and others, AIR 1995 SC 215

[277] *See* Rakesh Chandra Narayan v. State of Bihar, 1986(2) Scale 739

[278] Rakesh Chandra Narayan v. State of Bihar, 1994(3) Scale 1034

[279] 2008(1) BCR 719 (Bombay)

[280] The Juvenile Justice Act, 1986, Section 41

under the Mental Health Act, 1987. Therefore, only if a Court dealing with a matter under the Mental Health Act, 1987 is of the opinion that the parent/person is mentally ill could the Child Welfare Committee under the JJ Act, 1986 be justified in concluding that the child of such a parent is abandoned and therefore eligible for adoption under the relevant provisions of the Juvenile Justice Act, 1986.

- ## Supreme Court Legal v. State of M.P.[281]

In this case, the Supreme Court condemned the practice of chaining of patients with mental illness in the Gwalior Mental Asylum as a gross violation of right to life guaranteed under Article 21 of the Constitution. Some of the patients were found without a piece of clothing on them. The Supreme Court directed the authorities to take immediate action to remedy the deplorable situation.

- ## Ravinder v. Government of NCT & Ors.[282]

The Delhi High Court in this case directed the payment of Rs. 2 lakhs as compensation by the government to a 71 year old person for confining him in the Institute of Human Behaviour and Allied Sciences, Delhi (IBHBAS) because he had lost his temper in Court. It is to be noted that he was admitted without citing of any provision under the Mental Health Act, 1987. The Delhi High Court condemned this incident as an act of sheer negligence on the part of the doctors at IHBAS, Delhi and an absolute violation of the fundamental rights of the person confined, including his right to life. The Court *inter alia* made reference to the judgement of the US Supreme Court in *O'Connor v. Donaldson*[283]wherein it was held that the sole finding of mental illness of a person cannot be a reason to keep him/her in confinement.

---

[281] 1994(5) SCC 27
[282] W.P. (CRL.) 3317/2017
[283] 422 US 563 (1975)

- **Dr. Sangamitra Acharya & Anr. v. State (NCT of Delhi) & Ors.**[284]

In this case, the High Court of Delhi held that involuntary admission under special circumstances under Section 19 of the Mental Health Act, 1987 is only viable when the patient is mentally ill and the medical officer in charge of the mental health institution has reached a satisfaction to that effect. Admission under special circumstances for the mere observation of the patient amounts to a violation of the right to life, liberty and dignity of the person so admitted. The fundamental criteria to be fulfilled, therefore, must be that the person so admitted should be unable to express his/her willingness to get admitted and such an admission should be in the best interest of the person. To be satisfied of the existence of the above conditions, the medical officer in charge of the mental health institution should personally interact with the person and make observations regarding the condition of the person thereafter.

The Hon'ble High Court held that such a decision cannot be taken by a mere conversation on the phone or through a WhatsApp message, even if the person conveying the message was a qualified mental health professional. The Court reiterated the intent of the Parliament while framing such a law, being that when a person is brought by someone else, claiming that the person is mentally ill, the provisions of law entail a duty on the medical officer in charge of the mental health institution to be personally satisfied that the person is mentally ill, and is therefore not in a position to express willingness to be admitted as an in-patient.

> *"A person brought to a mental health institution without her consent, and sought to be admitted faces a serious infraction of her life and liberty. This dictates the mandatory nature of the safeguards under the MHA having to be scrupulously followed."*[285]

A violation of the above mandate, the Court observed, will not only cause irreparable harm to the person but will also seriously violate his/her constitutional rights. The Court also recommended the setting up of a Code of

---

[284] W.P. (CRL.) 1804/2017 & CM No. 9963/2017

[285] Dr. Sangamitra Acharya & Anr. v. State (NCT of Delhi) & Ors., W.P. (CRL.), Para. 123

Ethics for Psychiatrists to follow, a code which would reinforce the law; and directed the Delhi Police to prepare a manual stating in details how to deal with cases under the Mental Health Act, 1987 and thereafter the Mental Healthcare Act, 2017.

SUMMARIZING: This Chapter is significant for this research because it draws an insight into the decisions of the Supreme Court of India and the various High Courts in the country pertaining to mental healthcare issues. It can be concluded by stating that the Courts in India have time and again tried to draw a balance between the *"best interest"* of the person with mental illness involved, keeping in mind the gravity of the medical necessity in his/her mental healthcare. The Courts have also always upheld the right to life, dignity and equality of persons with mental illness at par with the other citizens of the country. It can be said that the 2017 Act upholds the ethos of these tenets and principles laid down by the Indian Courts.

Chapter IX

IX. INDIA'S NATIONAL MENTAL HEALTH POLICY, 2014 AND ITS REFLECTION IN THE MENTAL HEALTHCARE ACT, 2017

The aims and objectives of the National Mental Health Policy of India, 2014 and its recommendations find place in the provisions of the Mental Healthcare Act, 2017. Having discussed the 2017 Act and various judicial decisions of the Indian Courts pertaining to mental healthcare in India, it becomes very important to critically analyse the National Mental Health Policy of India, 2014 to comprehensively complete this research pursuit.

1. OBJECTIVES OF THE NATIONAL MENTAL HEALTH POLICY OF INDIA, 2014:

A Policy Group to recommend a National Mental Health Policy was set up in 2011. The National Mental Health Policy was passed in 2014[286] and was made in consonance with WHO Resolution WHA 65.4 approved by the 65th World Health Assembly on *"The global burden of mental disorders and the need for a comprehensive, coordinated response from health and social sectors at the country level."*[287] The goals and objectives, which the National Mental Health Policy of India, 2014 aims to achieve are:

- Reduce the disability, distress, mortality, etc. relating to mental health issues;
- Create awareness and enhance the level of understanding pertaining to mental health in the country;
- Strengthen the leadership in the mental health sector at various levels, including Center, State and District;
- Enable universal access to mental health care in the country;
- Enhance and increase the capacity to utilize mental health services by persons with mental health problems (Such services would include preventive services, services for treatment, care and support);
- Increase access of mental health services to the vulnerable sections of the society (for example: homeless persons, socially/economically/educationally backward sections of the Indian society);
- Reduce the occurrence of suicides and attempts to commit suicide;
- Reduce the stigma surrounding mental illness in the country;

---

[286] National Mental Health Policy of India (2014), Available at https://www.nhp.gov.in/sites/default/files/pdf/national%20mental%20health%20policy%20of%20india%202014.pdf (Last visited on April 5, 2018)
[287] WHO Resolution WHA 65.4, Available at http://apps.who.int/gb/DGNP/pdf_files/A65_REC1-en.pdf (Last visited on December 15, 2017)

- Reduce the prevalence of risk factors associated with mental health problems;
- Provide appropriate interventions by identifying the social, psychological and biological determinants of mental health issues; etc.

The fundamental principles to which the National Mental Health Policy of India adheres to are enumerated in the chart below:

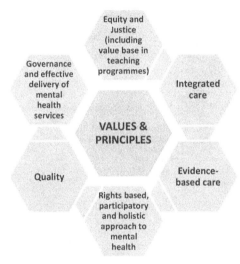

Table (5): Fundamental values and principles of the 2014 Policy

The 2014 Policy emphasizes on the importance of proper funding and availability of the same across departments for the proper fulfillment of the vision envisaged in the Policy. It is vital that new activities relating to rehabilitation of persons with mental illness and continuance of mental healthcare facilities should be coupled with adequate amount of funding from the Government.

The 2014 Policy recognizes the role that families of persons with mental illness play. *"The emotional and social costs of providing care for a family member with*

mental illness cannot be quantified but exacts a huge toll on the family."[288] The
Policy recommends that the family members be provided:

- Access to information;
- Guidance in getting access to services for their family member with
  mental illness; and
- Support to carry on with their role as care-givers.

The Policy calls for inter-sectoral collaboration and acknowledges the fact that
the Government and the non-government (private and non-profit organizations)
sectors should work hand in hand for the proper redressal of justice.

The recommendations of the 2014 Policy have been broken down into seven
broad categories, namely[289]:

**Table (6): Strategic Directions and Recommendations of Action (2014
Policy)**

---

[288] The 2014 Policy, Para 4.5
[289] The 2014 Policy, Para 5

147

2. ANALYSING THE STRATEGIC DIRECTIONS AND RECOMMENDATIONS OF THE 2014 POLICY:

i.   Effective governance and accountability[290]:

One of first steps towards addressing the concerns of mental healthcare in India are developing relevant laws, policies and laws in consonance with the National Mental Health Policy, 2014 with proper implementation and mechanisms to monitor the implementation. The Mental Healthcare Act 2017 is very much in consonance with the spirit of the 2014 Policy and is a positive step towards the realization of the goals envisaged in the Policy. However, availability of sufficient funds and proper planning is another major necessity to ensure the proper implementation of the recommendations of the Policy.

ii.   Promotion of mental health[291]:

The Policy recommends the redesigning of Anganwadi Centres to look after the early child care, emotional and development needs of children below the age of six years. Life Skill Education should be provided to school children and college going students by skilled trainers and skilled teachers catering to the context and the age of the students. Programmes should also be floated to assist adults in handling the stress in their life which can be done by counselling and appropriate workplace policies at workplace. The Policy recommends the inclusion of Ayurveda and Yoga professionals to be included in the list of activists promoting mental health. Gender sensitization of healthcare providers is another important measure recommended by the Policy. Reducing poverty and decreasing disparity in incomes is recommended through sensitization of the policy makers of the Government, because alleviating these factors will be instrumental in improving the mental health results. These recommendations are vital for the proper implementation of the 2017 Act too. The Act being in

---

[290] The 2014 Policy, Para 5.1
[291] The 2014 Policy, Para 5.2

consonance with the spirit of the Policy demands proper promotion of mental health which can effectively nip the issue in its bud.

iii. Prevention of mental illness and reduction of suicide and attempts to commit suicide[292]:

("Addressing stigma, discrimination and exclusion"[293])

The 2014 Policy recommended the decriminalization of attempt to commit suicide,[294] which has been incorporated in Section 115 of the 2017 Act. The Act of 2017 requires the appropriate Government to design and plan public health programmes for reducing suicides and attempts to commit suicide.[295] The 2017 Act decriminalizes attempt to commit suicide. It is stated that notwithstanding the provisions of Section 309 of the Indian Penal Code, any person who attempts to commit suicide should be presumed to be under severe stress and should not be tried or punished under the Indian Penal Code for the attempt to commit suicide.[296]The 2017 Act also makes it a duty of the Appropriate Government to provide care, treatment and rehabilitation to a person who attempts to commit suicide, the reason being that the person who so attempts is under severe stress and care, treatment and rehabilitation is vital to reduce the chances of any further attempts to commit suicide by the person.[297]

The 2014 Policy recommends the encouragement of persons with mental illness to be actively involved in the social and economic walks of life, to create a conducive environment for their growth without discrimination of any kind. This finds its resonance in Chapter V of the Act of 2017 which enumerates the rights of persons with mental illness. Removal of discrimination is only possible through eradicating the stigma relating to mental illness in the country. Sensitizing various sections of the society, particularly the police and the judicial officers is a very vital step towards the fulfillment of the same. Section 30 of the

---

[292] The 2014 Policy, Para 5.3
[293] Id.
[294] Id.
[295] The 2017 Act, Section 29(2)
[296] The 2017 Act, Section 115
[297] Id.

2017 Act requires the Appropriate Government to take all possible measures to ensure that various programmes to reduce stigma relating to mental illness should be planned, funded, enforced and implemented effectively. One of the major features of such programmes being, generating of awareness by disseminating information and making various sections of the society sensitive to the issue of mental illness.

iv.   Access to mental healthcare to be universal:[298]

The 2014 Policy requires mental healthcare facilities to be universally accessible. Comprehensive services that address treatment, care and rehabilitation of persons with mental illness should be readily available to all sections of the society, across territories, communities, sections and strata. This right has been enumerated in Section 18 of the 2017 Act which states that every person has the right to access to mental health services which are run by the government or are funded by it. The 2014 Policy also requires the development of standards and periodical improvisation of the quality of these facilities. Programmes should be implemented that facilitate the screening and early identification of symptoms of mental illness and provide treatment for the same.

The 2014 Policy also advocates the idea of *"Assisted Living Services"*[299] which is a form of domiciliary care for persons with long term or chronic mental illnesses. A combination of the *'institutional'*, *'community'* and *'family'* care and rehabilitation dependent on the situation, nature of illness and requirements of the person with mental illness should be incorporated for every such person with mental illness to be able to stand back in the society.

---

[298] The 2014 Policy, Para 5.4
[299] *Id.*

v.   Increasing the availability of adequately trained mental health human resources[300]:

Mental health professionals for the purposes of this recommendation of the 2014 Policy include psychiatrists, psychologists, medical psychiatric social workers, counsellors, psychiatric nurses, etc. The same is reiterated in the definition of a mental health professional under the 2017 Act.[301] The Policy emphasizes upon the need to increase the availability of more and more mental health professionals in the country to facilitate the universal access to mental healthcare. Integrating the training pertaining to mental health in other fields is necessary to facilitate the person with mental illness to be directed to a mental health professional from a general practitioner. The Policy recommends setting up of more psychiatric nursing courses or mental health courses and the skill upgradation of auxiliary nursing midwives in mental healthcare.

vi.   Community participation[302]:

The 2014 Policy requires the Government to promote the full participations of persons with mental illnesses in all aspects of life, which includes housing, education, employment, social welfare, etc. The Policy recommends the involvement of such persons in Village Health, Water and Nutrition Committees, Patient Welfare Committees in order for them to be able to participate in the planning and the monitoring of the public health system in India.

vii.   Research[303]

The National Health Policy of India, 2014 harps upon the importance of comprehensive and collaborative research to improve mental healthcare facilities in the country. It is recommended that the comprehensive research agenda should also incorporate epidemiological, health and clinical research systems along with sociological, ethnographic and other research methods

---

[300] The 2014 Policy, Para 5.5
[301] The 2017 Act, Section 2(s)
[302] The 2014 Policy, Para 5.6
[303] The 2014 Policy, Para 5.7

151

recognizing the important role of diverse methodologies and disciplines including that of participatory research method. It is recommended that Centres of Excellence for Mental Health should foster partnerships with the Medical Colleges of Psychiatry, District Mental Health Programmes and NGOs working in this arena and various research institutions. Research should also be conducted to evaluate the scope and potential of alternative therapies, traditional knowledge and practices in addressing mental health problems.

The WHO Resource Book on Mental Health, Human Rights and Legislation (2005) discusses about the significance of the coordinate interface between mental health legislation and mental health policy. It is stated that mental health legislation can help in achieving the goals laid down in the Policy and sometimes the legislation can be instrumental in making the policy makers to formulate a Policy to further the cause of the legislation and facilitate the proper enforcement of the laws, and the same is true vice-versa.[304]

It can be concluded by saying that even though the National Health Policy of India, 2014 does not address the concerns of mental healthcare of women separately the Policy is a progressive step towards better mental healthcare in the country, resultantly protecting the rights of women with mental illness too. The recommendation for universal access to mental healthcare, community care and comprehensive research is a positive development in mental healthcare discourse. The beacon of the propositions of the Policy has been taken forward by the 2017 Act, which if properly implemented can lead to the realization of the aims of the 2014 Policy and the protection of the rights of women with mental illness. The strategic recommendations and directions of the 2014 Policy can always act as the basic tenets to rely on for fulfilling the aims and objectives of the 2017 Act.

---

[304] THE WHO RESOURCE BOOK ON MENTAL HEALTH, HUMAN RIGHTS AND LEGISLATION (2005)

Chapter X

X. INTERNATIONAL INSTRUMENTS

This Chapter analyses the various international instruments, declarations and standards pertaining to mental healthcare and rights of persons and women with mental illness. This Chapter is divided into two broad parts that are: International Instruments by UN and WHO; and Regional and Organizational Developments pertaining to mental healthcare worldwide.

1. INTRODUCTION

This Chapter analyses the various international instruments, declarations and standards pertaining to healthcare and rights of persons and women with mental illness. It is divided into two broad parts that are: International Instruments by UN and WHO; and the regional and organizational developments pertaining to mental healthcare worldwide. The aim of this Chapter is to test the 2017 Act in the anvil of International mental healthcare standards. This Chapter also gives a bird's eye view of mental healthcare globally by analyzing the mental healthcare legal instruments and standards that are international, regional and organizational in nature.[305]

2. UNITED NATIONS AND THE WORLD HEALTH ORGANIZATION

i. Declarations and Conventions covering general rights

a. The Universal Declaration of Human Rights (1948) (UDHR)
UDHR[306] was proclaimed by the UN General Assembly on 10th December, 1948 which was also declared as the Human Rights Day to mark the occasion.

UDHR came into existence in the background and in the time of World War II, and was based on the idea *"that there are a few common standards of decency that can and should be accepted by people of all nations and cultures."*[307]UDHR is a yardstick of measuring the progress of a nation in the true sense of the term.[308] The document describes itself as a *"common standard"* towards which *"every individual and every organ of society"* should *"strive."*

---

[305] *See* also JEAN MCHALE, ET. AL., HEALTH CARE LAW: TEXT AND MATERIALS (2007)
[306] UDHR, Available at http://www.un.org/en/udhrbook/pdf/udhr_booklet_en_web.pdf (Last visited on November 5, 2017)
[307] Mary Ann Glendon, *The Rule of Law in the UDHR,* 2 Nw. J. Int'l Hum. Rts. 1 (2004)
[308]*Id.*

With respect to the basic character of UDHR, Eleanor Roosevelt[309], stated that:

"In giving our approval to the declaration today, it is of primary importance that we keep clearly in mind the basic character of the document. It is not a treaty; it is not an international agreement. It is not and does not purport to be a statement of law or of legal obligation. It is a declaration of basic principles of human rights and freedoms, to be stamped with the approval of the General Assembly by formal vote of its members, and to serve as a common standard of achievement for all peoples of all nations."

It is to be noted that even though UDHR as such is not binding, most of its rights had already received a significant degree of recognition by 1948 in the Constitutions of many nations[310]; and over the years most of its rights have been incorporated into the domestic legal systems of almost all countries.[311]

UDHR being the foremost International instrument towards the protection of human rights of one and all is relevant to the discussion pertaining to the international perspective of women with mental illness. Laying down provisions for equality and dignity, irrespective of status, sex, etc, UDHR can be said to be the international foundation to the protection of rights of one and all, which would include women with mental illness. The Preamble to UDHR begins by recognizing the need to protect the inherent dignity of all human beings and the inalienable and indispensable human rights. Equal rights of men and women being one of the pillars towards the promotion of social progress and better standards of life at large are pivotal for UDHR.[312] Enumerated herein in the

---

[309] Elena Roosevelt presided over the drafting process as chair of the U.N.'s first Human Rights Commission.
[310] Mary Ann Glendon, *The Rule of Law in the UDHR,* 2 Nw. J. Int'l Hum. Rts. 1 (2004)
[311] *Id.*
[312] *See* ANITA ABRAHAM, NATIONAL LAW SCHOOL OF INDIA UNIVERSITY, BANGALORE, HUMAN RIGHTS LAW –ESSENTIAL NATIONAL AND INTERNATIONAL DOCUMENTS (2004)

table below are those provisions of UDHR which are pertinently relevant with respect to the rights of women with mental illness:

Sr. No.	Article of UDHR	Right
i.	Article 1	Freedom and equality in dignity of rights; Spirit of brotherhood;
ii.	Article 2	Every person is entitled to the rights and freedoms enumerated in UDHR irrespective of race, colour, sex, language, religion, political or other opinion, national or social origin, property, birth or other status;
iii.	Article 3	Right to life, liberty and security of person;
iv.	Article 5	No one to be subjected to torture or treatment which is cruel or degrading;
v.	Article 6	Right to recognition everywhere as a 'person' before law;
vi.	Article 7	All are equal before the law and are therefore, entitled to the equal protection of law;
vii.	Article 8	All have the right to effective remedy for the violation of the rights guaranteed to them;
viii.	Article 9	No one to be subjected to exile, detention or arrest which is arbitrary in nature;
ix.	Article 12	No one should be made arbitrarily subject to interference with his/her privacy, family, home or

		correspondence, or to any attack to his/her person, honour or reputation. The law should protect every person from any interference of this kind;
x.	Article 16	Men and women of full age have the right to marry and to found a family. Everyone is entitled to equal rights pertaining to marriage, during marriage and at its dissolution;
xi.	Article 19	Every person has the right to freedom of opinion and expression;
xii.	Article 25	Right to a standard of living which is adequate not only for the well-being but also the good health of the family, which includes clothing, food, medical care, etc. Motherhood and childhood being entitled to special care and assistance facilities.
xiii.	Article 28	All persons are entitled to a social and international order in which the rights and freedoms in this Declaration can be fully realized;
xiv.	Article 29	Exercise of one's rights entails the duty to respect and protect the rights of others. A person's rights can be subjected only to such further limitations as are necessary to protect the rights of others, public order, morality and the general welfare of the society at large.

b. The International Covenant on Civil and Political Rights (ICCPR) and the International Covenant on Economic, Social and Cultural Rights (ICESCR)

After UDHR, the Human Rights Commission came up with two instrumental Covenants, both of which entered into force in the year 1976, namely: ICCPR[313] and ICESCR[314].

UDHR, ICCPR and ICESCR together make the International Bill of Rights. Both ICCPR and ICESCR have their foundation in UDHR and comprise rights and duties of persons and the responsibilities of the State parties in furtherance of the provisions of UDHR. India acceded to ICCPR[315]and ICESCR[316] on 10th April, 1979. Most of the rights in the Bill of Rights were already there in the provisions of the Indian Constitution and some others have been recognized by the Courts in India while interpreting the fundamental rights in Part III of the Constitution of India.

---

[313] ICCPR, Available at http://www.ohchr.org/en/professionalinterest/pages/ccpr.aspx (Last visited on November 5, 2017)

[314] ICESCR, Available at http://www.ohchr.org/EN/ProfessionalInterest/Pages/CESCR.aspx (Last visited on November 20, 2017)

[315] Some landmark Judgements of the Supreme Court of India that refer to the ICCPR:
PUCL v. Union of India, (1997) 1 SCC 301; D.C. Saxena (Dr.) v. Honourable Chief Justice of India, (1996) 5 SCC 216; Kirloskar Brothers Ltd., v. ESI Corpn., (1996) 2 SCC 682; Kubic Darusz v. Union of India, (1990) 1 SCC 568; Francis Coraile Mullin v. Administration, Union Territory of Delhi, (1981) 1 SCC 608.

[316] Some landmark Judgements of the Supreme Court of India that refer to the ICESCR:
LIC of India v. Consumer Education Research Centre (1995) 5 SCC 482; Regional Director, ESI Corpn. v. Francis Decosta, 1993 Supp (94) SCC 100; CESC Ltd. v. Subhash Chandra Bose, (1992) 1 SCC 441.

Sr. No.	Rights	UDHR	ICCPR	ICESCR	Fundamental Right under the Constitution of India
i.	Right to life	Article 3	Article 6	-	Article 21
ii.	Right to personal liberty	Article 3	Article 9	-	Article 21
iii.	Right to health	Article 25	-	Article 12	Article 21 Parmanand Katra v. Union of India;[317] Paschim Banga Khet mazdoor Samity & ors v. State of West Bengal & ors.[318]
iv.	Right against discrimination	Article 2	Article 2 & Article 4	Article 2	Articles 14, 15, 23 and 30
v.	Right to privacy	Article 12	Article 17	-	Article 21 Justice K.S. Puttaswamy (Retd.) v. Union of India[319]

---

[317] AIR 1989 SC 2039
[318] (1996) 4 SCC 37
[319] (2017) 10 SCC 1

vi.	Right to family	Article 16	Article 23	-	Article 21 Lata singh v.state of Uttar Pradesh;[320] Shakti Vahini v. Union of India and Ors.;[321]Jasvir Singh and anr. v. State of Punjab and Ors.[322]
vii.	Right to protection of: a. persons with disability b. women c. children	Article 25	Article 24	Article12.2	Article 15
viii.	Right to equal protection before law	Article 7	Article 26	-	Article 14
ix.	Right to legal remedy	Article 8	Article 14	-	Article 14 and 32
x.	Right against torture, cruel, inhuman treatment or	Article 5	Article 7	-	Articles 14, 17, 21 and 23

---

[320] AIR 2006 SC 2522
[321] W.P. Civil No. 231 of 2010 (Supreme Court of India)
[322] (2015) 1 RCR (Criminal) 509

161

	punishment				
xi.	Right to work	Article 23	-	Article 6 & Article 7	Article 19(1)(g)

c. Convention on Elimination of Discrimination Against Women (CEDAW)

The need to protect the rights of women in particular was recognized by the United Nations Organization and enacted in the form of CEDAW[323]. India signed and ratified on 30th July, 1980 and 9th July 1993 respectively.[324]

The basis of the Convention is to prevent discrimination on the ground of gender and thereby promote and protect equality between men and women alike. State parties to CEDAW undertake to take measures towards facilitating the exercise of rights and protection of freedoms of women in their country. This Convention is the only human rights treaty which not only protects the rights of women but also targets to reform traditions and cultures which influence the gender roles and family relations in the society.[325] Article 1 of CEDAW defines *"discrimination against women"* and thereby elaborates upon the vices this Convention aims to address.[326]CEDAW condemns *"all forms of discrimination*

---

[323] CEDAW, Available at http://www.ohchr.org/Documents/ProfessionalInterest/cedaw.pdf (Last visited on January 10, 2018)

[324] Some landmark Judgements of the Supreme Court of India that refer to provisions of CEDAW:
Gita Hariharan (Ms.) v. RBI, (1992) 2 SCC 228; Apparel Export Promotion Council v. A.K. Chopra (1999) 1 SCC 759; Vishaka v. State of Rajasthan, (1997) 6 SCC 241; C. Masilamani Mudaliar v. Idol of Sri Swaminathaswami Mudaliar Thirukoil (1996) 8 SCC 525; Madhu Kishwar v. State of Bihar, (1996) 5 SCC 125

[325]UN Women, *United Nations Entity for Gender Equality and the Empowerment of Women, Convention on the Elimination of All forms of Discrimination Against Women*, Available at http://www.un.org/womenwatch/daw/cedaw/ (Last visited on January 10, 2018)

[326] The term *"discrimination against women"* is defined in Article 1 of CEDAW to mean *"any distinction, exclusion or restriction made on the basis of sex which has the effect or purpose of impairing or nullifying the recognition, enjoyment or exercise by women, irrespective of their marital status, on a basis of equality of men and women, of human rights and fundamental freedoms in the political, economic, social, cultural, civil or any other field."*

162

against women", in all degrees and forms and entails the State parties to take appropriate measures through policies and laws thereby embodying the principle of the equality of men and women including sanctions prohibiting any form of discrimination against women.[327]Legal protection of women should be on an equal basis with men. The parties to the Convention should take all appropriate steps to eliminate discrimination against women by any person, organization or enterprise.[328] State parties should work in all fields, including social, political, cultural, economic, to ensure through legislations and policies, the full advancement and development of women.[329] This includes appropriate measures to:

- Modify social and cultural patterns discriminating between men and women;
- Ensure family education, to facilitate a proper understanding of maternity as a social function and the need to acknowledge the common responsibilities of men and women;[330]
- Eliminate discrimination against women in the field of education[331] and employment[332];
- Eliminate discrimination against women in the field of health care to facilitate equal access to health care services, including appropriate services pertaining to pregnancy;[333]
- Eliminate discrimination against women in the economic and social life, which includes equal access to family benefits, bank loans, mortgages, recreational activities, sports, etc.;[334]

---

[327] CEDAW, Article 2
[328] *Id.*
[329] CEDAW, Articles 3 and 5
[330] CEDAW, Article 5
[331] CEDAW, Article 10
[332] CEDAW, Article 11
[333] CEDAW, Article 12
[334] CEDAW, Article 13

- Eliminate discrimination against women in all family matters and decisions pertaining to marriage and its dissolution;[335]

CEDAW also requires the parties to address the particular problems of women in the rural areas and address the concerns with appropriate policy measures.[336] State parties should ensure that men and women are equal before law and have equal legal capacity, including in particular civil rights, enter into contracts, administer properties, etc.[337]

CEDAW is particularly relevant to the present research. Women with mental illness are more vulnerable as compared to men with mental illness, for the sheer existence of vulnerabilities of women, who are susceptible to discrimination in the society, family and in matters relating to healthcare. Elimination of discrimination also requires positive action towards empowering the women to be on an equal standing to exercise their rights just like men. Mentally ill women are discriminated not only on the ground of their incapacities caused by their illness but also because of the patriarchal setup where the plights of women are often ignored. CEDAW therefore, is a guiding light towards making sure that mental healthcare laws are gender sensitive and eliminate discriminations of any form on the basis of gender, ensuring equality in access to mental healthcare facilities, treatment, care and exercise of rights.

d.   Other important UN Conventions:

The Convention on the Rights of the Child (CRC)[338] is relevant to our discussion from the perspective of female children with mental illness. Proclaiming that childhood requires special care and assistance, CRC protects the rights and duties of all members of the human family, including the

---

[335] CEDAW, Article 16
[336] CEDAW, Article 14
[337] CEDAW, Article 15
[338] CRC, Available at http://www.ohchr.org/EN/ProfessionalInterest/Pages/CRC.aspx (Last visited on January 10, 2018)

children.[339] State parties to the Convention recognize that every child has the inherent right to life and the maximum possible facilities for survival and development. Among myriad other rights, Article 24 of the Convention elaborates upon the right to healthcare of every child, that is the right of every child to enjoy the highest attainable standards of health, treatment during illness and rehabilitation. Other relevant and important United Nations instrument is the Convention against Torture and Other Cruel, Inhuman or Degrading Treatment or Punishment[340] which requires the parties to the Convention to take effective measures, legislative, administrative, judicial, etc., to prevent acts of torture in any territory under its jurisdiction.

ii.   Declarations and Conventions covering rights of persons with mental illness in particular

a.   Declaration on the Rights of Disabled Persons (1975)

This Declaration was adopted by the UN General Assembly in 1975 to protect the rights and ensure the welfare of persons who are physically and/or mentally disadvantaged and for their rehabilitation and integration to a normal life.[341] The term *"disabled person"* is defined to mean a person who is incapable, because of deficiency in his/her mental capabilities, of ensuring and living a normal individual and/or social life.

---

[339] *'Child'* is defined for the purposes of the Convention of the Rights of the Child, Article 1 as *"every human being below the age of eighteen years unless under the law applicable to the child, majority is attained earlier."*
[340] Available at http://www.ohchr.org/EN/ProfessionalInterest/Pages/CAT.aspx (Last visited on January 3, 2018)
[341] UN Declaration on the Rights of Disabled Persons (1975), Available at http://www.ohchr.org/EN/ProfessionalInterest/Pages/RightsOfDisabledPersons.aspx (Last visited on January 3, 2018)

- Disabled persons have the *"inherent right to respect for their human dignity"* and to the equal exercise of the fundamental rights and the same civil and political rights as are available to others;[342]
- They should be able to exercise as normal a life as possible and be enabled to become as self-reliant as feasible;
- They have the right to equal physical, mental and physiological treatment as others;
- The special needs of persons with disability should be borne in mind at every stage of social and economic planning;
- Disabled persons should be facilitated to be able to live with their families and foster parents;
- If the disabled person has to stay at a specialized establishment because of his/her condition, the conditions at the establishment should be as close to a normal lifestyle as possible;
- Disabled persons should be protected from exploitation, discriminatory and abusive treatment;
- They should be entitled to and have access to qualified legal aid;
- Whenever the rights of disabled persons are being considered, organization of disabled persons should be consulted about the same;

This Declaration was one of the first international documents concerning persons with disabilities. Despite the fact that the principles in this Declaration are more generic in nature and are not limited to healthcare only, this Declaration has been a guiding light for such similar instruments that came about later.

---

[342] *Id.*

b. UN Principles for the Protection of Persons with Mental Illness and for the Improvement of Mental Health Care (1991)

The UN Principles for the Protection of Persons with Mental Illness and for the Improvement of Mental Health Care were adopted by the UN General Assembly in 1991 in its plenary meeting vide Resolution A/RES/46/119.[343]

The Principles recognize *"mental health care"* to include diagnosis and analysis of the mental condition of a person, and treatment, care and rehabilitation for a mental illness or a suspected mental illness. The twenty-five principles succinctly provide for equality and well-being in mental healthcare. Some of the pertinent points covered in the principles are discussed herein below:

- Referring to the basic rights and fundamental freedoms, it is stated that best available mental health care should be made available to all without discrimination.

- The need to be treated with respect upholding the dignity of the person, and protecting him/her from economic exploitation, sexual exploitation, physical abuse, etc. is also upheld by the principles.

- Determination of the mental illness of any person should be according to the medical standards internationally accepted.

- Past medical history should never be considered the sole factor to determine the mental illness of a person.

- Classification of a person as a person with mental illness will never be made except for matters pertaining to mental healthcare.

- Except according to the respective domestic law, no person can be compelled to undergo medical examination to determine whether he/she has a mental illness.

- Confidentiality should be protected as a right to all the persons to whom these Principles apply.

---

[343] UN Principles for the Protection of Persons with Mental Illness and for the Improvement of Mental Health Care (1991) Available at http://www.un.org/documents/ga/res/46/a46r119.htm (Last visited on December 15, 2017)

- Every person in need of mental healthcare has the right to be first and as far as feasible to be treated in his/her community; and when the treatment is undergone at a mental health facility, the person shall be treated at a mental health facility nearest to his/her home.
- The environment of treatment in mental health care should be as less restrictive as possible. The patient should be protected from any form of unnecessary medication, abuse or harm by other patients or staff at the healthcare facility, and from any other acts or situations of discomfort.
- Treatment involved in mental healthcare should be patient centric, and should be based on a prescribed plan which is prepared for each patient individually. In pursuance of the treatment international norms of medical ethics should be strictly adhered to.[344] The treatment of each patient should strive towards enhancing the personal autonomy of the person as far as possible.
- Medication should only be administered for treatment and therapeutic purposes and never in the form of a punishment or for the convenience of someone. Medication records of the patient should be maintained and the treatment should be prescribed by a legally authorized mental health practitioner.
- The importance of informed consent for treatment in mental healthcare is also discussed in detail.
  - Obtaining the informed consent of the patient is a pre-requisite for the treatment to commence.
  - Informed consent should be a free consent without any duress or fraud, and the information provided should be in the language in which the patient is conversant.
  - The information should include the diagnosis, purpose, duration and method of the treatment process, side effects and risks of the

---

[344] *See* SHAUN D. PATTINSON, MEDICAL LAW AND ETHICS (2009); J.K. MASON, ET. AL., MASON AND MCCALL SMITH'S LAW AND MEDICAL ETHICS (2006)

treatment. The patient should also be apprised of the alternative treatment.

o The patient should be given the right to request the presence of person or persons of his/her choice while giving the informed consent. However, the obtaining of informed consent, may become difficult in some cases, and the treatment can be proceeded with without obtaining the consent of the patient, under the following circumstances:

  ▪ The patient is an involuntary patient at the time of the treatment; or

  ▪ An independent authority decides that the concerned treatment is in the medical interest of the patient;

However, if the personal representative of the patient is there, he/she should be the one to give the consent to the treatment. In case of a medical emergency, the qualified mental health practitioner may proceed with the treatment without obtaining the patient's informed consent, if the treatment is vital to prevent immediate or plausible harm to the patient. However, as far as possible, every attempt should be made to explain the patient about the details of the treatment administered during mental healthcare. The medical record of the patient has to be updated regularly, and should specify whether a treatment has been administered voluntarily or involuntarily.

• Involuntary seclusion and physical restraint of the patient should never take place except according to the officially approved procedures, and should be employed only as a means of last resort and when it is the only way possible to prevent any harm to the patient or others. Some of the important points to be taken note of here are:

  o The restraint shall not be continued beyond the period necessary;

  o The personal representative of the patient should be given instant notice of such a restraint or confinement;

- The instances of such restraints, the reasons for the same, the nature and duration are to be mentioned in the patient's medical record;
- A patient in seclusion or under restraint shall be kept in conditions which are humane; and
- The patient shall be under the careful supervision of the qualified staff.

- It is forbidden to carry out sterilization as a treatment for mental illness.
- Psychosurgery or any other irreversible or intrusive treatments are not to be undertaken upon an involuntary patient. In case of a voluntary patient, informed consent of the patient is mandatory along with an approval of an independent external body that the said treatment is necessary and that the consent has been freely obtained.
- No major surgical or medical procedure shall be conducted on a person with mental illness if the same is not permitted by the domestic law of the country. The same can be undertaken only when the same is necessitated for the best interest of the person and he/she has given informed consent for the same. If the patient is not in a state to give an informed consent, the procedure will only be executed if approved by an independent review by a competent body.
- Experimental treatment and/or clinical trials cannot be undertaken without the informed consent of the patient for the same. If the patient is not in a state to give an informed consent, the procedure will only be executed if approved by an independent review by a competent body.
- If there is violation of any of the aforementioned mandates, the patient or his/her representative or any interested person for that matter will have the right to appeal against the treatment meted out to the patient, before a judicial or other independent authority appointed for the purpose in the concerned country.

c. WHO, Mental Health Care Law: Ten Basic Principles (1996)

Based on a concerted and comparative analysis of the laws pertaining to mental health in forty-five countries and taking que from the United Nations Principles for the Protection of Persons with Mental Illness and for the Improvement of Mental Health Care, 1991, WHO adopted the Ten Basic Principles of Mental Health Care Law were adopted in 1996.[345] These principles are ancillary to the basic principles of health care in general, like confidentiality, informed consent, etc.

The Principles are enumerated herein below:

i.   Promotion of mental health of all and prevention of mental disorders;

ii.   Accessibility to mental health care;

iii.   Mental Health Assessments to adhere to the principles internationally accepted;

iv.   Mental Healthcare to be least restrictive;

v.   Right to self-determination;

vi.   Right to be assisted to exercise one's self-determination;

vii.   Availability and accessibility to review procedure;

viii. Periodical review mechanism which is automatic;

ix.   Qualified decision maker; and

x.   Respect of and adherence to Rule of Law.

These Principles contain the basic tenets to which the mental healthcare laws of countries should adhere too. Based on the legal system of each country, these principles might not find place in one single compiled law but in different legal instruments combined together. The 2017 Act of India does stand tested and pass under the anvil of this test.

---

[345]WHO, Ten Basic Principles of Mental Health Care Law (1996), Available at http://www.who.int/mental_health/policy/legislation/ten_basic_principles.pdf (Last visited on April 1, 2018)

d. UN Convention on Rights of Persons with Disability (2006) & Optional Protocol

UNCRPD was introduced with the intention to promote respect for the inherent dignity of all persons with disabilities, by making sure that they get equal access to enjoy all human rights and fundamental freedoms. The term *"persons with disability"*, for the purposes of UNCRPD, includes *"those who have long-term physical, mental, intellectual or sensory impairments which in interaction with various barriers may hinder their full and effective participation in society on an equal basis with others."*[346]

Article 3 enumerates the general principles or tenets to which UNCRPD adheres to, namely:

- Autonomy of the individual, inherent dignity, freedom of choice;
- Non-discrimination;
- Inclusion in the society and the opportunity to active and full participation in the societal affairs;
- Respecting diversity and accepting human diversity as an inherent aspect of humanity;
- Equality of opportunity and accessibility;
- Respecting the evolving capacity of children with disabilities and respecting their right to preserve their identity; and
- Equality between men and women.

UNCRPD was instrumental into the coming into existence of the 2017 Act in India. The Preamble of the 2017 Act states *inter alia* that the Act was introduced to align and to harmonize the existent mental healthcare laws in the country to UNCRPD.

Women with Disability: UNCRPD is an exhaustive instrument covering various rights of persons with disabilities. It is stated that every person with

---

[346] UNCRPD, Article 1

disability is entitled to respect for his/her physical and mental integrity, on an equal basis and at par with the others in the society. This was the first instrument of its kind pertaining to persons with disabilities which specifically mentions about women with disabilities, the vulnerabilities faced by them and directs the member states to take necessary steps to obviate such vulnerabilities and discrimination. UNCRPD recognizes the fact that women and girls who have disabilities are more often than not at a greater risk of injury or abuse, negligent treatment, violence, exploitation and maltreatment, both within their homes and outside. Article 6 of UNCRPD discusses about women with disabilities and the need to address the predicaments faced by them. It is stated that women and girls having disabilities face discriminations which are multiple in number and nature. State parties to UNCRPD therefore, should work towards ensuring equal and full enjoyment by them of all fundamental freedoms and human rights. Appropriate measures should also be made in order to ensure the advancement, empowerment and development of women in order to guarantee their enjoyment of various human rights and fundamental freedoms. State parties are also directed to put into place effective and appropriate legislations and policies, including women-centric and women-focused laws and policies to ensure identification of instances of violence, exploitation and abuse of persons with disabilities, and that such instances are investigated upon and prosecuted further thereto. State parties are also directed to ensure access by persons with disabilities, in particular women and girls who have disabilities, to programmes for social protection and poverty reduction.

Rights and freedoms: Some of the other important points of concern addressed by UNCRPD include bringing about awareness pertaining to the rights of persons with disabilities, ensuring the equality and accessibility of persons with disabilities and equal recognition before the law. The right to life is recognized as an inherent right of every individual and all the required measures should be undertaken by the member states to ensure that the persons with disabilities are able to enjoy their right to life at par with others.

The right to equal recognition before the law, access to justice, liberty of person and security of person are some other important rights recognized in the UNCRPD. Apart from the above, UNCRPD recognizes the following rights and freedoms of persons with disability:

- Freedom from torture or degrading, inhuman or cruel punishment or treatment;
- Freedom from abuse, violence and exploitation;
- Integrity of person;
- Liberty of nationality;
- Liberty of movement;
- Freedom to live independently and the right to be included in the community;
- Freedom of speech, expression, opinion and access to information;
- Personal mobility in the time and manner of one's choice and at an affordable cost;

- Freedom from torture or degrading, inhuman or cruel punishment or treatment;
- Freedom from abuse, violence and exploitation;
- Integrity of person;
- Liberty of nationality;
- Liberty of movement;
- Freedom to live independently and the right to be included in the community;
- Freedom of speech, expression, opinion and access to information;
- Freedom from torture or degrading, inhuman or cruel punishment or treatment;

For the pursuance of the above, state parties to UNCRPD, have undertaken to collect information, both research data and statistical data to be able to formulate and implement policies to bring their legal framework in consonance with the principles laid down in UNCRPD. For the fulfillment of the said purpose the importance of international cooperation is also recognized. UNCRPD also sets up a Committee on the Rights of Persons with Disabilities for the fulfillment of the aims and purposes of the Convention. It is to be noted that the 2017 Act of India was introduced with the aim to make the laws pertaining to mental healthcare in India in consonance and harmony with UNCRPD.

e.   WHO Mental Health Action Plan 2013-2020[347]

The 65th World Health Assembly in its resolution WHA65.4, in May 2012, on addressing the global burden pertaining to mental disorders, recognized the need for a coordinated and comprehensive response from the social and health sectors of all member nations at the national level. On the basis of the resolution culminated the WHO Mental health Action Plan of 2013-2020 after exhaustive and comprehensive consultation with all the member states, the civil society and the international stake holders. The Action Plan aims towards multifarious factors pertaining to mental healthcare, namely prevention, rehabilitation, promotion, recovery and care.

The background in which the Action Plan culminated is discussed at length in the Action Plan itself:

- Scarcity of resources to meet the needs of mental healthcare
- Inequitable distribution of resources
- Inefficient usage of available resources

GLOBAL DATA BY WHO:[348]

1. Globally: Annual spending on mental health < US$ 2
2. Low availability of basic medicines for mental healthcare in primary healthcare facilities and less usage of the same because of lack of trained medical professional
3. Low-income countries: Annual spending on mental health < US$ 0.25;
4. Low income countries: only 36% covered by   mental health legislation;
5. High income countries: 92% covered by   mental health legislation

---

[347] Available at http://apps.who.int/iris/bitstream/10665/89966/1/9789241506021_eng.pdf?ua=1 (Last visited on February 5, 2018)
[348] WHO Mental Health Action Plan 2013-2020

The Mental Health Action Plan proceeds on six cross-cutting binding principles in the fulfillment of the goals of the Act, namely:

i.   Universal Health Coverage
ii. Protection of Human Rights
iii. Evidence-based practice
iv. Life course approach
v.   Multi-sectoral approach and
vi. Empowerment of persons with mental illness and psychological disabilities.

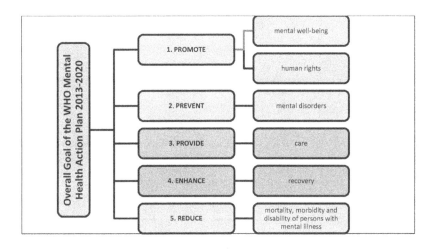

Table (7): Overall Goal of the WHO Mental Health Action Plan 2013-2020

The WHO Action Plan aims to fulfill the following targets by the year 2020:

- 80% countries of the world to update/develop their policies pertaining to mental health and bring the same in consonance with various regional and international human rights instruments;

- 50% countries of the world to update/develop their laws relating to mental health and bring the same in consonance with various human rights instruments of regional and international nature;
- Increasing at least by 20% service coverage for severe mental disorders;
- 80% countries of the world to have at least two promotion and prevention programmes functioning at the national and multi-sectoral level pertaining to mental health;
- Reducing the world wide rate of suicides by 10%;
- 80% countries should be collecting and reporting regularly, a core set of mental health indicators at least every two years through their information systems.

The WHO Action Plan also elucidates upon the options for implementation of the afore-mentioned targets and plans in great detail. With respect to universal health coverage pertaining to mental health, it is stated that persons with mental disorders should be in a position to access basic mental health care without running the risk of impoverishment and irrespective of differentiating factors like sex, age, race, sexual orientation, etc. Mental health treatment, strategies and inventions should be in compliance with the provisions of the United Nations Convention on Rights of Persons with Disabilities, and universally recognized best standards and practices. Apart from promoting the mental well-being, the WHO Action Plan targets towards prevention of mental disorders, providing adequate care, enhancing chances and scope for recovery, reducing the disability, morbidity and mortality of persons with mental illness and also protecting their human rights.

The WHO Action Plan takes the life course and the multi-sectoral approaches. As per the *"life course approach"*,[349] it is necessary for the policies, services and plans pertaining to mental health to take into account the social and healthcare needs at all the respective stages of life course, namely: infancy,

---

[349] *Id.*

childhood, adolescence, adulthood and old age. As per the *"multi-sectoral approach"*,[350] for a comprehensive fulfillment of mental healthcare requirements, there is a need of concerted cooperation among the public sectors pertaining to health, housing, social, education, employment and the private sector in pursuance with the specific requirements and situations of each of the member states respectively. It is very important for the fulfillment of the above goals and the proper implementation of the mental health action plan that the persons with mental disorders of with psychological disabilities are empowered and are actively involved in mental health policy, legislation, services, advocacy, monitoring, evaluation and research.

f.   Sixty-fifth World Health Assembly (Geneva, 2012): Resolution WHA 65.4

In the background of WHO Resolution WHA55.10[351] and the United Nations General Assembly Resolution 65/95,[352] and recalling the same, WHO Resolution WHA 65.4[353] was passed after considering WHO Report of 2011[354] titled *"The global burden of mental disorders and the need for a comprehensive, coordinated response from health and social sectors at the country level."*

WHO Resolution WHA 65.4 passed in 2012 in Geneva on *"The global burden of mental disorders and the need for a comprehensive, coordinated response from health and social sectors at the country level"* urged its member states to take specific positive steps to alleviate the global burden of mental disorders. WHO Resolution WHA65.4 was passed taking into account the work already done

---

[350] *Id.*

[351] Available at http://www.who.int/substance_abuse/en/WHA55.10.pdf (Last visited on December 15, 2017)

[352] Available at http://www.un.org/en/ga/search/view_doc.asp?symbol=A/RES/65/95&referer=http://www.un.org/en/ga/65/resolutions.shtml&Lang=E (Last visited on December 15, 2017)

[353] Available at http://apps.who.int/gb/DGNP/pdf_files/A65_REC1-en.pdf (Last visited on December 15, 2017)

[354] WHO, Report by the Secretariat, *The global burden of mental disorders and the need for a comprehensive, coordinated response from health and social sectors at the country level* (2011), Available at http://apps.who.int/iris/bitstream/handle/10665/23741/B130_9-en.pdf?sequence=1 (Last visited on December 15, 2017)

and undertaken by WHO, particularly in pursuance of the Mental Health Gap Action Programme, 2008.[355] The Resolution suggested the increase in the investment in mental health for the well-being of its citizens. Investment should not be limited to national investments but also multi-lateral treaties working towards the goal. The Resolution also acknowledges that mental illness culminates from attitudinal and behavioural impediments by the members of the society, and therefore to facilitate equal participation of persons with mental illness with others in the society in the background of the World Report on Disability 2011[356] which *inter alia* elaborates on the steps to facilitate the participation and the inclusion of persons with mental disabilities in the society.[357]

WHO Resolution WHA 65.4 urged its member states to collaborate with its Secretariat to work towards a comprehensive mental health action plan and *inter alia* to take the following specific positive steps:

- To develop policies and strategies to promote policies and strategies promoting mental health, early identification, support, care and treatment followed by recovery;

- To include in such policies the promotion and protection of the human rights of persons with mental illness particularly to tackle the issue of stigma surrounding this form of illness in the society;

- To address through these Policies, major risks pertaining to poverty and homelessness by promoting awareness among the general masses, creating opportunities for rehabilitation of persons with mental illness, enabling them to become self-sufficient by generating their own income

---

[355] Available at http://www.mhinnovation.net/sites/default/files/downloads/resource/mhGAP%20Mental%20Health%20Gap%20Action%20Programme%20English.pdf (Last visited on April 6, 2018)
[356] Available at https://www.ncbi.nlm.nih.gov/books/NBK304079/ (Last visited on April 6, 2018)
[357] *See* also UN Standard Rules on the Equalization of Opportunities for Persons with Disabilities (1993), Available at https://www.un.org/development/desa/disabilities/standard-rules-on-the-equalization-of-opportunities-for-persons-with-disabilities.html (Last visited on January 1, 2018)

and providing them with housing and such facilities to be able to be rehabilitated in the society;

- To identify through surveillance frameworks, various social determinants of health and thereby evaluate the existent trends in mental health issues in one's country;
- To give appropriate priority to mental health and to works towards streamlining mental health by:
  - Promoting mental health;
  - Prevention of mental disorders;
  - Provision for support, care and treatment in programmes relating to health and development in the country; and
  - Allocate appropriate funds to facilitate the same.

It is noteworthy that the National Mental Health Policy of India[358] was passed by the Government of India in 2014 in consonance with and in furtherance of WHO Resolution WHA 65.4.

3. REGIONAL AND ORGANIZATIONAL DEVELOPMENTS PERTAINING TO MENTAL HEALTH

i. World Congress of Psychiatry -The Hawaii Declaration (1977)

The Hawaii Declaration was adopted by the 6th World Congress of Psychiatry which had assembled at Honolulu in Hawaii in 1977.[359] The Declaration was later amended by the 7th World Congress of Psychiatry in 1983 in Vienna, Italy.[360]

The Guidelines laid down in the Hawaii Declaration are considered as the minimum ethical standards which the psychiatrists across the countries should

---

[358] National Mental Health Policy of India (2014)

[359] World Psychiatric Association, The Declaration of Hawaii, Available at http://www.codex.vr.se/texts/hawaii.html (Last visited on April 6, 2018)

[360] Available at http://www.wpanet.org/detail.php?section_id=5&content_id=27 (Last visited on April 6, 2018)

adhere to.[361] Some of the important guidelines enlisted in the Declaration are discussed herein below:

- It is the foremost duty of every psychiatrist to treat a patient to best of his/her capability, with the accepted latest scientific knowledge while adhering to the principles of ethical standards.

- Respecting the privacy and dignity of the patient is vital. The treatment should be based on mutual agreement, cooperation and trust. If establishing the same with the patient is difficult, the mutual understanding should be established with a relative or someone near to the patient.

- The patient should be informed about and presented with the opportunity to choose among the available options of treatment options and procedures.

- No treatment should be administered without the will and consent of the patient. However, if there is need for an immediate treatment to be administered to the patient and he is not in a condition to consent, then treatment can be proceeded with without the will of the patient. Whenever the conditions for compulsory treatment cease to exist, such treatment should stop; and the psychiatrist is to proceed with any further kind of treatment only once the voluntary consent is obtained.

- The psychiatrist is supposed to respect and protect the dignity of his/her patients and their human rights and should not misuse this fiduciary relationship to cause harm to the patient or exploit him/her in any way.

- When a patient is presented before a class for research and analysis, informed consent of the patient is mandatory.

- All information divulged by the patient to the psychiatrist should be kept confidential by the latter, unless the disclosure of the same becomes necessary to prevent harm to the patient or someone else. The research

---

[361] *See* also S.A.M. MCLEAN AND J.M. MASON, LEGAL AND ETHICAL ASPECTS OF HEALTHCARE (2003); SUDHIR ANAND, ET. AL., PUBLIC HEALTH, ETHICS AND EQUITY (2009)

subject/ patient should be free to withdraw the consent at any given point of time

ii. Latin America -The Caracas Declaration of Latin America (1990)[362]

In 1990 there was a Regional Conference on *"Restructuring of Psychiatric Care in Latin America within the Local Health Systems Model"* in Caracas. The Declaration states the importance of the consonance of the following approaches for psychiatric care for Latin America (countries which included Brazil, Colombia, Chile, Ecuador, Venezuela, and Panama) namely:

- Decentralized;
- Preventive and
- Participative.

The Declaration states the significance to protect the civil and human rights of persons in need of psychiatric care. Every attempt should be made to avoid relocation of such persons so that they can be treated and can live in their community or ordinary place of residence. The Declaration proposed reforming the laws pertaining to mental healthcare in various Latin American countries to bring them in consonance with the aims, objectives and principles of the Declaration.

iii. Europe: The WHO European Region

The WHO European Region includes 53 member states comprising a population of around 900 million people. Majority of the member states have mental health laws and policies and have been making advancement towards community-based services in health.[363]

---

[362] Available at http://www1.paho.org/hq/dmdocuments/2008/DECLARATIONOFCARACAS.pdf (Last visited on February 10, 2018)
[363] The European Mental Health Action Plan 2013-2020, Available at
http://www.euro.who.int/__data/assets/pdf_file/0020/280604/WHO-Europe-Mental-Health-Acion-Plan-2013-2020.pdf (Last visited on April 15, 2018)

The WHO European Ministerial Conference on Mental Health held in Helsinki in 2005 addressed the challenges facing mental healthcare in Europe and passed the Mental Health Declaration, which was co-signed cosigned by the European Commission and the Council of Europe and endorsed by the Regional Committee. It was acknowledged that there is *"no health without mental health."* The member states of the WHO European Region, in this Ministerial Conference, passed the Mental Health Declaration for Europe in 2005, wherein it was committed to follow *inter alia* the below-mentioned measures, tailored to the needs and constitutional framework of the member states:

- Enforcing legislation and policies pertaining to mental health;
- Access impact of government's action on mental health;
- Eliminate stigma surrounding mental health;
- Affording people with mental health the choice to make decisions pertaining to their own care;
- Ensure that the legislations are anti-discrimination and sensitive;
- Aim at averting risk factors pertaining to mental health, for example by introducing sensitive and inclusive work environment;
- Enhance the role of primary healthcare in mental healthcare;
- Promote community based services;
- Provide for basic care facilities to persons with mental illness, for example, relating to health, education, employment, etc.;
- Promote development in specialized expertise in mental healthcare;

The Council of Europe and the European Commission was requested to support this Declaration passed in Helsinki.

Following is the list of various Policies and Declarations pertaining to mental health passed by European nations over the years:

- The European Pact for Mental Health and Well-being passed by the European Commission in 2008;

- Mental Health Gap Programme, 2008;
- European Union Health Programme funded Joint Action on Mental Health and Well-being in 2013;
- The European Mental Health Action Plan, 2013-2020.

It is important to analyse the European Mental Health Action Plan 2013-2020[364], which holds immense importance to the present discussion. It adheres to the basic tenets of healthcare including gender and equity, social determinants, etc. It is further acknowledged that disorders relating to depression occur twice as common in women than in men. The Action Plan emphasizes upon the need to respect the human rights of persons with mental illness and providing them with sufficient opportunities giving them the scope to enjoy a quality life, free of discrimination and stigma. Effective, appropriate and safe treatment for mental illness is an entitlement to be available to one and all. The Plan acknowledges the need to work in close coordination with other sectors like education, research, etc.

iv. World Psychiatric Association (WPA)

WPA is an international organization of 140 psychiatric societies across 120 nations, representing more than two lakh psychiatrists.[365] The World Psychiatric Association works for the following missions:[366]

- Work towards attaining highest possible standards pertaining to clinical practice;
- Disseminate information, skills and knowledge pertaining to mental disorders, steps to prevent the same, values based practice and evidence-based therapy;
- Promote mental health for all;
- Promote the highest attainable ethical standards for psychiatric practices;

---

[364] Id.
[365] Available at http://www.wpanet.org/detail.php?section_id=5&content_id=4 (Last visited on February 5, 2018)
[366] Id.

- To espouse the cause for protecting and upholding the rights of patients with mental illness, their families and psychiatrists;
- Reaching out to the isolated and impoverished sections of the society.

WPA organizes the World Congress of Psychiatry after a period of every three years. It is one of the major international scientific events in the field of psychiatry.[367] The World Congress of Psychiatry has been held by far at Madrid (1996), Hamburg (1999), Yokohama (2002), Cairo (2005), Prague (2008), Buenos Aires (2011), Spain (2014) and Berlin (2017).

v.   **World Federation of Mental Health (WFMH)[368]**

WFMH is an international membership organization. It was founded in 1948 with the aim to promote among peoples and nations:
- The advancement of mental health;
- Prevention of mental and emotional disorders;
- Appropriate treatment and care of persons with such disorders, and the promotion of mental health;
- Focus on best practices in mental healthcare globally;
- Disseminate public awareness and necessary information relating to mental healthcare among the people at large; and
- To improve the mental healthcare facilities and standards worldwide.

WFMH observed the World Mental Health Day for the first time on 10th October, 1992 as an annual event with the aim to promote *"mental health advocacy and educating the people on relevant issues."*[369] In the year 1996 when the fifth World Mental Health Day was celebrated, the theme was Women and Mental Health with the aim to address the concerns and vulnerabilities of women with

---

[367] *Id.*

[368] Available at https://wfmh.global/ (Last visited on February 5, 2018)

[369] World Mental Health Day, WFMH, Available at https://wfmh.global/world-mental-health-day/ (Last visited on February 5, 2018)

mental illness. The World Mental Health Day, 2018 will be focusing on *"young people and mental health in a changing world."*[370]

SUMMARIZING: This Chapter holds significance for this research work because it shows the global perspective pertaining to mental healthcare. International standards, regional and organizational developments relating to mental healthcare, give the analysis of the 2017 Act a positive boost. The 2017 Act emerges from this Chapter as being globally viable, being abreast with the latest relevant legal developments world-wide, and an appropriate piece of legislation with larger aims which can be fulfilled on its implementation if the same is done word for word.

---

[370] World Mental Health Day, 2018, WFMH, Available at https://wfmh.global/world-mental-health-day-2018/ (Last visited on May 5, 2018)

XI. DELVING INTO THE MENTAL HEALTHCARE LAWS OF SIX OTHER COUNTRIES

To be able to evaluate the Indian legal scenario it was very important to weigh the Indian legal framework with the World standards and requirements. This Chapter delves into the legal framework pertaining to mental healthcare and the position of women with mental illness in six countries, namely: United Kingdom, South Africa, Bangladesh, Indonesia, New Zealand and Brazil. It is a fair combination of developed and developing nations and thereby helps in drawing an analysis as to how the laws of countries with various socio-political and economic setups address mental healthcare in their territories, respectively. The ultimate aim of this Chapter is to widen the horizon of discussion and appreciate the Indian situation.

1. INTRODUCTION

To be able to evaluate the Indian legal scenario it was very important to weigh the Indian legal framework with the World standards and requirements. This Chapter delves into the legal framework pertaining to mental healthcare and the position of women with mental illness in six countries, namely: United Kingdom, South Africa, Bangladesh, Indonesia, New Zealand and Brazil. It is a fair combination of developed and developing nations and thereby helps in drawing an analysis as to how the laws of countries with various socio-political and economic setups address mental healthcare in their territories, respectively. The ultimate aim of this Chapter is to widen the horizon of discussion and appreciate the Indian situation.

	Country	**Mental Healthcare Legislation**
1.	United Kingdom	The Mental Health Act, 1983 as amended by the Mental Health Act, 2007; and The Mental Capacity Act, 2005
2.	South Africa	The Mental Health Care Act, 2002
3.	Bangladesh	The Mental Health Act, 2014
4.	Indonesia	The Mental Health Law of 2014
5.	New Zealand	The Mental Health (Compulsory Assessment and Treatment) Act 1992
6.	Brazil	Ministerial Decrees of 1991, 1992, 1999, 2000, 2001 and Law No. 10.216 of 2001

2. UNITED KINGDOM

The United Kingdom, located in northern part of Europe, comprises England, Scotland, Wales and the Northern Island. It is a Constitutional monarchy and is considered as one of the few largest economies in the world.

The Guardian in an article titled *"Mental illness soars among young women in England"*[371] blamed the drastic increase in chronic mental illness among women in England on sexual violence, peer pressures, childhood traumas and pressures from the social media. According to the Government funded Adult Psychiatric Morbidity survey, one in four women in England aged between 16 years to 24 years has harmed herself because she experiences mental health problems.[372] In the light of the same the laws pertaining to mental healthcare in the United Kingdom are discussed herein below.[373]

The Mental Health Act, 2007[374] of the United Kingdom was introduced in 2007. It amended the Mental Health Act 1983, the Domestic Violence, Crime and Victims Act 2004 and the Mental Capacity Act 2005 with respect to mentally disordered persons.

The Mental Health Act, 2007 defines mental disorder to mean any disorder or disability of the mind. The main aim of the 1983 Act which the 2007 Act amends

---

[371] Denis Campbell and Haroon Siddique, Mental illness soars among young women in England – survey, The Guardian (Sep. 2016), Available at
https://www.theguardian.com/lifeandstyle/2016/sep/29/self-harm-ptsd-and-mental- illness-soaring-among-young-women-in-england-survey (Last visited on October 14, 2017)
[372] *Id.*;
See also Adult Psychiatric Morbidity Survey: Survey of Mental Health and Wellbeing, England (2014), Available at
http://webarchive.nationalarchives.gov.uk/20180328140249/http://digital.nhs.uk/catalogue/PUB2 1748 (Last visited on October 14, 2017)
[373] *See* JOAN RAPHAEL-LEFF AND ROSINE JOZEF PERELBERG, FEMALE EXPERIENCE- THREE GENERATIONS OF BRITISH WOMEN PSYCHOANALYSTS ON WORK WITH WOMEN (1997)
[374] The Mental Health Act, 2007, Available at
http://www.legislation.gov.uk/ukpga/2007/12/pdfs/ukpga_20070012_en.pdf (Last visited on November 1, 2017)

is to ensure that a person with mental disorder is not detained for treatment without his/her free consent. It also enumerates the safeguards to be in place and the procedures to be followed to ensure that proper treatment is meted out to the patients and that no treatment is proceeded with in the absence of his/her consent.[375] The Mental Health Act, 2007 was passed in response to the Bournewood Judgement[376] of the European Court of Human Rights where a man with autistic illness was kept in the Bournewood Hospital without his consent and against his wishes and the wishes of his caretakers. The Court held this as a violation of the principles of the European Convention on Human Rights.[377]

In order to address the issue of capacity/incapacity to give consent to medical treatment, the following legislations were passed[378]:

- Adults with Incapacity (Scotland) Act 2000
- Mental Capacity Act 2005 (England and Wales)
- Mental Capacity Act (Northern Ireland) 2016

It is to be noted that the Mental Health Act, 2007[379] and the Mental Capacity Act, 2005 work in parity with each other, complementing each other in various aspects. Mental Health Act, 2007 is limited to treatment and assessment for mental disorder whereas the Mental Capacity Act, 2005 addressed the concern of capacity to consent for treatment whether physical or mental.

The Mental Health Act, 1983[380] as amended by the Mental Health Act, 2007 lays down the provisions pertaining to mental healthcare in the United Kingdom.

---

[375] Id.
[376] HL v. UK (Application No.45508/99)
[377] ECHR, Article 5
[378] Tony Zigmond, Mental Health Law across the UK 41(6): 305–307BJPsych Bull. (2017), Available at https://www.ncbi.nlm.nih.gov/pmc/articles/PMC5709677/#R5 (Last visited on March 3, 2018)
[379] See PAUL BOWEN, BLACKSTONE'S GUIDE TO THE MENTAL HEALTH ACT, 2007 (2007)
[380] The Mental Health Act, 1983, Available at https://www.legislation.gov.uk/ukpga/1983/20/contents (Last visited on March 3, 2018)

Admission to hospital is categorized into compulsory admission to hospital and application for admission to hospital. Compulsory admission to hospital is further categorized into admission for the purpose of assessment, admission for the purpose of treatment, and admission for the purpose of assessment in cases of emergency. An application for admission to hospital may be made for the admission of a patient to a hospital under this Act. Permission granted in response to this application is considered as enough authority for the applicant, or any person authorised for this purpose by the applicant, to take the patient and convey him to the hospital if the situation so demands.

An application may be made in respect of a patient already in the hospital and if the application is made it shall be deemed that the admission has taken place from the date of the application. Any surgical operation pertaining to brain tissue or such other form treatment as may be prescribed by regulations, can be executed only on obtaining the consent of the person with mental illness and after getting a second opinion of a medical practitioner for the said purpose. There is a Mental Health Review Tribunal to consider applications and references made by patients. An approved mental health professional may be appointed by a local social service authority, and the professional has the power to enter and inspect at reasonable hours, premises in which a patient is living, if he/she has reason to believe that the patient is not be properly taken care of. Ill treatment of a patient under this Act is an offence. Any person being, an officer/staff/manager at a hospital or care home, who ill-treats or neglects a patient undergoing treatment is subject to, on summary conviction to imprisonment for a term not exceeding six months or to a fine not exceeding the statutory maximum, or to both, and on conviction on indictment, to imprisonment for a term up to 5 years or to a fine of any amount, or to both.

The laws pertaining to mental healthcare in UK are therefore, abreast with time and are organized enough to cater to various issues relating to mental healthcare that arise or are likely to arise in the country.

3. THE REPUBLIC OF SOUTH AFRICA

The Republic of South Africa is situated in the southern-most tip of the African continent. The Constitution[381] of the Republic of South Africa prohibits unfair discrimination of people with mental or other disabilities.[382] The Mental Health Care Act, 2002[383] is the principal statute governing mental healthcare in South Africa which provides for treatment, care and rehabilitation of mentally ill persons.

The Mental Health Care Act, 2002 defines the term *"mental health status"* to mean *"the level of mental well-being of an individual as affected by physical, social and psychological factors and which may result in a psychiatric diagnosis."* The objects of the Act are:

- to regulate mental health care by
    - o providing for the best possible healthcare, treatment and rehabilitation facilities,
    - o ensuring access to mental healthcare and
    - o integrating mental healthcare services into services available for general health;
- enumerating the rights and duties of mental health care users and the obligations of mental health care providers, respectively and
- regulating matters pertaining to the property rights of persons with mental illness.

The Act requires various organs of the State to come together and ensure that mental healthcare and rehabilitation reaches at all levels of healthcare that are,

---

[381] The Constitution of the Republic of South Africa, Available at
http://www.justice.gov.za/legislation/constitution/SAConstitution-web-eng.pdf (Last visited on March 13, 2018)
[382] The Constitution of the Republic of South Africa, Article 9(3)
[383] Available at
http://www.hpcsa.co.za/Uploads/editor/UserFiles/downloads/legislations/acts/mental_health_car
e_act_17_of_2002.pdf (Last visited on March 13, 2018)

primary, tertiary and secondary. It promotes community based approach and aims towards protecting the rights of the mentally ill persons, thereby improving their mental health status. Mental health care is categorized into involuntary, voluntary and assisted mental healthcare keeping in mind the facts and circumstances of each case. For the fulfillment of the aims of the Act, the Mental Health Review Boards have been set up at various levels.

The Act enumerates the following rights and duties pertaining to mental health care users:

1.	Respect human dignity and privacy	<ul><li>Aiming towards improving mental capacity of the user;</li><li>Facilitate his/her reintegration into the community;</li><li>Intrusion by the healthcare to be proportionate to the mental status of the user.</li></ul>
2.	Consent by the mental health care user	<ul><li>Care;</li><li>Treatment;</li><li>Rehabilitation services;</li><li>Admission to mental health establishment;</li></ul>
3.	No unfair discrimination	Receive health care, treatment and rehabilitation services according to the standard applicable to any other healthcare user.
4.	Not to be exploited and abused	Every person, organization or body providing mental health care should ensure: <ul><li>that the users of mental healthcare are</li></ul>

		not exploited or abused,
		• that they are not subject to forced labour and
		• are not punished for the convenience of others.
5.	Determining the mental health status	To be based on factors exclusively relevant for the mental health status of the user of mental healthcare
6.	Non-disclosure of information	Non-disclosure of information which the mental health user is entitled to keep private and confidential
7.	Limitation to adult intimate relationship	Only if the ability to consent of the mental healthcare user is diminished due to mental illness
8.	Right to representation	The mental healthcare user is entitled to representation including legal representation
9.	Right to get discharge report	The user has the right to get discharge report from the establishment where he/she was admitted for mental healthcare, treatment or for availing rehabilitation services.
10.	Knowing one's rights	A health care provider must inform the user of his/her rights under the Mental Health Care Act, 2002.

Table (8): Rights and Duties pertaining to mental health care users under the Mental Health Care Act, 2002

The disparity in the letter of the law and the ground level situation is however, humongous. Mental health is an impeding and vital public health issue in the country.[384] A study reported in 2014 at a South African local newspaper stated that one-third of South Africa's population suffers from mental illness and over seventy-five percent of them do not receive or have access to mental healthcare facilities.[385] Juveniles receiving treatment at these facilities have been raped or run the risk of being raped.[386] Establishments are under-staffed and the facilities for rehabilitation of these patients are not strong enough for them to recoup into the normal life.[387]Implementation of the law and proper enforcement mechanism, it is submitted, can help in obviating such a situation and in fulfilling the aims of the 2002 Act. Funding and support of the State in this regard is indispensable.

---

[384] Catherine E Draper, Et. al., *Mental Health Policy in South Africa: development process and content*, 24. 342-356 (2009)Health Policy and Planning, Available at https://academic.oup.com/heapol/article/24/5/342/586799 (Last visited on March 3, 2018)

[385] SA's Sick State of Mental Health , Sunday Times (6th July, 2014), Available at http://www.sadag.org/index.php?option=com_content&view=article&id=2178:sa-s-sick-state-of-mental-health&catid=74&Itemid=132 (Last visited on March 3, 2018)

[386] *Id.*

[387] Catherine E Draper, Et. al., *Mental Health Policy in South Africa: development process and content*, 24. 342-356 (2009)Health Policy and Planning, Available at https://academic.oup.com/heapol/article/24/5/342/586799 (Last visited on March 3, 2018)

4. PEOPLE'S REPUBLIC OF BANGLADESH[388]

Bangladesh is a country located in southern part of Asia. It shares its geographical boundaries with India and Myanmar. There is a higher prevalence of mental disorders among the economically weaker sections of Bangladesh, particularly more in women than in men more so because women are considered the more vulnerable sex of the society.[389] Social stigma attached to mental illness, many a time prevents these women to come out and accept their mental illness and get treated for the same.[390]

An article published in 2014 in the BMC Psychiatry, discusses *inter alia* how the mental healthcare dynamics in Bangladesh are very similar to its neighbouring countries, particularly India and Pakistan.[391] It also states that Bangladesh being essentially a male dominated nation, the women with mental illness are more likely to remain neglected and thereby do not receive the required mental healthcare and treatment.[392] Despite having a three-tier healthcare system, inadequate mental health professionals coupled with lesser infrastructural support in this sphere, comes in the way of the mental healthcare delivery.[393]

---

[388]*See also* WHO, *WHO-AIMS Report on Mental Health System in Bangladesh* (2007), Available at http://www.who.int/mental_health/bangladesh_who_aims_report.pdf (last visited on March 17, 2018)

[389]*See* M.E.KARIM, M.M. ZAMAN, NATIONAL INSTITUTE OF MENTAL HEALTH & HOSPITAL (BANGLADESH), WHO BANGLADESH: PREVALENCE, MEDICAL CARE, AWARENESS AND ATTITUDE TOWARDS MENTAL ILLNESS IN BANGLADESH (2007)

[390]*See also* A.K. Chowdhury, M.N. Alam, Dasherkandi Project Studies. *Demography, morbidity and mortality in a rural community of Bangladesh.* Chowdhury AK, Bangladesh Med Res Counc Bull. (1981)

[391] M.D. Hossain, Et. al., *Mental Disorders in Bangladesh: A Systematic Review,* BMC Psychiatry (2014), Available at https://www.ncbi.nlm.nih.gov/pmc/articles/PMC4149198/ (Last visited on March 5, 2018)

[392]*See also* N.A. Jahan, *Women's Mental Health- their problems, their disorders,* Bang J Psychiatry (2001)

[393] M.D. Hossain, Et. al., *Mental Disorders in Bangladesh: A Systematic Review,* BMC Psychiatry (2014), Available at https://www.ncbi.nlm.nih.gov/pmc/articles/PMC4149198/ (Last visited on March 5, 2018)

The Mental Health Act, 2014[394] is the principal statute governing mental healthcare in Bangladesh which provides for treatment, care and rehabilitation of mentally ill persons. The Act repeals the Mental Health Act 1986.

The Mental Health Act, 2014 lays down the legislative scheme for the treatment of persons with mental illness and their assessment; establishes the Mental Health Tribunal and the Mental Health Complaints Commissioner; and appoints the chief psychiatrist. The term used in the Act is *'consumer'* for any person who has received or is receiving mental health services or has sought or is seeking such services. It aims towards providing treatment and care in the least restrictive way thereby respecting the rights of the persons receiving the treatment. Informing such persons of their rights is therefore of vital importance. Treatment is encouraged to be participative so that the person undergoing treatment can exercise his/her decision making right.

The Act lays down the following *"mental health principles"* which the mental health care providers are duty-bound to adhere to when administering treatment/care under this Act:

- Treatment to be in the least restrictive way possible, respecting the rights, dignity and autonomy of the person receiving mental health services;[395]
- Mental health services should aim towards bringing out the best possible therapeutic outcome for the person receiving mental health services;
- Active involvement in the decision-making process pertaining to treatment and healthcare by the person receiving mental health services and his/her carers;

---

[394] The Mental Health Act, 2014, Available at http://www.astss.org.au/wp-content/uploads/2016/01/14-026aa-authorised.pdf (Last visited on March 13, 2018)
[395] *See* also The Daily Star, Draft Bangladesh Mental Health Act, 2014: Rights Perspective (2015), Available at http://www.thedailystar.net/draft-bangladesh-mental-health-act-2014-rights-perspective-51534 (Last visited on March 12, 2018)

- The medical and other health needs and the individual needs of the persons receiving mental health services should be respected and protected;
- Particular care should be taken to address the interests of children or young persons receiving mental health services;

The Act introduces two concepts namely, that of "statement of rights" and "advance statements". A statement of rights is a document that lays down the rights of the person being assessed or receiving treatment under the Act and comprises the process of such assessment or treatment as the case may be. It is the duty of an authorized psychiatrist to ensure that when the statement of rights is handed to such a person he/she is given an oral explanation of what is contained in the statement of rights. An advance statement is a document that sets out a person's preferences with respect to treatment under the Act, in the event that he/she becomes a patient in need of mental healthcare in the future. An advance statement has to be in writing, signed by the person making the statement, should be dated and should also signed by an authorized witness who attests to the fact that the person making the statement has the capacity to understand his/her statement presently. An advance statement may be revoked by the person making the statement. Making of a new advance statement also has the effect of revoking the previous statement.

The 2014 Act is therefore, a beacon of hope for the mental health delivery system in Bangladesh. By providing for consent, autonomy and active involvement in the decision-making process by the person receiving the mental health services, the 2014 Act gives scope for justice and equality in the mental healthcare system in Bangladesh.

5. REPUBLIC OF INDONESIA

Republic of Indonesia is a trans-continental sovereign island state located predominantly in South-East Asia having some territories in Oceania. It comprises over thirteen thousand islands.

In 2016 Human Rights Watch came out with a report titled, *"Indonesia: Treating Mental Health with Shackles"*[396]which bore open to the world the harsh reality of the mentally ill in Indonesia, who have been confined inside walls, shackled with chains, abused and treated worse than animals. This was followed by reports from the CNN,[397] Al Jazeera,[398] the Guardian,[399] TIME,[400]Huffpost[401] and multiple articles in various legal and health journals across the globe.

According to HRW around 57000 people in Indonesia with mental illness or perceived mental illness had been confined and put into shackles at least once in their lifetime. Pasung, the practice of restraining or confining mentally ill persons, though banned in Indonesia in 1977, was found prevalent even now.[402] The entire country has only 48 mental health institutions and around

---

[396] HRW, *Indonesia: Treating Mental Health with Shackles* (2016), Available at https://www.hrw.org/news/2016/03/20/indonesia-treating-mental-health-shackles (Last visited on February 10, 2018)

[397] Kathy Quiano, *Living in chains: In Indonesia, mentally ill kept shackled in filthy cells* CNN (2016), Available at https://edition.cnn.com/2016/03/20/asia/indonesia-mental-health/index.html (Last visited on February 10, 2018)

[398] Mentally ill in Indonesia shackled and locked up, Al Jazeera English (2016), Available at https://www.youtube.com/watch?v=-Vkvulgc2s4 (Last visited on December 12, 2017)

[399] Sam Jones, *'Living in hell': mentally ill people in Indonesia chained and confined,* The Guardian (2016) Available at https://www.theguardian.com/global-development/2016/mar/21/living-in-hell-indonesia-mentally-ill-people-chained-confined-human-rights-watch-report (Last visited on December 12, 2017)

[400] Thousands of Mentally Ill Indonesians Are Imprisoned in Shackles, Report Says, TIME, Available at http://time.com/4265623/indonesia-mental-illness-chains-pasung-hrw/ (Last visited on December 12, 2017)

[401] Kathryn Snowdon, *Indonesia's 'Horrifying' Mental Health Services Exposed By Human Rights Watch* (2016) Available at http://www.huffingtonpost.co.uk/entry/indonesias-horrifying-mental-health-services-exposed-by-human-rights-watch_uk_56efeed6e4b0cc1ede8c53f2 (Last visited on December 12, 2017)

[402] *See* Harry Minas & Hervita Diatri, Pasung: *Physical restraint and confinement of the mentally ill in the community,* International Journal of Mental Health Systems (2008) Available at

600-800 psychiatrists. Due to lack of access to mental health facilities, families land up shackling their relatives with mental illness within the confines of their homes.[403] Fear of stigma and embarrassment by the family, leads such confinements, more than often, to be absolute in nature and perpetual in duration.[404]

There is over-crowding in the mental health institutions raising the risk and incidences of exploitation and sexual abuse, especially of women patients. Female wards are mostly open, and staff members, including the male staff have access to the wards 24 hours thereby making female patients very vulnerable and victims of sexual perpetration and violence.[405] Patients are almost everywhere forced to eat, sleep, urinate and excrete in the same confined place, making life for them a living hell. Treatment administered ranges from that by *"magical herbs"*, religious recitations and involuntary electro-convulsive therapy without anesthesia.[406]Not a single patient present in these institutions claimed to be a voluntary patient, most of them had been dumped by their families or were found abandoned, and were languishing in these institutions against their will.[407]

---

https://ijmhs.biomedcentral.com/articles/10.1186/1752-4458-2-8 (Last visited on January 15, 2018)

[403] Kriti Sharma, *Break the Shackles of Stigma on Mental Healthcare in Indonesia,* Human Rights Watch (2014) Available at https://www.hrw.org/news/2014/09/16/break-shackles-stigma-mental-health-care-indonesia (Last visited on October 19, 2017)

[404] Human Rights Watch, *Indonesia: Treating Mental Health with Shackles* (2016), Available at https://www.hrw.org/news/2016/03/20/indonesia-treating-mental-health-shackles (Last visited on February 10, 2018)

[405] *See also* Movement for Global Mental Health, *'Living in Hell'* : mentally ill people in Indonesia chained and confined, Available at http://www.globalmentalhealth.org/category/country/indonesia (Last visited on October 19, 2017)

[406] HRW, *Indonesia: Treating Mental Health with Shackles* (2016)

[407] *See also* The ASEAN Secretariat, *ASEAN Mental Health Systems* (2016), Available at http://asean.org/storage/2017/02/55.-December-2016-ASEAN-Mental-Health-System.pdf (Last visited on February 10, 2018)

The Mental Health Law of 2014 of Indonesia lays down a national mental health policy and various local mental health policies to address the concerns of mental healthcare of persons with mental illness and protect their human rights. The promotion of mental health is aimed at:

- Improving the level of community health;
- Eliminating stigma, human rights violations;
- Improving understanding, awareness and community participation;
- Increasing public acceptance and participation towards mental healthcare.

The law requires preventive measures to be implemented in the family, community and various institutions, to have a holistic approach to the entire issue. The mental health curative efforts should aim towards recovery, reduction of suffering and controlling the disability. The law sets up the Mental Health Service system which includes basic mental health services and referral mental health services. Human resource planning should be conducted by the Government according to the law, through procurement of human resources in the field of mental health in the government and community level through education, training and sensitization.[408]

There is a dearth of literature analyzing the impact of the introduction of the 2014 Act in Indonesia. It can be stated that implementation of the law and proper redressal of justice, still remain matters of concern pertaining to mental healthcare in the country.

---

[408] Available at
https://translate.google.co.in/translate?hl=en&sl=id&u=https://kabarlgbt.files.wordpress.com/201 6/02/uu_no_18_2014-2.pdf&prev=search (Last visited on July 23, 2017)

6. NEW ZEALAND

New Zealand is an island nation located in the south-western Pacific Ocean. It includes the South Island, the North Island and six hundred small islands. New Zealand is very rich in biodiversity, being one of the last pieces of lands discovered by humans. It is a high-income economy.

The New Zealand Bill of Rights Act, 1990[409] enumerates the rights of the people of New Zealand including their right to life and security. The rights also include the right to refuse medical treatment. An exception to the same has been drawn with respect to persons with mental illness in need of treatment under the Mental Health (Compulsory Assessment and Treatment) Act 1992[410].

The 1992 Act is the primary legislation pertaining to mental healthcare in New Zealand.[411] The main aims of the Act as stated in the Guidelines to the Mental Health (Compulsory Assessment and Treatment) Act 1992 are[412]:

- defining the circumstances under which compulsory assessment and treatment may occur;
- ensuring that vulnerable persons are protected from any form of harm;
- ensuring that the public at large is protected from any harm;
- protecting the rights of patients and proposed patients;
- assessment and treatment should be done in the least restrictive manner possible;
- ensuring good clinical practice;
- ensuring accountability for actions taken by virtue of the Act.

---

[409] Available at http://www.legislation.govt.nz/act/public/1990/0109/latest/DLM224792.html (Last visited on April 3, 2018)

[410] Available at http://www.legislation.govt.nz/act/public/1992/0046/latest/DLM262176.html (Last visited on January 3, 2018)

[411] *See* also the Health and Disability Commissioner (Code of Health and Disability Services Consumers' Rights) Regulations 1996, Available at http://www.hdc.org.nz/your-rights/about-the-code/code-of-health-and-disability-services-consumers-rights/ (Last visited on April 5, 2018)

[412] Available at https://www.health.govt.nz/system/files/documents/publications/guide-to-mental-health-act.pdf (Last visited on January 3, 2018)

Section 2 of the Act defines mental disorder in relation to a person.

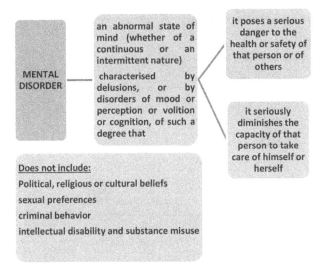

Table (9): Definition of "mental disorder" under the Mental Health (Compulsory Assessment and Treatment) Act 1992

A person can request a mental health assessment of any person under the Act. The same has to be supported by the recommendation of the registered medical practitioner and the person's general practitioner. A specialist psychiatrist must conduct the clinical assessment for the pursuance of the same. Registered Duly Appointed Officers oversee the functioning of this provision of this Act to avert any miscarriage of justice under the Act. Period of assessment may be for 5 days initially and then extended to a further period of 14 days if need be. Despite the provision for compulsory treatment it is mandatory to obtain the consent of the patient at the earliest if he has the ability to consent.[413] A patient may be declared as a restricted patient presenting special difficulties by a declaration by the Director of Mental Health Services on reference by the Judge before whom the matter is pending.

The Act lays down various rights of patients undergoing treatment under the Act, namely:

- General right to information;
- Respect for their cultural identity;
- Right to appropriate treatment;
- Right to be informed about the treatment;
- Right to get psychiatric advice which is independent;
- Right to get legal advice;
- Right to company and seclusion;
- Right to receive letters, postal articles and also visitors;
- Right to make phone calls; and
- Right to make complaints in case of breach of rights.

If a complaint is made by or on behalf of a patient that any of his/her rights under the Act have been breached, the matter has to be referred to a district inspectors under the Act have been breached, the matter has to be referred to a district inspector under the Act have been breached who will proceed with the investigation and arrive at a decision under this Act accordingly.

In addition to the Mental Health (Compulsory Assessment and Treatment) Act 1992, the Health and Disability Commissioner (Code of Health and Disability Services Consumers' Rights) Regulations 1996[414] protects the rights of persons with mental illness. It is mandatory to treat patients undergoing mental treatment with respect, dignity and independence. Such persons have the right to be not discriminated against, to get certain standards of care and to get the

---

[413] The Mental Health (Compulsory Assessment and Treatment) Act, 1992; and Guidelines to the Mental Health (Compulsory Assessment and Treatment) Act, 1992

[414] Available at http://www.hdc.org.nz/your-rights/about-the-code/code-of-health-and-disability-services-consumers-rights/ (Last visited on April 5, 2018)

opportunity to make informed choices, etc.[415] Patients also enjoy the right to privacy including the privacy pertaining to one's medical information under the Privacy Act, 1993.[416]It can be concluded that the laws in New Zealand are well-placed and cater to various aspects of mental healthcare in the country quite aptly.

7. FEDERATIVE REPUBLIC OF BRAZIL

Brazil is a country in the continent of South America, and spreads over an area of around 8.5 million kilometers square. It is a stark example of contrasts, reason being that it is one of the prospering economies in the world according to its GDP, and it is at the same time also classified as a lower middle income country by the World Bank on the basis of its HDI.[417]

In 1990 there was a Regional Conference on *"Restructuring of Psychiatric Care in Latin America within the Local Health Systems Model"* in Caracas.[418] The Declaration states the significance to protect the civil and human rights of persons in need of psychiatric care. Following the Caracas Declaration, Brazil

---

[415] Ian Soosay and Rob Kydd, *Mental Health Law in New Zealand*, BJPsych Int. 13(2): 43–45 (2016), Available at https://www.ncbi.nlm.nih.gov/pmc/articles/PMC5619622/ (Last visited on April 10, 2018)

[416] The Privacy Act, 1993, Available at http://www.legislation.govt.nz/act/public/1993/0028/latest/DLM296639.html (Last visited on April 5, 2018)

[417] Mario D Mateus, *The mental health system in Brazil: Policies and future challenges,* International Journal of Mental Health Systems 2:12 (2008), Available at https://www.researchgate.net/publication/23241126_The_Mental_Health_System_in_Brazil_Pol icies_and_Future_Challenges (Last visited on July 23, 2017)

[418] Available at http://www1.paho.org/hq/dmdocuments/2008/DECLARATIONOFCARACAS.pdf (Last visited on February 10, 2018)

has since 1991 undertaken quite a few positive steps towards restructuring its psychiatric care regime.[419]

Discussed herein below are some of those significant legal reforms in Brazil[420]:

- **Ministerial Decree No. 189 (1991):** The Decree aimed at improving the quality of attention that was being meted out to persons with mental illness by funding instrumental mental health services and programmes including therapeutic workshops.
- **Ministerial Decree No. 224 (1992):** This Decree required psychiatric care to incorporate multi-professional teams, ensuring that service and healthcare is continuous and consistent at all stages.
- **Ministerial Decree No. 1077 (1999):** This Decree provides for access to basic drugs and facilities for mental healthcare thereby requiring the states and also authorities at the municipal level to have a permanent programme to make basic mental health drugs available at all times.
- **Ministerial Decree No. 106 (2000):** This Decree established the Residential Therapeutic Services for Mental Health under Brazil's National Health System. The Residential Therapeutic Services provides for houses in the premises of communities where the persons with mental illness who do not have a family to go back to can live, including persons who have been released from long-term stay at hospitals for mental healthcare treatment.
- **Ministerial Decree No. 799 (2000):** This decree establishes the mechanism for auditing of the various mental health services in the country, including regular supervision of mental healthcare facilities in hospitals.

---

[419] Mónica Bolis, *The Impact of the Caracas Declaration on the Modernization of Mental Health Legislation in Latin America and the English-speaking Caribbean,* Available at http://citeseerx.ist.psu.edu/viewdoc/download?doi=10.1.1.525.8287&rep=rep1&type=pdf (Last visited on December 5, 2017)
[420] *Id.*

- **Law No. 10.216 (2001):** This Law mandates the State to ensure the protection of the rights of persons with mental health system and also reorients the mental healthcare regime in the country on the following lines, namely:
  - Non-discrimination on the grounds of race, sex, colour, nationality, family, etc.;
  - Rights of persons requiring mental healthcare and their families, including the access to best possible health care, protection from abuse, informed consent, therapeutic treatment involving less invasive treatment, etc.
  - Role of the State to develop the national mental health policy and play a positive role in furtherance of the policy;
  - Regulating involuntary admissions for mental healthcare in hospitals;
  - Rehabilitation and psychological assistance to be provided long-term patients of mental healthcare in hospitals;
  - Psychiatric hospitalization should be preceded by well-researched findings;
  - Regulating admission to hospitals for mental healthcare respecting the decision-making power of the person and the opportunity of the family to play a role in the same, the need for hospitalization, etc.[421]

The *"return home programme"* existent in Brazil provides for rehabilitation of persons with mental illness and their social inclusion during and after recovery. Patients who have had a long stay at hospitals for mental healthcare are provided with a monthly benefit to rehabilitate them and facilitate them towards

---

[421] *See* also WHO-AIMS Report on Mental Health System in Brazil, Available at http://www.who.int/mental_health/evidence/who_aims_report_brazil.pdf (Last visited on July 23, 2017)

self-dependence over time.[422] It is submitted that the rehabilitation policy in Brazil, is something that the Indian legal system could take cue from.

8. CONCLUDING

The Mental Healthcare Act, 2017 of India came into force very recently, that is, from 29th May, 2018[423]in furtherance of the aims of the UNCRPD. After having delved into the legal framework of the afore-discussed six countries in this Chapter, and after having analysed the provisions of the Mental Healthcare Act, 2017 in Chapters V, VI and VII of this research, one is bound to appraise the provisions of the 2017 Act. It can therefore be concluded by stating that the 2017 Act is a compilation of the best practices pertaining to mental healthcare laws across the world and it stands fairly passed on the anvil of juxtaposition to the laws on mental healthcare of the six countries that were discussed in this Chapter.

---

[422] Mario D Mateus, *The mental health system in Brazil: Policies and future challenges,* International Journal of Mental Health Systems 2:12 (2008), Available at https://www.researchgate.net/publication/23241126_The_Mental_Health_System_in_Brazil_Pol icies_and_Future_Challenges (Last visited on July 23, 2017)
See also Sônia Barros and Mariana Salles, Mental health care management in the Brazilian National Health System, Rev. esc. enferm. USP vol.45 no.spe2 São Paulo Dec. (2011), Available at http://www.scielo.br/scielo.php?pid=S0080-62342011000800025&script=sci_arttext&tlng=en (Last visited on July 23, 2017)
[423] Notification No.: S.O. 2173(E), Ministry of Health and Family Welfare, Government of India (29th May, 2018)

XII. COMPILATION OF THE EMPIRICAL RESEARCH WORK

As the Secondary Empirical Data relied upon as a part of this Research comprises the NCW and NIMHANS Report (2016) and HRW Report (2014) both of which have been discussed in detail and analysed in the previous section of this research, this Chapter is only a compilation and analysis of the primary empirical data collected by the researcher herself. It is noteworthy, that the primary empirical research undertaken by the researcher is not claimed as representative of the entire country. It is to compliment the data collected in the 2016 and the 2014 Reports respectively and thereby further authenticate the viability of these two well-researched and comprehensive reports.

1. AIM OF THE EMPIRICAL RESEARCH UNDERTAKEN

The empirical work taken up in the pursuance of this research aimed at gauging the situation at the ground level. Being a student of law, the researcher was not well-equipped enough to understand the intricacies of a mental health establishment or the mental healthcare from the medicinal perspective. It was also necessary to analyse the general understanding of the people at large relating to the issue of mental healthcare, especially the situation of women with mental illness. Awareness about the 2017 Act and the concepts introduced by the Act among the general public was also something that had intrigued the researcher in the pursuance of this research.[424]

During the course of the research, the researcher was provided with the most authentic data possible pertaining to women with mental illness in India, that is the NCW and NIMHANS Report on *"Addressing concerns of women admitted to psychiatric institutions in India: An in-depth analysis"* published in 2016. The report was exhaustive, elaborate and was performed by a team of skilled researchers and professionals with adequate resources thereby forming an important source of secondary data of empirical nature for this research.[425] The research also refers to report by a renowned NGO, Human Rights Watch, titled *"Treated Worse than Animals- Abuses against Women and Girls with Psychological and Intellectual Disabilities in Institutions in India"* published in 2014[426] which was instrumental in NCW and NIMHANS coming together to pursue its research culminating in their 2016 Report mentioned above. These two Reports have been analysed in detail in Chapters III and IV of this research respectively, nevertheless it is important to acknowledge the same as vital sources of secondary empirical data relied upon by the researcher.

---

[424] *See* ROBERTA MORRIS, ET. AL., DOING LEGAL RESEARCH- A GUIDE FOR SOCIAL SCIENTISTS AND MENTAL HEALTH PROFESSIONALS (1997)
[425] *See* Chapter IV
[426] *See* Chapter III

The Empirical Research Work which forms a part of this research can be categorized as follows:

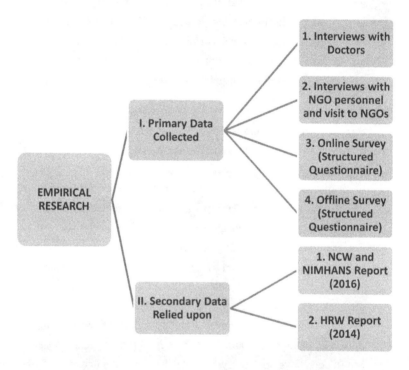

Table (10): Categories of Empirical Research undertaken or relied upon

A. PRIMARY DATA Collected:

a. Interviews with Doctors

b. Interviews with NGO personnel and visit to NGOs

c. Online Survey (Structured Questionnaire)

d. Offline Survey (Structured Questionnaire)

B. SECONDARY DATA Relied upon:

1. Report by NCW and NIMHANS published in 2016, titled: *"Addressing concerns of women admitted to psychiatric institutions in India: An in-depth analysis"*[427]

2. Report by HRW published in 2014, titled: *"Treated Worse than Animals-Abuses against Women and Girls with Psychological and Intellectual Disabilities in Institutions in India"*[428]

As the Secondary Empirical Data relied upon as a part of this Research comprises the NCW and NIMHANS Report (2016) and HRW Report (2014) both of which have been discussed in detail and analysed in the previous section of this research, this Chapter is only a compilation and analysis of the primary empirical data collected by the researcher herself. It is noteworthy, that the primary empirical research undertaken by the researcher is not claimed as representative of the entire country. It is to compliment the data collected in the 2016 and the 2014 Reports respectively and thereby further authenticate the viability of these two well-researched and comprehensive reports.

---

[427] Available at http://ncw.nic.in/pdfreports/addressing_concerns_of_women_admitted_to_psychiatric_institutions_in_india_an_in-depth_analysis.pdf (Last visited on October 10, 2017)

[428] Available at https://www.hrw.org/report/2014/12/03/treated-worse-animals/abuses-against-women-and-girls-psychosocial-or-intellectual (Last visited on April 5, 2018)

2.   INTERVIEW WITH PSYCHIATRISTS

As part of the research, the author had the opportunity to interview five psychiatrists each of who have had multiple years of experience in the practice of psychiatry. All the interviews were focused interviews, the questions asked were open-ended. The discussion revolved around one or more of the following areas:

- General analysis of the Mental Healthcare Act, 2017;
- Stigma pertaining to mental illness of women;
- Psychiatric advance directives;
- Vulnerabilities of women with mental illness;
- De-criminalization of attempt to commit suicide;
- Human Rights of persons with mental illness, etc.

Psychiatrist 1

Name: Dr. Om Prakash Singh

Specialization: Psychiatrist

Date of interview: 16-12-2017

About him: Dr. Om Prakash Singh has more than fifteen years of experience as a practicing doctor of Psychiatry in Kolkata. He is the Honorary Editor at the Indian Psychiatric Society.

Summary of the interview:

- "India is not prepared as a country to go for advance directives." Since there is no concept of <u>advance directive</u> for any major physical illness, how can the same be introduced for mental illness. India lacks in infrastructure to maintain records of psychiatric advance directives, for the treating doctor to have access to the advance directives of all his/her patients respectively. It increases the burden of the Psychiatrist because he/she will have to delve into whether the advance directive is good for the well-being of the patient or not. A blanket ban on any kind of treatment through an advance directive, for example, could prove to be very harmful to the patient in need of treatment. While making the advance directive, the patient cannot be sure what kind of treatment will be available when the advance directive becomes enforceable, for example, 5 years down the line there can be improvements in mental healthcare which one is not aware of while making the advance directive. Therefore, rather than treating the patient, recourse to fulfilling the formalities of the advance directive will become an unnecessary concern for the treating doctor. Psychiatric advance directive doesn't matter. *"It will not change much. Hardly few people are going to make advance directives."* Now that there is the concept of nominated representative (relative), he/she can give consent on behalf of the patient. That is better than advance directive.

Psychiatrist 2

Name: Dr. Saikat Baidya
Specialization: Psychiatrist
Date of interview: 17-12-2017
About him: Dr. Saikat Baidya is a faculty member at the Department of Psychiatry at the Medical College and Hospital, Kolkata. He is a member of the Mental Health Innovation Network (MHIN).

Summary of the interview:
- *"Influence of stigma is more for women than men. Prevalence of stigma is much higher in our society amongst women."* Though the level of stigma has reduced to a great extent, more people are coming to Doctors for treatment, but the stigma is still very much prevalent for

216

women. Most of the women when they get victimized in any form, they don't want to disclose it to their near and dear ones. They think that if they disclose, then they might be stigmatized or may be isolated totally. That is one of the main causes why so many women do not seek psychiatric help. Stigma is prevalent across all sections of society for women with mental illness, even in the western world, particularly United States and Japan. Psychiatrists need to be more aware of this stigmatization. Psychiatrists generally listen to their symptoms and prescribe medicine; the patients are not counselled. Counselling has to go hand in hand with psychiatric treatment. Government should also have more role to play, there should be anti-stigma campaign. Celebrities should endorse the cause and help in creating awareness about mental illness. Psychiatrists and psychologists should be more careful about this stigmatization.

- Most of the patients in the Medical College come from village areas. Many of them are illiterate and have no idea of mental illness. First of all they go to the local faith healers, local quacks, only after that they come to the doctors. Awareness programmes should be in all strata of society, particularly in village areas.

- Both the ideas of psychiatric advance directives and of nominated representatives are very good, but in a country like ours where there is illiteracy, most of our patients do not have any idea about psychiatric illness, then how they would predict a future mental illness. If awareness is brought about then maybe implementation of the advance directive will be more rational in that case.

- If a person is brought from the streets by the police stating that he/she suffers from mental illness, the first thing that the psychiatric team does is the Mental Status Examination (MSE) of the person. If as per the MSE the patient is fine, the doctors inform the police that the person does not need any treatment. The Police then try to locate the family or home of the person and send him/her back to the family.

217

- Patients are abandoned in hospitals by the family. Even after their recovery, when the patient is ready for discharge, nobody is willing to take the patients back. Some of these patients are absolutely okay but because no one is coming to take them back, they occupy a bed in the hospital. *"We try to get them involved in psychiatric rehabilitation."*
- "Bio-psycho-social-spiritual." Psychiatric rehabilitation is a major concern. In a psychiatric hospital or a psychiatric unit the treatment part is made much attention. Rehabilitation is mainly done by NGOs. *"I think in any psychiatric hospital or any psychiatric unit in any general hospital itself, there must be the provision for psychiatric rehabilitation…For complete cure of a psychiatric patient, holistic approach is always mandatory."* Medicine can remedy to some extent. Psycho-therapy, psychiatric rehabilitation, care-givers all have to come together for complete cure of the psychiatric patient. *"In our country only the medicine part is taken care of but all other parts are neglected."* Bio-psycho-social-spiritual model should be taken up. This is the holistic approach that is required for complete cure of the patient.
- Psychiatric to patient ratio is very less in our country. *"Not only psychiatrists, psychiatric social workers, psychologists, nurses trained in psychiatry, there is deficit everywhere."* Training the general physician in basic psychiatry in remote village areas in India where psychiatrists are not available can be an important step to address this concern. Integration of mental healthcare with primary healthcare and decentralization of mental healthcare is the way ahead.

Psychiatrist 3

Name:	Dr. Mahesh R Gowda
Specialization:	Psychiatrist
Date of interview:	23-08-2016 (Since the interview was before the passing of the 2017 Act, the discussion is pertaining to then

	Mental Healthcare Bill, 2016 which was later passed in the Parliament in the form of the Mental Healthcare Act, 2017)
About him:	Dr. Mahesh R Gowda is a Consultant Psychiatrist at Spandana Nursing Home, Rajajinagar, Bangalore and the Managing Director of Spandana Health Care, Nandini Layout, Bangalore. With around eighteen years of experience in the field of psychiatry, Dr. Gowda specializes in general adult psychiatry, rehabilitation and de-addiction.

(The researcher was given a tour of the Spandana Nursing Home by one of the resident Doctors and was given the opportunity to passively observe the functioning of the Nursing Home.)

Summary of the interview:

- Law has generally been very gender neutral. Apart from mention of reproductive rights the provisions of the mental healthcare law are gender neutral.

- For the implementation of a law like Mental Healthcare Bill, 2016, at least around 40,000 psychiatrists in India are needed whereas only 6000 psychiatrists are there in India. In the 40 years of NIMHANS being instrumental in creating mental health professionals, the country has been able to develop only 6000 psychiatrists. Also, we lack in the judicial or financial resources. The Bill did not have any input from NIMHANS. The concepts in the Bill are very western. India lacks the resources to implement the provisions of the Bill.

- The concept of psychiatric advance directives can be compared to a will. The provision of making a will exists in the country, yet very few people make a will, because nobody apprehends death. Similarly, with respect to psychiatric advance directive, it will be very rare when an individual will come up and say how they want to be treated when they become mentally ill. An advance directive should be a tri-partite agreement involving the patient, the family member or care giver and the treating psychiatrist. The treating psychiatrist should be able to decide whether the advance directive would be good or bad for the health of the patient making the directive. Admission of the patient to a hospital for mental healthcare should be for his/her benefit; and should be valid based on the consent of the legal guardian/care giver/family member of the patient. If the practice of advance directive comes to fore, every hospital will require a legal team to look into the legality of each advance directive before it.

- 90% of the patients that we treat are difficult patients, who are unable to gauge what is good for them at that point of time. Compulsory treatment in such situations should be accommodated. The family members/ care givers should be given the right by the law to get such a person treated and cured.

- Many of the patients are not capable to differentiate what is good for them from what is bad for them. They don't want to bathe or keep themselves clean. Bed bugs and lice would develop and various dermatological issues would become prevalent if some force is not used to make them clean and tidy and if proper hygiene is not maintained.

- The stigma surrounding mental illness is waning because of awareness among people and the generation of sensitivity in the society about mental illness. More and more people are coming to hospitals and psychiatrists for psychiatric treatment.

- The Act is completely silent about the rights of the care-givers. The care-givers receive the brunt of the violence and incapacity of the patient when he/she is unable to differentiate her good from his/her bad.

- Referring to the vulnerability of women, it can be said that when a husband falls sick the wife is more accepting. This is not always the case when the wife falls sick. Husbands sometimes on their own accord, and sometimes under the influence of parents, want to go for a divorce with a woman who develops mental illness. Presently four patients at Spandana have divorce petitions filed against them by their husbands, respectively, in Courts and a Doctor has to appear as one of the witnesses in the Court pertaining to the same regularly.

- Every time there is an attempt to commit suicide, a psychiatrist should be made to get involved to find out the causes which lead to such an attempt by the person. Through counselling and proper treatment the person should be helped to recover. If the attempt to commit suicide is repeated, there should be a compulsory treatment, if need be through admission in a psychiatric hospital or in the psychiatric unit of a general hospital. Decriminalization of attempt to commit suicide is a welcome change to help such a person to get back to a normal state of mind and live a normal life as a member of the society.

- Hysterectomy does not take away the physical aspect of sex. It only disables the woman from bearing a child. A woman with mental illness who is unable to take care of herself, how can one expect her to mother a child? So, hysterectomy in extreme situations should be allowed.

Psychiatrist 4

Name:	Dr. Suresh Bada Math
Specialization:	Psychiatrist
Date of interview:	05-08-2016 (Since the interview was before the passing of the 2017 Act, the discussion is pertaining to then Mental Healthcare Bill, 2016 which was later passed in the Parliament in the form of the Mental Healthcare Act, 2017)
About him:	Additional Professor of Psychiatry, In-charge of Legal Aid Clinic, In-charge of Telemedicine, Consultant, Forensic Psychiatry & OCD clinic, Department of

Psychiatry, National Institute of Mental Health and Neuro Sciences, Bangalore.

Summary of the interview:

- Most of the patients that come are with family members. <u>Advance directive</u> might antagonize the caring family by making the situation anti-family, leading to hostility or abandonment of the patient itself. This may lead to multiple litigations unnecessarily. Psychiatric advance directives could be viable twenty years down the line when the country has the capacity to set up the infrastructure for the same. It will unnecessarily create impediments for the treating psychiatrist for whom the treatment of the ailing patient is a matter of primary concern at this point of time.

- <u>Autonomy</u> of the patient is difficult to gauge here because the patient is not in a fit state of mind. Scope of misuse is there in every circumstance. Just because of the 2% chance of misuse by a care-giver in mental healthcare decision making for a person with mental illness, we cannot stop the 98% good work that is being done for the welfare of the patients.

- For <u>safety of women</u> with mental illness in NIMHANS, there is always sufficient security to avert any scope of infiltration. The complete staff is female and male doctors can visit only with supervision.

- Under the new law there is provision for registration of hospitals. There are checks which can be put to place to ensure that torture is not meted out. However, one cannot ignore the fact that there are <u>dargahs and temples</u> where faith healing goes on and law enforcement agencies cannot enter such places to check for violation of any law because these are sensitive zones and the question of culture and religion comes into the picture.

- The <u>rights</u> introduced in the new law are a welcome change. However, these rights need to be accompanied with duties, and for fulfilling the same India requires funding and infrastructure.

Psychiatrist 5

Name:	Dr. Malay Kumar Ghoshal
Specialization:	Psychiatrist
Date of interview:	6-1-2018
About him:	Prof. Dr. Malay Kumar Ghoshal is a Professor of Psychiatry at the Department of Psychiatry at the Medical College and Hospital, Kolkata. He is the Chairperson of a Sub-Committee of the Eastern Zonal Branch of the Indian Psychiatric Society.

Summary of the interview:

- Psychiatric advance directive is not feasible in India presently. India does not have the infrastructure for psychiatric advance directive to operate smoothly.
- The human rights aspect of the 2017 Act is a welcome change. Proper implementation of the provisions can go a long way in promoting and protecting the interests and welfare of patients with mental illness.
- Women with mental illness are more vulnerable than men with mental illness. Mental illnesses that are more common in women than in men are depression, particularly unipolar depression and alzheimer's disease.
- The process of recovery of a patient should go through four main phases, namely:
  - i) Identification of the mental illness
  - ii) Acceptance of the fact of the mental illness
  - iii) Medical Treatment
  - iv) Reformative action and rehabilitation.

Mere treatment does not solve the issue. Helping the patient stand back and become an active part of the society should be the ultimate aim.

COMPARING AND ANALYSING ALL THE FIVE INTERVIEWS:

There was an acknowledgement among all the five psychiatrists interviewed in the pursuance of this research, about the comparative vulnerability of women with mental illness in the country. They all acknowledged the prevalence of stigma and the tendency to go to traditional faith healers before approaching the psychiatric professionals. Abandonment of patients in mental hospital was also a common phenomenon reported by them. Decriminalizing attempt to commit suicide was considered a necessary change. There was however, difference of opinion about the viability of introducing psychiatric advance directives. Four of the psychiatrists interviewed were of the opinion that introduction of psychiatric advance directives would be a hassle for the family members and care-givers; would unnecessarily add complications for the mental healthcare team and would open the window for unnecessary litigations. Awareness regarding psychiatric advance directives and proper implementation would result in a positive change according to one psychiatrist. The concerted opinion of all the psychiatrists was therefore, that the societal and legal set up of India was not yet conducive for the introduction of psychiatric advance directives. Concern over rehabilitation for the holistic treatment and care of persons with mental illness was recognized and emphasized upon by all the five psychiatrists interviewed.

3.   NGOs AND HALF-WAY HOMES WORKING FOR WOMEN WITH MENTAL ILLNESS IN INDIA

In the pursuance of this research, the researcher interviewed personnel of three NGOs and half-way homes working for rehabilitation of women with mental illness in the country, namely:

1. Paripurnita Halfway Home (Kolkata)
2. The Banyan (Chennai)
3. Anjali (Kolkata)

The interviews were focused interviews and had a semi-standardized format. The questions asked were mainly open-ended in nature. The aim was to get an idea about the nature of the work being undertaken by each of these NGOs for rehabilitation of women with mental illness and mental healthcare in general.

i.   Paripurnita Halfway Home –Centre for Psychological Rehabilitation for women with mental illness

Paripurnita is a non-profit organization.[429] It is a Centre for Psychological Rehabilitation for women with mental illness. It was established in Calcutta in 1992 and was the first half-way home for women in eastern India.

> "In our Halfway Home, so called, because it is the mid-point in a person's journey from her place of confinement to her home, in a family like ambience, individuals are guided to pick up the lost pieces of their lives, which prepares them for their natural home and help them integrate in to their community and the wider society, so that they once again can lead a productive and meaningful life."

The researcher visited Paripurnita on 31st March, 2018 during the day. She interviewed Mr Briti Sundar Bhattacharjee, Psychiatric Social Worker at Paripurnita and Mr. Prabir Basu, Honorary Secretary at Paripurnita. Mr.

---

[429] Paripurnita Halfway Home, *See* http://www.paripurnata.org/index.php (Last visited on April 2, 2018)

Bhattacharjee also showed the researcher the various parts of the Paripurnita building and accompanied her along with a female attendant to one of the wards.

Paripurnita is only limited to female patients from Calcutta Pavlov Hospital. The half-way home has thirty beds. It is a small rehabilitation centre which aims at helping these women recoup with life. The screening process on the basis of which Paripurnita shortlists a patient for admission as a resident includes:

- Female patients only;
- Economic condition is poor;
- The patient suffers from chronic illness and has been in the hospital for many days;
- The patient is not pregnant; and
- The patient does not suffer from any physical ailment and can carry out her own daily chores.

After a patient clears the screening, she is asked for her consent for admission into Paripurnita. She is informed that she will have to take care of her own needs, which include making her own bed, helping in cooking/serving food, attending of signing/dancing/stitching/block printing classes. If the patient happily consents to the aforementioned conditions, she is then admitted as a resident in Paripurnita.

Residential programmes at Paripurnita:

i. Rehabilitation programme: for marginalized women (for period of nine to twelve months)

ii. Recuperation programme: for ex-residents who have relapsed because of either not taking medicine or attitude of indifference by family members (for period of two to three months)

iii.   Short-stay programme: for women admitted at Paripurnita directly by their family members (four to six months)

In the year 2016-17, nine residents who had been inducted from Calcutta Pavlov Hospital were rehabilitated with their family members, eight re-lapsed former residents were treated and discharged; and twenty-six short-stay patients were treated at Paripurnita.

The rehabilitation process at Paripurnita includes:

- Pharmaco-therapy
- Psychologocal counselling
- Physical check-ups
- Socio-cultural therapy
- Occupational therapy
- Informal education
- Outings and picnics
- Cognitive therapy

The residents here help in cooking cleaning, making their bed, etc. They decide the menu and also plan special events for festivals. The work being done at Paripurnita is respected by the local people of the area. Many a time, these residents have been invited to inaugurate an event or a Durga Puja celebration in the local neighbourhood. Occupational therapy for residents at Paripurnita includes classes for painting, block-printing, singing, stitching and dancing. Residents also have a time of the day fixed for yoga, for watching television, for reading the newspaper (or a book of her choice) respectively.

Follow-up with former residents is carried out through home visits by the Paripurnita team, family meets and ex-residents meet at Paripurnita on a regular basis. OPD facilities for ex-residents are also provided for regularly. Since its existence, Paripurnita has been instrumental in reintegrating more than two hundred residents with their families.

ii.   Emergency Care and Recovery Centre (ECRC), the Banyan, Chennai

Since its origin in 1993 in Chennai, the Banyan has worked towards *"holistic mental health solutions"*[430] The Banyan aims to create sustainable models of treatment care and welfare for persons with mental illness which includes emergency requirements, acute medical, psychological, psychiatric and social care provided through their street based services, shelter based services, hospitals, outpatient care which is community based, etc.

ECRC is a flagship programme of the Banyan which provides *"critical services to homeless women with mental illness since 1993."* [431]It is part of the hospital and shelter bases services provided at the Banyan, Chennai. The integrated care offered at ECRC seeks recovery in all the four following spheres:

a) Clinical recovery   c) Social recovery

b) Functional recovery   d) Personal recovery

ECRC located in Mogappair, Chennai is a hundred and ten beds Care and Recovery Centre for homeless women with mental illness. The team at ECRC comprises the Director and Assistant Director (who is the Head of the Department of Psychiatry at ECRC), the nursing head with training in psychology, social workers, clinical psychologists, case managers, psychologists and four psychiatrics.   There are eight departments functional at ECRC, namely:

a) Primary care   e) Occupational therapy

b) Psychology   f) Vocational training

c) Medical and Psychiatric   g) Community   in-patient
Care   services

d) Health care workers   h) Re-integration and after-
                                                    care

---

[430] The Banyan, Available at http://thebanyan.org/aboutus/ (Last visited on April 5, 2018)
[431] ECRC, The Banyan, Available at http://thebanyan.org/ecrs/ (Last visited on April 5, 2018)

The researcher interviewed Mr. Rishabh Anand, Head of the Re-Integration Department at ECRC on 3rd February, 2018. Mr. Anand is also the Programme lead of the Project on Maharashtra Promotion of Mental Health Facilities in Tribal Areas.

Stages of the journey of a client (the term ECRC uses for the patients) at ECRC were explained to the researcher elaborately by Mr. Anand. A succinct summary of the same is as follows:

Stage 1: On being informed about a woman who is in need of care and protection and who needs immediate mental healthcare, the ECRC team at the Banyan visits the rescue spot. Before going to the rescue spot, brief assessment is done of the informant and the information provided by him/her. After assessing the gravity of the situation, the decision to rescue/not to rescue culminates. The rescue team comprises a social worker and two members of the staff who take along with them, clothes/food/first aid facilities, thereby preparing for whatever that the woman could possibly need immediately at the time of the rescue.

Stage 2: Rescue team is part of the primary care development at ECRC. On reaching the woman, an assessment is done of her, by observing the rescue spot, people around her, their opinion about the situation and most importantly the condition of the woman. To make her feel safe and comfortable, the ECRC team talks to her. She is given food and proper clothing to cover herself on the spot, if need be. Chances are that she might be scared or in a stage of shock and be unable to comprehend as to what is happening. Thus, sufficient time is given to her to feel comfortable with the rescue team. Only after the team gets her confidence and consent, is she rescued from the spot. Mr. Anand called it a two-way process of co-operation by the ECRC team and the woman to be rescued and/or the informant.

Stage 3: The woman is then taken to the local police station in the jurisdiction of which the rescue spot is located. The police also interact with her and assess her situation, after which the official police memo is prepared. This forms the first Official Document of association of the woman with ECRC.

Stage 4: On arriving at ECRC the client is first taken to the Emergency Rescue Room. She is provided with a welcome kit comprising clothes, toiletries, etc. for her personal use. Within 24-48 hours of arrival, her physical assessment is done, wherein her blood tests and other medical tests are conducted to understand her physical fitness. Most of the women who first come to ECRC are anemic. Some of them have high blood pressure, diabetes, etc. and some are even HIV+. The client is also checked for rashes, maggots, worms, wounds, fractures and is checked for signs of tuberculosis, leprosy and pregnancy. In case of a medical emergency, the patient is transferred to the nearest hospital at the earliest.

Stage 5: The woman is then produced before the Magistrate (within whose jurisdiction the rescue spot is situated) within 48 hours of her rescue. Reception order is obtained from the Magistrate, which forms the second official document of association of the client with ECRC.

Stage 6: This period is the observation period and it continues for one to two weeks from the arrival of the woman (client) to ECRC. A social worker is appointed as the Case Manager for the woman, who looks after the improvement in her conditions and re-assesses her condition throughout her association with ECRC. Psychological Assessment of the client is done by the psychology department over the period of every 1-2 weeks. Mr. Anand also pointed out that sometimes these women have been rescued from such deplorable condition and have been victim to such exploitation, situations and abuse that they are in a state of shock and require time to recuperate to normalcy.

Medicine is not started immediately. Psychological tests are performed to gauge the mental status of the woman, the same is done through tests like; IQ Assessment, 16 Personality Factor Questionnaire (16-PF), Rorschach test, etc.

The progress is assessed throughout the three phases of treatment and care which are: (i) pre-medication; (ii) under medication; and (iii) post-medication. The medicine is revised regularly, that is on a weekly and monthly basis as the case may be.

Stage 7: Occupational therapy and vocational therapy involving vocations like: weaving, candle making, tailoring, baking, embroidery, etc. are provided to the clients. Positive peer culture, financial incentives and personal accountability are the positive outcomes of this therapy which has always produced very good results among the clients.

Stage 8: Reintegration and after-care is the final phase of a client's journey at ECRC. The reintegration team works to find out the native homes of the clients. After being reintegrated with their family, the clients do not lose contact with ECRC. The re-integration and after-care team remains in contact with the clients and their family members to ensure that the previous condition of the client does not relapse and that there is continuity of care.

iii.   Anjali –Mental Health Rights Organization (Kolkata)

Anjali is a Mental Health Organization at Kolkata working with the aim of mainstreaming mental illness within the health discourse.[432] Anjali's mission is to progress from institutionalization towards the full rehabilitation of the mentally ill. Anjali works in close coordination with the Pavlov Mental Hospital, Lumbini Park Mental Hospital, and Bahrampur Mental Hospital.

The researcher interviewed Ms. Zara Sengupta on 29th March, 2018 at Kolkata. She is the Programme Manager of ARC (Advocacy, Research and Campaign) at Anjali, Kolkata. Ms. Sengupta apprised the author about the multi-faceted work Anjali undertakes which is instrumental towards the welfare of women with mental illness.

---

[432] Anjali – Mental Health Rights Organization, *See* http://www.anjalimentalhealth.org/ (Last visited on March 25, 2018)

Anjali's Voices (hospital) program is built with the vision of independence and citizenship for every individual, especially for people living with psychosocial disabilities in government mental institutions who are unable to claim their basic rights and freedoms. Women are faced with an even greater degree of vulnerability and are more likely to be abandoned in institutions than men. While only 29% of the people admitted are women, they constitute 67% of those who have to remain as long stay residents. The women who are admitted are also usually brought in when their illness is at a chronic stage, when they are dysfunctional, while men are admitted for early treatment.

Life-skills training at Anjali include:

a) Cognitive therapy

b) Creative therapy

c) Recreation and Relaxation therapy

d) Occupational therapy

d) Psychotherapy

e) Economic empowerment

f) Organizing shelter facilities

g) Reconnecting with the real world

The organization brings in the human rights, gender and sexuality discourse to mental health treatment, care, and policy development through a combination of right-based programmes. Anjali aims to secure large-scale systemic changes in the mental health field, by making mental health institutions and systems inclusive. In the last two years, the organization has also initiated employment opportunities, provided legal support and brought in a sexuality discourse pertaining to women with psycho-social disabilities.

SUMMARIZING:

The 2017 Act lays down provisions for half-way homes, sheltered accommodation and supported accommodation, and the Mental Healthcare (Rights of Persons with Mental Illness) Rules, 2018[433]lay down rules for the

---

[433] Notification No.: G.S.R. 509(E), Ministry of Health and Family Welfare, Department of Health and Family Welfare, Government of India (29th May, 2018)

setup of such services. Cue can be taken from these three NGOs which have been relentlessly and successfully working towards rehabilitation of women with mental illness. Their efforts have been acknowledged in the NCW and NIMHANS Report (2014)[434] which also recommends the setting up of half-way homes, shared and sheltered accommodations by the Government in the light of such ventures by these organizations.

---

[434] Available at
http://ncw.nic.in/pdfreports/addressing_concerns_of_women_admitted_to_psychiatric_institution s_in_india_an_in-depth_analysis.pdf (Last visited on October 10, 2017)

4. ONLINE SURVEY

The researcher conducted an online survey by circulating a structured questionnaire. The questionnaire comprised twelve questions, out of which six questions were close-ended and six questions were open-ended. The questionnaire was circulated online and received a total of hundred and ten responses.

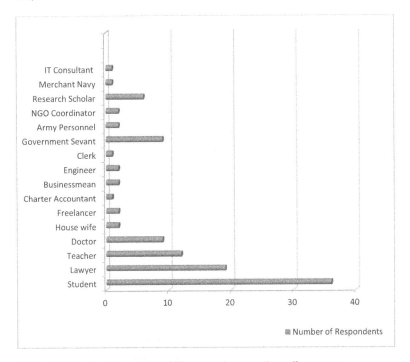

Table (11): Designations of the 110 respondents to the online survey

Questions in the online survey:

The questionnaire comprised twelve questions, out of which six questions were close-ended and six questions were open-ended.

Close-ended questions:

i) Is there a stigma surrounding mental illness in the Indian society? (Yes/No)

ii) Are you aware of the Mental Healthcare Act, 2017? (Yes/No)

iii) Are women with mental illness more vulnerable than their male counterparts? (Yes/No)

iv) Is India ready for the concept of psychiatric "advance directives"? (Yes/No)

v) Do many Indians still believe in traditional forms of healing for mental illness? (Yes/No/May be)

vi) Are the provisions pertaining to admission, treatment and discharge under the Mental Healthcare Act, 2017 an improvement from the relevant provisions from the Mental Health Act, 1987? (Yes/No/No comments)

Open-ended questions:

i) Chapter V of the Mental Healthcare Act, 2017 enumerates the rights of persons with mental illness. What steps can be taken to protect these rights of women with mental illness?

ii) What would be the implications of introducing psychiatric advance directives on women in need of mental healthcare?

iii) What, according to you, are the parameters that should be kept in mind to determine the free and informed consent for mental healthcare of women with mental illness?

iv) What according to you, can be done to ensure that mental healthcare is sensitive to the vulnerabilities of women with mental illness?

v) What role can psychiatric institutions and the psychiatric fraternity play to ensure that mental healthcare is gender sensitive?

vi) What role can the law play in ensuring the rehabilitation of women with mental illness in the society?

In addition to the above questions, there was also space allotted for any additional comments by the respondents of the questionnaire. The 110 responses received, included Indians from all walks of life who have access to the internet. They were either minimum graduates or were pursuing their studies.

Analysis of the Responses to the Questions in the online survey:

It is important to note that the online link to the Mental Healthcare Act, 2017 was given in the beginning of the questionnaire for the respondents to make reference to while answering the online questionnaire. Herein next, is the question-wise analysis of the 110 responses received to the online survey:

Question 1: Is there a stigma surrounding mental illness in the Indian society? (Yes/No)

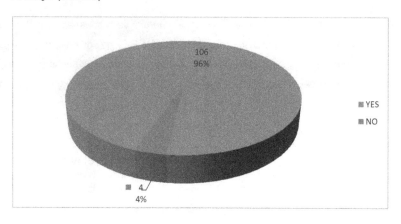

	YES	NO
Number of respondents	106	4
Percentage	96%	4%

Out of the 110 respondents who filled the questionnaire, a thumping majority of 106 persons, that is, 96% of the respondents agreed that there is stigma pertaining to mental illness in the country. Reasons associated with the stigma are manifold, including inconvenience and danger to others caused by persons with mental illness, association of mental illness with sins or evil spirits and general perception that persons with mental illness become an obligation and a monetary burden to the family. Name calling, branding, general ostracizing and abandonment are some of the resultant effects of associating stigma to mental illness in India.

Question 2: Are you aware of the Mental Healthcare Act, 2017? (Yes/No)

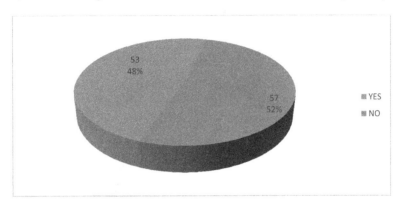

	YES	NO
Number of respondents	53	57
Percentage	48%	52%

Only half (53) of the 110 respondents who filled the questionnaire were aware of the Mental Healthcare Act, 2017 and a little more than half (57) were not aware of the new 2017 Act. The new Act has multifarious facets that have the potential to change mental healthcare in India drastically. The respondents of the online survey were all educated professionals and students. Lack of awareness among more than half of them about the 2017 Act is a matter of great concern. Disseminating awareness is a vital step which should precede the implementation of the Act for the process of implementation to be smooth and successful.

Question 3: Are women with mental illness more vulnerable than their male counterparts? (Yes/No)

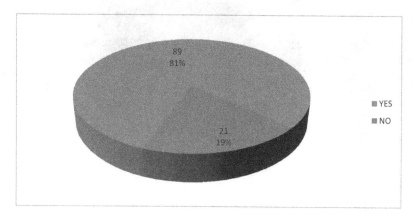

	YES	NO
Number of respondents	89	21
Percentage	81%	19%

Out of the 110 respondents who filled the questionnaire, a majority of 89 persons that is 81% of the respondents agreed that women with mental illness more vulnerable than their male counterparts. This justifies the asking of the *"woman question"* pertaining to mental healthcare. In the social-economic setup prevalent in the country, it is a known fact that women happen to be the vulnerable sections of the society. Women with mental illness sometimes become victims of twin disabilities, that of *'gender'* and *'mental illness'*. The gravity of the same has been addressed in the NCW Report (2016) and HRW Report (2014).

Question 4: Chapter V of the Mental Healthcare Act, 2017 enumerates the rights of persons with mental illness. What steps can be taken to protect these rights of women with mental illness?

The responses to this question were manifold, however all of them recommended steps that can be taken by the Government towards the protection of the rights of women with mental illness in the country. Herein below are some of the primary responses received to this question:

- Generate awareness;
- Set up special homes;
- Sensitization of mental healthcare professionals;
- Justice redressal system should be cheaper;
- Setting up of guidelines to protect the rights of women with mental illness;
- Ensuring the support of the family; and
- Proper implementation of the provisions of the law.

Question 5: Is India ready for the concept of psychiatric "advance directives"? (Yes/No)

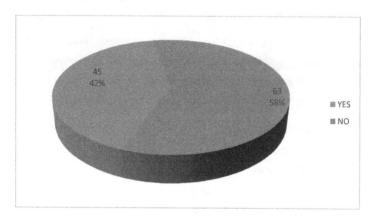

	YES	NO
Number of respondents (108)	45	63
Percentage	42%	58%

There was a difference of opinion regarding the viability of introducing the concept of psychiatric advance directives in India. Two respondents chose to not answer this question. 45 out of the 108 respondents said yes, whereas 63 of them said no. The apprehensions addressed by some of the respondents whom the researcher met in person were relating to awareness about the concept and that the concept would introduce unnecessary formalities in healthcare when the imminent requirement is the treatment of the patient. However, the ones in support of the concept of psychiatric advance directives considered it a welcome change which will give the persons with mental illness the freedom of choice and the right to exercise their autonomy over their own body. It is important to note that the online link to the 2017 Act was given in the beginning of the questionnaire for the respondents to make reference to while answering the online questionnaire. Therefore, the respondents were well-informed in advance about the concept of psychiatric advance directive before answering the questionnaire.

Question 6: What would be the implications of introducing psychiatric advance directives on women in need of mental healthcare?

42% of the respondents had stated that India is ready for the concept of psychiatric advance directive and 58% had said no. The online link to the 2017 Act was given in the beginning of the questionnaire for the respondents to make reference to while answering the online questionnaire. Therefore, the respondents were well-informed in advance about the concept of psychiatric advance directive before answering the questionnaire. The responses to this question were mixed. Herein below are some of the pertinent responses received to this question:

- Psychiatric advance directives will give more autonomy to the patient with mental illness about his/her treatment;
- Chances of misuse;
- Lack of awareness about the concept;
- Unnecessary complications for the treating Doctor;
- A patient with mental illness may not differentiate between what is good and what is bad for him/her; and
- Opening gates for unnecessary litigations.

Question 7: Do many Indians still believe in traditional forms of healing for mental illness? (Yes/No/May be)

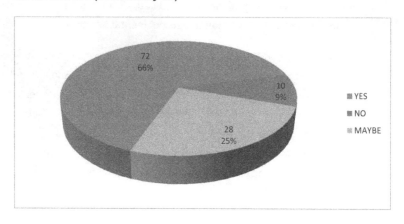

	YES	NO	May be
Number of respondents	72	10	28
Percentage	66%	9%	25%

66% of the respondents to this question agreed to the fact that many Indians still believe in traditional forms of healing for mental illness. 25% of the respondents were not sure and only 9% disagreed to the proposition. Traditional forms of healing include faith healers, visits to dargahs, temples and other forms of religious and cultural activities associated with the cure for mental illness in the country. It is relevant to note that the psychiatrists interviewed by the researcher had also acknowledged the fact that many of the patients who come to them already try traditional healing methods for mental healthcare before approaching them for mental healthcare and treatment.

Question 8: What, according to you, are the parameters that should be kept in mind to determine the free and informed consent for mental healthcare of women with mental illness?

All the respondents were in favour of ensuring the obtaining of informed consent of the person with mental illness before proceeding with any form of treatment. The respondents recommended that the information provided before obtaining the consent should be communicated in the language and manner which the patient can decipher. If the patient is unable to understand and is not in a state to give consent, the same information should be provided to and consent be obtained from the nominated representative/guardian/family member of the patient. It is important to ensure that the consent obtained is free and that there is no fraud/force/coercion/misrepresentation involved in obtaining the same.

Question 9: What according to you, can be done to ensure that mental healthcare is sensitive to the vulnerabilities of women with mental illness? Question 10: What role can psychiatric institutions and the psychiatric fraternity play to ensure that mental healthcare is gender sensitive?

81% of the respondents had agreed to the proposition that women with mental illness are more vulnerable than men with mental illness in this country. The responses to questions 9 and 10 were almost same and therefore have been clubbed together for the purpose of analysis and compilation. While answering these two questions, the respondents proposed multiple suggestions. The list herein below exhaustively enumerates the suggestions put forth by the respondents while answering this question:

- Increasing the number of women personnel in mental health care;
- Sensitization of mental health care providers;
- Making women with mental illness aware of their rights; and
- Making family members sensitive to the situation and rights of women with mental illness in the country.

Question 11: Are the provisions pertaining to admission, treatment and discharge under the Mental Healthcare Act, 2017 an improvement from the relevant provisions from the Mental Health Act, 1987? (Yes/No /No Comments)

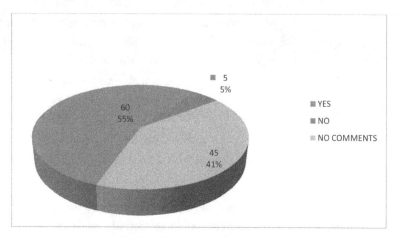

	YES	NO	NO COMMENTS
Number of respondents	60	5	45
Percentage	55%	5%	41%

Answering this question with a 'yes' or a 'no' was not mandatory because a third option of "no comments" was also provided with. The same was done knowing that it would be impractical to expect all the respondents to the survey to be aware of the provisions of both the 2017 Act and the Mental Health Act, 1987. It is noteworthy that the persons who responded were therefore aware of the provisions of both the legislations and their implications. According to 55% of the respondents the provisions pertaining to admission, treatment and discharge under the 2017 Act are an improvement from the relvant provisions of the Mental Health Act, 1987.

Question 12: What role can the law play in ensuring the rehabilitation of women with mental illness in the society?

This question received many positive responses from the respondents with suggestions that are very much viable. The pertinent suggestions put forth in the responses were:

- Setting up of more shelter homes and half-way homes;
- Making mental healthcare a journey towards independence;
- Ensuring the financial independence of the women with mental illness;
- Support from the family and care-givers;
- Educating the society;
- Gender sensitization; and
- Vocational and occupational training.

5.   OFFLINE SURVEY

The researcher conducted an offline survey by circulating a structured questionnaire. The questionnaire comprised nine questions, out of which five questions were both close-ended and open-ended in nature; and four questions were open-ended only. There was the option of "Any additional comments" at the end of the questionnaire. The questionnaire received a total of seventy-five responses. The respondents comprised 53 lawyers, 18 students, 2 research scholars and 2 medical officers.

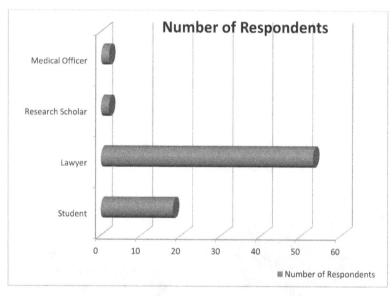

Table (12): Designations of the 75 respondents to the offline survey

Herein below are the questions asked in the questionnaire of this offline survey:

1. Are you aware of the following developments in law pertaining to mental healthcare?

The Mental Healthcare Act, 2017	❑ Yes	❑ No
The National Mental Health Policy, 2014	❑ Yes	❑ No
The Mental Health Act, 1987	❑ Yes	❑ No
The United Nations Convention on Rights of Persons with Disability	❑ Yes	❑ No

2. Is there a stigma surrounding mental illness in the Indian society?

        ❑ Yes   ❑ No

Reasons for the same (comments if any):

_____
_____
_____
_____
_____
_____

3. Are women with mental illness more vulnerable than their male counterparts?

        ❑ Yes   ❑ No

Reasons for the same (comments if any):

_____
_____
_____
_____
_____
_____

Chapter III of the Act introduces the concept of **psychiatric advance directives** and Chapter IV comprises provisions pertaining to the nominated representative of the person with mental illness. The Act states that any person, not being a minor, has the right to make an **advance directive in writing specifying, the way the person wishes to be cared for and treated for a mental illness**; the individual or individuals, in order of precedence, he wants to appoint as nominated representative.

4. **Is India ready for the concept of psychiatric *"advance directives"*?**

   ❑ Yes   ❑ No

Comments if any:

_____
_____
_____
_____
_____

5. **Do many Indians still believe in traditional forms of healing for mental illness?**
   ❑ Yes   ❑ No

Comments if any:

_____
_____
_____
_____
_____

The 2017 Act defines **informed consent** to mean "consent given for a specific intervention, without any force, undue influence, fraud, threat, mistake or misrepresentation, and obtained after disclosing to a person adequate information including risks and benefits of, and alternatives to, the specific intervention in a language and manner understood by the person."

6. **What, according to you, are the parameters that should be kept in mind to determine the free and informed consent for mental healthcare of women with mental illness?**

_____
_____
_____

Rights of persons with Mental Illness (Chapter V of the 2017 Act):

i.	Right to access mental healthcare	vii.	Restriction on release of information in resp
ii.	Right to community living		of mental illness
iii.	Right to protection from cruel, inhuman and degrading treatment	viii.	Right to access medical records
iv.	Right to equality and non-discrimination	ix.	Right to personal contacts and communicati
		x.	Right to legal aid
v.	Right to information	xi.	Right to make complaints about deficiencies provision of services
vi.	Right to confidentiality		

7. Chapter V of the Mental Healthcare Act, 2017 enumerates the rights of persons with mental illness. What steps can be taken to protect these rights of women with mental illness?

_____
_____
_____
_____
_____

8. What according to you, can be done to ensure that mental healthcare is sensitive to the vulnerabilities of women with mental illness?

_____
_____
_____
_____

9. What role can psychiatric institutions and the psychiatric fraternity play to ensure that mental healthcare is gender sensitive?

_____
_____
_____
_____
_____

10. Any additional comments:

_____

1. Are you aware of the following developments in law pertaining to mental healthcare?

The Mental Healthcare Act, 2017   ❑ Yes   ❑ No

The National Mental Health Policy, 2014   ❑ Yes   ❑ No

The Mental Health Act, 1987   ❑ Yes   ❑ No

The United Nations Convention on Rights of   ❑ Yes   ❑ No
Persons with Disability

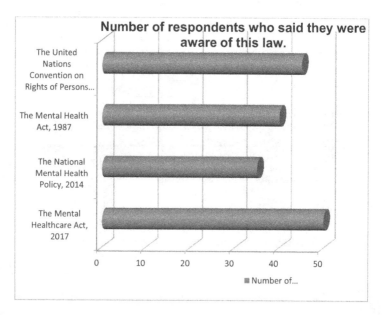

Legal instrument	Yes	No
1. The Mental Healthcare Act, 2017	50	25
2. The National Mental Health Policy of India, 2014	35	40
3. The Mental Health Act, 1987	40	35
4. United Nations Convention of Rights of Persons with Disability	45	30

2. Is there a stigma surrounding mental illness in the Indian society?

❑ Yes   ❑ No

Reasons for the same (comments if any):

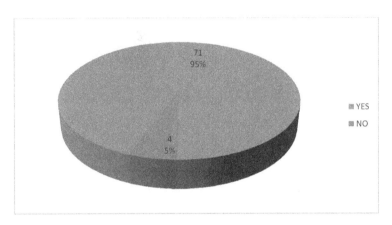

	YES	NO
Number of respondents	71	4
Percentage	95%	5%

Out of the 74 respondents who filled the questionnaire, a thumping majority of 71 respondents, that is, 95% of the respondents agreed that there is a stigma pertaining to mental illness in the country. Reasons associated with the stigma are manifold, including inconvenience and danger to others caused by persons with mental illness, association of mental illness with sins or evil spirits and general perception that persons with mental illness become an obligation and a monetary burden to the family. Name calling, branding, general ostracizing and abandonment are some of the resultant effects of associating stigma to mental illness in India.

3. Are women with mental illness more vulnerable than their male counterparts?

❑ Yes   ❑ No

Reasons for the same (comments if any):

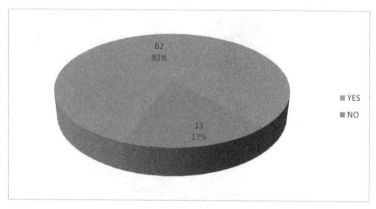

	YES	NO
Number of respondents	62	13
Percentage	83%	17%

Out of the 75 respondents who filled the questionnaire, a majority of 62 respondents, that is, 83% of the respondents agreed that women with mental illness more vulnerable than their male counterparts. This justifies the asking of the *"woman question"* pertaining to mental healthcare. In the social-economic setup prevalent in the country, it is a known fact that women happen to be the vulnerable sections of the society. Women with mental illness sometimes become victims of twin disabilities, that of *'gender'* and *'mental illness'*. The gravity of the same has been addressed in the NCW Report (2016) and HRW Report (2014).

4. Is India ready for the concept of psychiatric "advance directives"?

❑ Yes   ❑ No

Reasons for the same (comments if any):

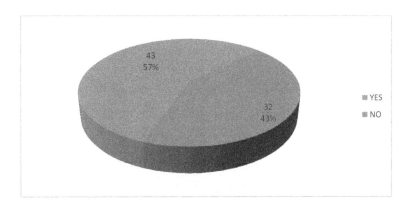

	YES	NO
Number of respondents	43	32
Percentage	57%	43%

There was a difference of opinion regarding the viability of introducing the concept of psychiatric advance directives in India. 43 out of the 75 respondents said yes, whereas 32 of them said no.

5. Do many Indians still believe in traditional forms of healing for mental illness?

❑ Yes   ❑ No

Reasons for the same (comments if any):

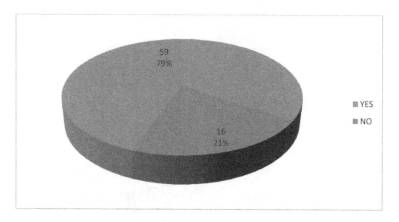

	YES	NO
Number of respondents	59	16
Percentage	79%	21%

79% of the respondents to this question agreed to the fact that many Indians still believe in traditional forms of healing for mental illness. 21% of the respondents disagreed to the proposition. Traditional forms of healing include faith healers, visits to dargahs, temples and other forms of religious and cultural activities associated with the cure for mental illness in the country. It is relevant to note that the psychiatrists interviewed by the researcher had also acknowledged the fact that many of the patients who come to them already try traditional healing methods for mental healthcare before approaching them for mental healthcare and treatment.

6. **What, according to you, are the parameters that should be kept in mind to determine the free and informed consent for mental healthcare of women with mental illness?**

The responses to this question in the offline survey were very similar to the responses to this question in the online survey. All the respondents were in favour of ensuring the obtaining of informed consent of the person with mental illness before proceeding with any form of treatment. The respondents recommended that the information provided before obtaining the consent should be communicated in the language and manner which the patient can decipher. If the patient is unable to understand and is not in a state to give consent, the same information should be provided to, and consent be obtained from the nominated representative/guardian/family member of the patient. It is important to ensure that the consent obtained is free and that there is no fraud involved in obtaining the same.

7. **Chapter V of the Mental Healthcare Act, 2017 enumerates the rights of persons with mental illness. What steps can be taken to protect these rights of women with mental illness?**

The responses to this question in the offline survey were very similar to the responses to the question in the online survey. Like the online survey, all the respondents to the question in the offline survey made recommendations towards the protection of the rights of women with mental illness in the country. Herein below are some of the primary responses received to this question:

- Generate awareness among the general public;
- Ensure that they are not abandoned in mental healthcare facilities;
- Rehabilitation;
- Sensitization of police, judiciary, mental healthcare professionals;
- Sensitization of the society;

- Proper enforcement mechanism should be in place;
- Support of the family;
- Vocational training of women with mental illness during their recovery;

8. **What according to you, can be done to ensure that mental healthcare is sensitive to the vulnerabilities of women with mental illness?**
9. **What role can psychiatric institutions and the psychiatric fraternity play to ensure that mental healthcare is gender sensitive?**

83% of the respondents had agreed to the proposition that women with mental illness are more vulnerable than men with mental illness in this country. The responses to questions 8 and 9 were almost same and therefore have been clubbed together for the purpose of analysis and compilation. While answering the two questions, the respondents proposed multiple suggestions. The list herein below exhaustively enumerates the suggestions put forth by the respondents while answering this question:

- Increasing the number of women personnel in mental health care;
- Sensitization of mental health care providers;
- Making it mandatory for the mental healthcare providers to obtain the informed consent of women with mental illness before administering any treatment to them;
- Making women with mental illness aware of their rights;
- Ensuring that only female staff should be present in women's wards at mental healthcare units and that no male member of the staff should visit the women's wards without the supervision of and in the absence of a female staff member; and
- Making family members sensitive to the situation and rights of women with mental illness in the country.

6. COMPILING THE RESULTS OF THE CLOSE-ENDED QUESTIONS OF THE ONLINE AND OFFLINE SURVEY

Question 1: Is there a stigma surrounding mental illness in the Indian society?

	YES	NO
Online survey (110)	106	4
Offline Survey (75)	71	4
TOTAL (185)	177	8
PERCENTAGE	95.6%	4.3%

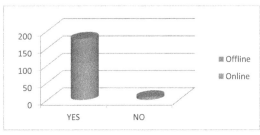

Question 2: Are you aware of the Mental Healthcare Act, 2017?

	YES	NO
Online survey (110)	53	57
Offline Survey (75)	50	25
TOTAL (185)	103	82
PERCENTAGE	55.6%	44.3%

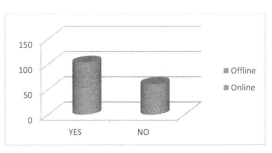

Question 3: Are women with mental illness more vulnerable than their male counterparts?

	YES	NO
Online survey (110)	89	21
Offline Survey (75)	62	13
TOTAL (185)	151	34
PERCENTAGE	81.6%	18.3%

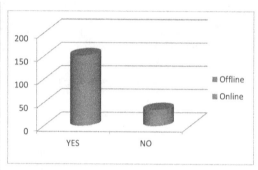

Question 4: Is India ready for the concept of psychiatric "advance directives"?

	YES	NO
Online survey (108)[435]	45	63
Offline Survey (75)	43	32
TOTAL (183)	88	95
PERCENTAGE	48.1%	51.9%

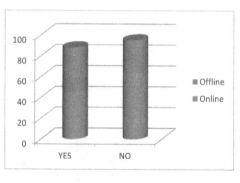

---

[435] Two respondents to the online survey chose not to answer this question.

Question 5: Do many Indians still believe in traditional forms of healing for mental illness?

	YES	NO	May be
Online survey (110)	72	10	28
Offline Survey (75)	59	16	--
TOTAL (185)	131	26	28
PERCENTAGE	70.8%	14.1%	15.1%

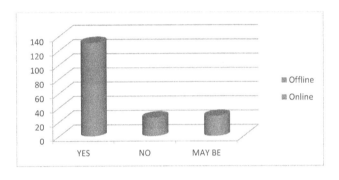

7. DECODING THE EMPIRICAL RESEARCH

The responses to the questions in both the online and offline survey were headed in the same direction. It can be discerned that the result of both the surveys is reliable because of the similarity in the answering trend evident in both of them. It is important to note that the results of the surveys, the interviews with the psychiatrists, the visits to NGOs are all in consonance with the findings of the NCW and NIMHANS Report (2016)[436] and HRW Report (2014)[437] which is the secondary source of empirical data relied upon in the pursuance of this research.

The results of the empirical research undertaken by the researcher also fulfil the aim of drawing a picture of the various aspects of mental healthcare and that of getting a better understanding of the roles of various personnel involved in mental healthcare in the country. Getting an idea of the temperament of the general public was also facilitated by the small exercise of the two surveys (online and offline) conducted by the researcher.

---

[436] Available at
http://ncw.nic.in/pdfreports/addressing_concerns_of_women_admitted_to_psychiatric_institutions_in_india_an_in-depth_analysis.pdf (Last visited on October 10, 2017)
[437] Available at https://www.hrw.org/report/2014/12/03/treated-worse-animals/abuses-against-women-and-girls-psychosocial-or-intellectual (Last visited on April 5, 2018)

Chapter XIII

XIII. Conclusion and Suggestions

1. THE CONSTITUTION OF INDIA -THE CONSTITUTIONALITY & LEGALITY OF THE MENTAL HEALTHCARE ACT, 2017

The Preamble to the Constitution of India upholds the ethos of dignity, equality and justice, in the background of which is the indispensable right to life and personal liberty guaranteed under Article 21 of the Constitution of India. Right to life entails within its ambit the right to live with dignity, the right to healthcare,[438] the right to privacy, the right to a home and family, the right not to be ill-treated or tortured and the right to make one's own decisions, etc.[439] Right to equality includes not only the right to be treated equally and be given equal opportunity but also the right not to be discriminated against arbitrarily. Equality includes equality of opportunity, of freedom, and an independent decision-making right in one's economic, social and cultural setup.

Persons with mental illness are the weaker sections of this society, sometimes requiring aid in decision-making and care-takers to address their needs.[440] This necessitates the need for the law to particularly protect the right to privacy of persons with mental illness and their right to autonomy to the extent exercisable.

The Hon'ble Supreme Court of India in the landmark Judgement of *Justice K.S. Puttaswamy (Retd.) v. Union of India*[441] upheld the right to privacy as a fundamental right covered under the right to life guaranteed under Article 21 of the Constitution of India, and discussed privacy from the context of the *"freedom of choice."* The Court held that the freedoms of an individual under Article 19(1) of the Constitution of India can only be fulfilled when the individual

---

[438] ANDREW CLAPHAM, ET. AL., REALIZING THE RIGHT TO HEALTH (2009)

[439] *See* Lata Singh v. State of Uttar Pradesh, AIR 2006 SC 2522; Shakti Vahini v. Union of India and Ors. W.P. Civil No. 231 of 2010 (Supreme Court of India); Paschim Bangal Khet Mazdoor Samity v. State of West Bengal, AIR 1996 SC 2426; Justice K.S. Puttaswamy (Retd.) v. Union of India, (2017) 10 SCC 1; State of Punjab v. Ram Labhaya Bagha, AIR 1998 SC 1703

[440] *See* MARC STAUCH MA, ET. AL., TEXT, CASES AND MATERIALS ON MEDICAL LAW AND ETHICS (2012)

[441] (2017) 10 SCC 1

has the right to choose his/her preferences pertaining to those freedoms.[442] Read with Article 21, the freedom and liberty envisaged in Article 19 of the Constitution of India entails with it the right of the person to choose factors pertaining to various facets of his/her life, including what to eat, where to live, how to live, who to live with, healthcare and various other vital life decisions. Right to privacy is indispensable for a person's dignity and thereby recognizes his/her autonomy to make choices that have the potential of affecting his/her life.[443] From the very crux of this Judgement of the Hon'ble Supreme Court in *Justice K.S. Puttaswamy (Retd.) v. Union of India*[444], the constitutionality of psychiatric advance directives under the Mental Healthcare Act, 2017 can be seen to ensue. The right of a person with mental illness to decide the way he/she wants/does not want to be cared for and treated is very much his/her *"freedom of choice"* to decide upon the vital factors about treatment and care during mental illness, in which because of the provision of psychiatric advance directive, he/she has the power and privilege to decide about the same in advance. The Hon'ble Supreme Court in its landmark Judgement *Common Cause (A Regd. Society) v. Union of India and Another*[445] delivered this year, upheld the constitutionality of passive euthanasia and laid down guidelines for advance directive pertaining to the same. Even though such an advance directive is different from the psychiatric advance directive issued under the 2017 Act, nevertheless they both are advance directives with respect to their basic feature (basic features being: issued by the person when he/she is of sound mind to be executed when he/she is unable to give consent); which implies the approval to the constitutionality of the concept of advance directives in general, given by the Hon'ble Supreme Court of India.[446]

---

[442] *See* MARY DONNELLY, HEALTHCARE DECISION-MAKING AND THE LAW –AUTONOMY, CAPACITY AND THE LIMITS OF LIBERALISM (2010)

[443] Justice K.S. Puttaswamy (Retd.) v. Union of India, (2017) 10 SCC 1

[444] (2017) 10 SCC 1

[445] W.P. (CIVIL) NO. 215 OF 2005

[446] Judgement Common Cause (A Regd. Society) v. Union of India and Another, W.P. (CIVIL) NO. 215 OF 2005

Rights of persons with mental illness are the same as that of any other persons, but the role of the State to respect and protect the rights of these persons is more active. The rights of persons with mental illness envisaged in Chapter V of the 2017 Act are in the reflection of the rights laid down in the United Nations Convention on Rights of Persons with Disabilities. It is also important to note that these rights take after the fundamental rights in Part III of the Constitution of India, either directly or through various landmark Judgements of the Hon'ble Courts in the country.[447]

The 2017 Act provides for the setting up of and assigning of duties to, Mental Health Authorities at the Central[448] and State[449] level, Mental Health Boards.[450] It lays down the duties of the appropriate government;[451] and provides for registration, recognition and regulation of mental health establishments[452] for the purposes of this Act and the admission, treatment and discharge of persons in need of mental healthcare[453]. Sections 107 to 109 of the Act provide for punishments and penalties for violation of various provisions of the Act respectively. These provisions, it is submitted, have the capacity to pave the way for proper implementation of the rights guaranteed under the 2017 Act in the time to come. However, it is pertinent to note that the implementation is possible successfully only if it is accompanied by massive flow of fund from the Central Government to various State Governments which are already grappling with inadequate medical infrastructure at district levels.[454]The National Health

---

[447] *See* Lata singh v.state of Uttar Pradesh, AIR 2006 SC 2522; Shakti Vahini v. Union of India and Ors. W.P. Civil No. 231 of 2010 (Supreme Court of India); Paschim Bangal Khet Mazdoor Samity v. State of West Bengal, AIR 1996 SC 2426; Justice K.S. Puttaswamy (Retd.) v. Union of India, (2017) 10 SCC 1; State of Punjab v. Ram Labhaya Bagha, AIR 1998 SC 1703
[448] The 2017 Act, Chapter VII
[449] The 2017 Act, Chapter VIII
[450] The 2017 Act, Chapter XI
[451] The 2017 Act, Chapter VI
[452] The 2017 Act, Chapter X
[453] The 2017 Act, Chapter XII
[454] Raghuraj Gagneja, *Mental Healthcare Bill: Despite the positive reform, a lot more needs to be done for the mentally ill,* FIRSTPOST (April 8, 2017), Available at

Policy, 2017[455] aims to raise the public healthcare expenditure from 1.4% to 2.5% of GDP. Public healthcare includes within its ambit mental healthcare and the National Health Policy, 2017 aims to consider the provisions of the National Mental Health Policy of India, 2014. The National Health Policy, 2017 could resultantly, prove to be pivotal in fulfilling the aims of the 2017 Act.

When undergoing treatment, a woman with mental illness is in the most vulnerable of states. The 2017 Act will play a pivotal role in ensuring that the vulnerabilities of such women requiring and undergoing mental healthcare are not exploited. The provisions of the Act are progressive and are a welcome change. Proper implementation of the legal provisions word for word will lead to the ultimate success of this legislation.[456]

2. TESTING THE MENTAL HEALTHCARE ACT, 2017 ON THE ANVIL OF THE WHO CHECKLIST ON MENTAL HEALTH LEGISLATION

Having tested the Mental Healthcare Act, 2017 on the anvil of the Constitution of India and the mandates of the United Nations Convention on the Rights of Persons with Disabilities, the final stage of critical evaluation of the new law was done in this research through evaluating its contents on the WHO Checklist on Mental Health Legislation[457](See Annexure 5.) The WHO Resource Book on

---

http://www.firstpost.com/india/mental-healthcare-bill-despite-the-positive-reform-a-lot-more-needs-to-be-done-for-the-mentally-ill-3373156.html (Last visited on May 10, 2017)

[455] The National Health Policy, 2017, Available at http://cdsco.nic.in/writereaddata/National-Health-Policy.pdf (Last visited on May 10, 2017)

[456] *See* DR. LILY SRIVASTAVA, LAW AND MEDICINE (2010)

[457] WHO Checklist on Mental Health Legislation, Annexure 1 of THE WHO RESOURCE BOOK ON MENTAL HEALTH, HUMAN RIGHTS AND LEGISLATION (2005), Available at https://ec.europa.eu/health/sites/health/files/mental_health/docs/who_resource_book_en.pdf (Last visited on April 5, 2018)

Mental Health, Human Rights and Legislation (2005)[458] comprises the WHO Checklist on Mental Health Legislation.[459] The Checklist is aimed at helping the law makers of various countries in evaluating the comprehensiveness of their mental health legislation and/or assists them in drafting a new legislation on the matter. The provisions of the Mental Health Care Act, 2017 were tested by the researcher through the checklist[460] and out of the 175 requirements mentioned in the checklist, the provisions of the 2017 Act cover 149 requirements. It is noteworthy that some of the requirements in the checklist, like reservation, education, etc. have been covered under the Rights of Persons with Disabilities Act, 2016 and hence do not find mention in the 2017 Act. As a whole the mental healthcare legal framework in India presently covers the requirements specified in the WHO Checklist fairly well.

3. ADDRESSING STIGMA, DISCRIMINATION AND EXCLUSION[461]OF WOMEN WITH MENTAL ILLNESS IN THE COUNTRY

Stigma is one of the worst aspects of mental illness that a woman faces because of her condition. Ostracizing, non-recognition, abandonment ensue from the stigma attached to mental illness in the society.[462] Paragraph 5.3.1 of the National Mental Health Policy of India, 2014 requires the government to

---

[458] THE WHO RESOURCE BOOK ON MENTAL HEALTH, HUMAN RIGHTS AND LEGISLATION (2005), Available at
https://ec.europa.eu/health/sites/health/files/mental_health/docs/who_resource_book_en.pdf
(Last visited on April 5, 2018)
[459] WHO Checklist on Mental Health Legislation, Annexure 1 of THE WHO RESOURCE BOOK ON MENTAL HEALTH, HUMAN RIGHTS AND LEGISLATION (2005), Available at
https://ec.europa.eu/health/sites/health/files/mental_health/docs/who_resource_book_en.pdf
(Last visited on April 5, 2018)
[460] See Annexure 5
[461] The 2014 Policy, Para 5.3.1
[462] Christie Hunter, *Understanding and reducing the stigma of mental illness in women*, Women's Health Research Institute, Available at
http://www.womenshealth.northwestern.edu/blog/understanding-and-reducing-stigma-mental-illness-women (Last visited on April 1, 2018)

address the stigma associated with mental illness in the Indian society, discrimination and exclusion meted out to persons with mental illness. Section 30 of the 2017 Act requires the Appropriate Government to take all possible measures to ensure that various programmes to reduce stigma relating to mental illness should be planned, funded, enforced and implemented effectively. One of the major features of such programmes being, generating awareness by disseminating information and making various sections of the society sensitive to the issue of mental illness.

Each of the above provisions requires a positive and active role of the government and the implementation authorities. The 2017 Act imposes a duty on the appropriate government not only to plan and design but also to implement programmes promoting mental health and preventing mental illness;[463] one of these programmes being those aiming at reducing suicides and attempted suicides in India.[464] In furtherance of the same, the Appropriate Government is required to take the following measures[465]:

- Giving wide publicity to the 2017 Act through public media at regular intervals, namely through television, radio, electronic and print media;
- Programmes to reduce stigma relating to mental illness to be planned, funded, enforced and implemented effectively;
- The Government officials including police officers and other officers to be periodically sensitized and be provided awareness and training on matters pertaining to this Act.

The 2017 Act read with the National Mental Health Policy of India, 2014, therefore, addresses the socio-cultural vice of stigma surrounding mental illness by disseminating information and creating awareness thereby aiming towards clearing the cobwebs of stigma relating to mental illness in the Indian society.

---

[463] The 2017 Act, Section 29(1)

[464] The 2017 Act, Section 29(2);
It is to be noted that Section 115 of the 2017 Act decriminalizes attempt to commit suicide. It is stated that notwithstanding the provisions of Section 309 of the Indian Penal Code, any person who attempts to commit suicide should be presumed to be under severe stress and should not be tried or punished under the Indian Penal Code for the attempt to commit suicide.

[465] The 2017 Act, Section 30

4. POSITIVE ROLE OF THE APPROPRIATE GOVERNMENT UNDER THE MENTAL HEALTHCARE ACT, 2017

The Appropriate Government[466] is required by the 2017 Act to increase the human resources in mental health services by developing education and training programmes in coordination with institutions of higher education. It is also important to improve the skill of existent human resources by updating them with the latest developments and advancements made in the area of mental healthcare. The Appropriate Government has to take up the responsibility to train the medical officers in public healthcare establishments and medical officers in prisons to be able to provide basic emergency mental healthcare services.[467] The Act requires the Appropriate Government to set up internationally acceptable guidelines within a period of ten years of the commencement of the Act.[468] The 2017 Act also acknowledges the coordinate role of various Ministries and Departments (including health, law, home affairs, employment, women, education, social justice, etc.) of the government, coordination of the same being instrumental in achieving the aim of the Act.[469]

5. THE MENTAL HEALTHCARE (RIGHTS OF PERSONS WITH MENTAL ILLNESS) RULES, 2018

The Mental Healthcare (Rights of Persons with Mental Illness) Rules, 2018[470] have been drafted by the Central Government in exercise of the powers

---

[466] The 2017 Act, Section 2(b)
[467] The 2017 Act, Section 31
[468] Id.
[469] The 2017 Act, Section 32
[470] Notification No.: G.S.R. 509(E), Ministry of Health and Family Welfare, Department of Health and Family Welfare, Government of India (29th May, 2018)

conferred by Section 121 of the 2017 Act.[471] The 2018 Rules are in furtherance of the cause of the mandates of UNCRPD, taken up by the 2017 Act. The provisions of the 2018 Rules if implemented completely can be instrumental in addressing the concerns of women with mental illness in the country.

Mental healthcare includes not only the diagnosis and treatment of mental illness but also the care and rehabilitation of the person back into the society.[472] It is therefore very important to understand the various elements that constitute mental illness to gauge this phenomenon.

The Rules lay down provisions for the setting up of *"half-way homes", "sheltered accommodation", "supported accommodation", "hospital and community based rehabilitation establishment" and "hospital and community based rehabilitation service",* respectively, thereby recognizing the pertinent role of rehabilitation for complete mental healthcare. The provisions are not myopic but rather look at mental healthcare holistically, with the ultimate aim of enabling the persons with mental illness to be able to get back to independent living and facilitate their reintegration into the society.

Clarity to the concepts pertaining to rehabilitation of persons with mental illness is provided by the various definitions enumerated in the 2018 Rules. Discussed herein below are some of the important definitions given under the 2018 Rules:

| Rule 2(c) | **Half-way home** | means: |
| | | *"a transitional living facility for persons with mental illness who are discharged as* |

---

[471] See also the Draft Central Regulations, 2017 under the 2017 Act, Available at https://mohfw.gov.in/sites/default/files/Final%20Draft%20Rules%20MHC%20Act%2C%202017%20%281%29.pdf (Last visited on April 27, 2018);
By virtue of the powers to make regulations under Section 122 of the 2017 Act Central Government has drafted the Draft Central Regulations, 2017 on behalf of Central Mental Health Authority. It is important to note that these Draft Central Regulations are subject to the modifications that may be made by the Central Mental Authority once it is constituted.
[472] The 2017 Act, Section 2(o)

		inpatient from a mental health establishment, but are not fully ready to live independently on their own or with the family."
Rule 2(d)	**Hospital and community based rehabilitation establishment**	means: "an establishment providing hospital and community based rehabilitation services"
Rule 2(e)	**Hospital and community based rehabilitation service**	means: "rehabilitation services provided to a person with mental illness using existing community resources with an aim to promote his reintegration in the community and to make such person independent in all aspects of life including financial, social, relationship building and maintaining."
Rule 2(h)	**Sheltered accommodation**	means: "a safe and secure accommodation option for persons with mental illness, who want to live and manage their affairs independently, but need occasional help and support"
Rule 2(i)	**Supported accommodation**	means: "a living arrangement whereby a person, in need of support, who has a rented or

		ownership accommodation, but has no live-in caregiver, gets domiciliary care and a range of support services from a caregiver of an agency to help him live independently and safely in the privacy of his home."

The 2018 Rules require the Appropriate Government under the Act of 2017 to establish such number of half-way homes, sheltered accommodations, supported accommodations, hospital and community based rehabilitation establishment and services at such places, as are necessary for providing services required by persons with mental illness and are to follow the required minimum standards specified in law.[473]

The Rules also elaborate in detail the *"right to access basic medical records."*[474] It is stated *inter alia* that a person with mental illness is entitled to receive the documented versions of his/her medical information relating to diagnosis, assessment, investigation and treatment as per the medical records.

After having discussed the essential features of the 2018 Rules, it can be said that these Rules are indeed a beacon of hope in fulfilling the aim of the 2017 Act. The rules pertaining to rehabilitation are meticulously framed. It is the implementation of these Rules and the positive action by the appropriate government and various authorities under the 2017 Act that can together facilitate the aims of the Act in the light of UNCRPD to not only provide for the treatment of the person with mental illness but also the reintegration and rehabilitation of the person into society to enable him/her to lead an independent life.

---

[473] 2018 Rules , Rules 3 and 4
[474] *Id.,* Rule 6

6. NEED TO INCORPORATE THE PROVISIONS OF THE DETAILED DRAFT MENTAL HEALTHCARE RULES, 2017

The 2018 Rules which have been notified on 29th May, 2018[475] were preceded by the Draft Mental Healthcare Rules, 2017. The Draft 2017 Rules were more elaborate and meticulously drafted. Many of the provisions of the Draft Rules have not been incorporated in the 2018 Rules. It is suggested that some of the essential provisions of the Draft 2017 Rules should be incorporated in the 2018 Rules as they provided detail and clarity. Discussed herein below are some of the relevant provisions of the Draft 2017 Rules:

Half-way homes: The Government is required to setup half-way homes for persons with mental illness. The half-way homes can function from within the community or outside the campus of any other mental health establishment. Half-way homes are to be registered as mental health establishments[476] and are to comply with the standards and requirements for the same. Admission to a half-way home can be taken by a person after his/her discharge from a mental health establishment or on advise by a mental health professional to be admitted in a half-way home instead of a mental health establishment. A half-way home runs programmes to help persons with mental illness in their transition journey while recuperating by learning life skills and moving towards an independent living and reintegration into the society. Services to inmates at a half-way home are to include social services, psychiatric services, medical services, educational services and such other services as are required for the holistic welfare of the inmates, including individual counselling and group counselling. In order to prepare the inmates for an independent living after being discharged from half-way homes, their stay at half-way homes should involve, performance of various chores, remuneration for which is also paid to appreciate and recognize the work put in by them, engaging in various

---

[475] Notification No.: G.S.R. 509(E), Ministry of Health and Family Welfare, Department of Health and Family Welfare, Government of India (29th May, 2018)
[476] The 2017 Act Section 65(1)

occupational activities, being trained in financial management and provided with employment counselling. Movement inside a half-way home for the inmates should be free. Inmates are to be facilitated outings from the half-way home under supervision or subject to some conditions. This helps in gradually finding themselves reintegrated in the society.

Sheltered accommodation: The sheltered accommodations as stated in the Draft Rules are to be owned, maintained, administered and run by a government agency. The persons with mental illness who are allotted admission in a sheltered accommodation can exercise the option of staying there with their parents, spouse or care-giver. The Draft Rules require a sheltered accommodation to have some of the following facilities, namely:
- o Communal areas having sports facilities, library, garden, jogging track, etc.;
- o Provision for common dining area and common laundry services;
- o Visiting area facilitating visits from friends and relatives;
- o Twenty-four hours emergency alarm in case of an emergency;
- o A manager and other staff members to look after the housekeeping and attending to situations of emergency.

A sheltered accommodation should comprise accommodation facilities ranging from shared rooms, independent rooms with kitchen and bath and apartments with private front door.

Supported accommodation: The concept of supported accommodation as envisaged in the Draft Rules entails structured assistance services from Government agencies for persons with mental illness who want to live in their own homes. This support is in addition to the unstructured support available to such a person from his/her friends and families and the treating mental health professional. These services should be flexible enough to cater to the individual needs of each person with mental illness respectively. Support services, which are a combination of some paid and some free services, may include assistance with respect to management of money, medical appointments, daily chores, etc.

Hospital & Community based Rehabilitation Services:[477] Hospital & Community Based Rehabilitation are to be made available to persons with mental illness at mental health establishments, community centres homes, including half-way homes. These services, depending on the needs of the persons with mental illness in that area, the local conditions and the availability of resources, are to include:

- o Medical treatment facilities;
- o Vocational rehabilitation services;
- o Family counselling;
- o Self-help groups;
- o Support in the recovery process;
- o Psychological interventions which includes psycho-education, psychotherapy and counselling; etc.

For the fulfillment of the above goal, the State Government is required to take steps towards providing training to rehabilitation workers and primary health care workers in psychological care; training persons who have recovered from mental illness and their family members to become resource persons for workers working in the area of rehabilitation; creating an inclusive environment congenial to the overall development of the person with mental illness ensuring the protection of his/her rights. The State Government is also required to arrange for awareness and sensitization drives in schools to alert students about the issue at a young age. Instilling awareness among the members of the society about the sensitivity of the issue is an important role involved herein along with making persons with mental illness and their care-givers aware of their rights.

---

[477] The Draft 2017 Rules, Schedule B

Capacity to consent for treatment:[478] The expert committee appointed by Central Mental Health Authority has to determine the factors to be considered to evaluate the capacity of a person with mental illness to consent for treatment.

The right to access basic medical records:[479] A person with mental illness has the right to receive documented medical information relating to his/her diagnosis and treatment. The person may request for a copy of the basic medical record by making an application in writing.

The right to free legal aid:[480] All mental health establishments are to put up on display on their notice board at a prominent place in a local language about the right of persons with mental illness to get free legal aid and the contact information of the local Legal Services Authority.

The provisions in the Draft 2017 Rules pertaining to rehabilitation have been meticulously framed, providing detail, clarity and precision. These Draft Rules and the positive action by the appropriate government and various authorities under the 2017 Act can together facilitate the aims of the Act in the light of UNCRPD to not only provide for the treatment of the person with mental illness but also the reintegration and rehabilitation of such persons into the society to enable them to lead an independent life. It is therefore, suggested that the afore-discussed provisions of the Draft 2017 Rules should be incorporated in the 2018 Rules.

---

[478] The Draft 2017 Rules, Rule 16
[479] The Draft 2017 Rules, Rule 19
[480] The Draft 2017 Rules, Rule 20

7. ANSWERING THE RESEARCH QUESTIONS

The research questions, finding answers to which was the primary aim of this research pursuit are:

- What is mental illness?
- Are women with mental illness vulnerable?
- What will be the implications of psychiatric advance directives on the autonomy of women with mental illness?
- Are the rights of women with mental illness adequately protected under the Mental Health Care Act, 2017?
- Are the provisions of the Mental Health Care Act, 2017 in consonance with the standards laid down in various International instruments?

	Research Questions	Answers
1.	What is mental illness?	*"Mental illness"* means *"a substantial disorder of thinking, mood, perception, orientation or memory that grossly impairs judgment, behavior, capacity to recognize reality or ability to meet the ordinary demands of life, mental conditions associated with the abuse of alcohol and drugs, but does not include mental retardation which is a condition of arrested or incomplete development of mind of a person, specially characterized by sub-normality of intelligence".*[481]

---

[481] The 2017 Act, Section 2(s)

		The definition given in the Mental Healthcare Act, 2017[482] is the appropriate definition of the term *"mental illness"*.
2.	Are women with mental illness vulnerable?	Yes.
3.	What will be the implications of psychiatric advance directives on the autonomy of women with mental illness?	Positive, subject to proper awareness and implementation.
4.	Are the rights of women with mental illness adequately protected under the Mental Healthcare Act, 2017?	Yes.
5.	Are the provisions of the Mental Health Care Act, 2017 in consonance with the standards laid down in international mental healthcare standards?	Yes, fairly.

Research Question 1: What is mental illness?

Chapter II of this research appraised the definition of mental illness as laid down in the Mental Healthcare Act, 2017 of India and the fact that the 2017 Act brings the Mental Healthcare legal framework in consonance with the mandates of UNCRPD.

---

[482] *Id.*

The definition given in the Mental Healthcare Act, 2017[483] is the appropriate definition of the term *"mental illness"*.

"Mental illness" therefore, means *"a substantial disorder of thinking, mood, perception, orientation or memory that grossly impairs judgment, behavior, capacity to recognize reality or ability to meet the ordinary demands of life, mental conditions associated with the abuse of alcohol and drugs, but does not include mental retardation which is a condition of arrested or incomplete development of mind of a person, specially characterized by sub-normality of intelligence."*[484]

Research Question 2: Are women with mental illness vulnerable?

The answer to this question is a 'yes'. Following is the research supporting the answer:

- The findings of Chapter III of the Research on Asking the "Woman Question" support the proposition that women with mental illness are very vulnerable.
- An analysis of the NCW and NIMHANS Report (2016) and HRW Report (2014) proved that women with mental illness are more susceptible to vulnerability and prone to abuse as compared to men with mental illness.
- All the five psychiatrists whom the researcher interviewed also agreed to the fact that women with mental illness are vulnerable.
- The personnel at the three NGOs whom the researcher had interviewed narrated the various ventures being undertaken by their organizations to address and remedy the vulnerabilities of women with mental illness.

---

[483] *Id.*
[484] The 2017 Act, Section 2(s)

- 81.6% of the 185 responses to the survey conducted by the researcher were in favour of the proposition that women with mental illness in India are more vulnerable than their male counterparts.
- It is also important to note that the WHO Checklist on Mental Health Legislation[485] recognizes women with mental illness as part of the vulnerable section of persons with mental illness.

Research Question 3: **What will be the implications of psychiatric advance directives on the autonomy of women with mental illness?**

The concept of psychiatric advance directives introduced by the 2017 Act in India is a new concept for the country. Even though questions can be raised pertaining to its implementation and viability, it is a positive step towards ensuring the protection of rights and autonomy of women with mental illness. It will give them the right and choice to decide about their mental healthcare. It is submitted that the checks to the viability of a psychiatric advance directive are sufficiently placed in the provisions of the 2017 Act and proper implementation of the law in its letters and spirit will help in fulfilling the goal with which this concept is being introduced in India.

The Draft Central Regulations, 2017[486]lay down the regulations pertaining to the manner of making an advance directive. It is stated that an advance directive for the purposes of the 2017 Act should be made according to Form CR-A of the Draft Central Regulations, 2017.

---

[485] WHO Checklist on Mental Health Legislation, Annexure 1 of THE WHO RESOURCE BOOK ON MENTAL HEALTH, HUMAN RIGHTS AND LEGISLATION (2005), Available at
https://ec.europa.eu/health/sites/health/files/mental_health/docs/who_resource_book_en.pdf
(Last visited on April 5, 2018)
[486] Draft Central Regulations, 2017 made by the Central Government in exercise of the powers conferred under Section 122 of the 2017 Act on behalf of the Central Mental Health Authority subject to modification by the Central Mental Authority on its constitution. Draft Central Regulations, 2017, Available at
https://mohfw.gov.in/sites/default/files/Final%20Draft%20Rules%20MHC%20Act%2C%202017
%20%281%29.pdf (Last visited on April 27, 2018)

Form CR-A of the Draft Central Regulations, 2017[487]

FORM –CR-A
Regulation 1 (a)
Advance Directive for Mental Illness Treatment
(U/S 122.2.a with 6)

Name (Enclosed copy of photo ID proof):_____

Age (Enclosed copy of age proof for being above 18 years of age) _____

Father's / Mother's Name: _____

Address (Enclosed copy of proof):_____

Contact number: _____

(Driving License/ Voter's Card/ Passport/ Aadhar card can serve as photo ID, address proof & age proof)

a) I wish to be cared for and treated as under:

_____
_____

b) I wish not to be care for and treated as under:

_____

c)I have appointed the following persons in order of precedence(Enclosed photo ID & age proof), who are above 18 years of age to act as my nominated representatives to make decisions about my mental illness treatment, when I am incapable to do so

1. Name: _____Age_____

Father's name: _____

Address: _____

Contact number/s_____

2. Name: _____Age_____

Father's name: _____

Address: _____

Contact number/s_____

[Any number of nominated representatives can be added in order of precedence]

Any history of allergies, known side effects, or other medical problems

_____
_____

Signature of the person................................. Date...................................

Signatures of nominated representatives

First nominated representative...............................Date...................

Second nominated representative.........................Date.................

Signatures of witnesses

....has made the advance directive of his/her own free will and has signed it in our presence.

Witness 1....................... ....Date...............

Witness 2....................... ....Date...............

Certificate of a Medical Practitioner:

Certified that ....has the capacity to make mental health care and treatment decisions at the time of making the advance directive.

Name and signature with stamp...

---

[487] Available at
https://mohfw.gov.in/sites/default/files/Final%20Draft%20Rules%20MHC%20Act%2C%202017%20%281%29.pdf (Last visited on April 27, 2018)

A nominated representative who is named in the advance directive should sign in the advance directive thereby consenting to the same.[488] The nominated representative may withdraw his/her consent at any time from the same by writing an application to that effect to the Mental Health Review Board and handing over a copy of the application to the person who made the advance directive.[489] All advance directives are to be countersigned by two witnesses stating that the advance directive was signed by the person making the same in their presence.[490] A person making the advance directive is required to keep a copy with himself/herself and give a copy to his/her nominated representative.[491] Release of a copy of the advance directive to the media or any unauthorized person is not permitted.[492] All advance directives are to be registered with the concerned Mental Health Review Board free of cost.[493] An advance directive should be made online by the Board within 14 days of receiving the same.[494] A person can change his/her advance directives any number of times, there are no restrictions on the number.[495] Each change in an advance directive is required to undergo the same process and regulations as an advance directive to be considered valid.[496] Every time a new advance directive is made, the person making the advance directive and/or his/her nominated representative must inform the treating mental health professional about the same.[497]

It is therefore, submitted that the checks to the viability of a psychiatric advance directive are sufficiently placed in the provisions of the 2017 Act and proper implementation of the law in its letters and spirit will help in fulfilling the goal

---

[488] Draft Central Regulations, 2017
[489] Id.
[490] Id.
[491] Id.
[492] Id.
[493] Id.
[494] Id.
[495] Id.
[496] Id.
[497] Id.

with which this concept is being introduced in India. The Draft Central Regulations, 2017 add further regulations and checks to ensure the smooth functioning and proper implementation of psychiatric advance directives. Subject to the implementation of the laws, psychiatric advance directives will have positive implications on the autonomy of women with mental illness and the exercise of their right to choice over the treatment meted out to them.

Research Question 4: Are the rights of women with mental illness adequately protected under the Mental Healthcare Act, 2017?

Yes, the rights of women with mental illness are adequately protected under the Mental Healthcare Act, 2017. Read with the National Mental Health Policy of India, 2014 and the Mental Healthcare (Rights of Persons with Mental Illness) Rules, 2018[498], the provisions of the Mental Healthcare have the potential to particularly address the vulnerabilities of women with mental illness. There are suggestions to facilitate this further (in the last section of this research, titled "SUGGESTIONS") which, it is humbly submitted, will further enable the fulfillment of this goal.

Research Question 5: Are the provisions of the Mental Healthcare Act, 2017 in consonance with the standards laid down in international mental healthcare standards?

Yes, the provisions of the Mental Healthcare Act, 2017 are in consonance with the standards laid down in International Mental Healthcare instruments. The three documents on the fulcrum of which the Mental Healthcare Act, 2017 has been tested to international mental healthcare standards are:

---

[498] Notification No.: G.S.R. 509(E), Ministry of Health and Family Welfare, Department of Health and Family Welfare, Government of India (29th May, 2018)

i) WHO, Ten Basic Principles of Mental Health Care Law (1996)

ii) The United Convention on Rights of Persons with Disability (UNCRPD) (2006)

iii) WHO Checklist on Mental Health Legislation (Annexure 1 to WHO Resource Book on Mental Health, Human Rights and Legislation (2005))

After having indulged in an in-depth analysis of i) WHO, Ten Basic Principles of Mental Health Care Law (1996) and ii) The United Convention on Rights of Persons with Disability (UNCRPD) (2006) in Chapter X of this research, it can be stated that the 2017 Act is in consonance with the standards laid down in these two international instruments.

The WHO Resource Book on Mental Health, Human Rights and Legislation (2005) comprises the WHO Checklist on Mental Health Legislation.[499] The Checklist is aimed at helping the law makers of various countries in evaluating the comprehensiveness of their mental health legislation and/or assists them in drafting a new legislation on the matter. The provisions of the Mental Health Care Act, 2017 were tested through the checklist[500] and out of the 175 requirements mentioned in the checklist, the provisions of the 2017 Act cover 149 requirements. It is noteworthy that some of the requirements in the checklist, like reservation, education, etc. has been covered under the Rights of Persons with Disabilities Act, 2016 and hence do not mention in the Mental Healthcare Act, 2017. As a whole the mental healthcare legal framework in India presently covers the requirements in the WHO Checklist fairly well.

---

[499] WHO Checklist on Mental Health Legislation, Annexure 1 of The WHO Resource Book on Mental Health, Human Rights and Legislation (2005), Available at
https://ec.europa.eu/health/sites/health/files/mental_health/docs/who_resource_book_en.pdf
(Last visited on April 5, 2018)
[500] *See* Annexure 5

6. TESTING THE HYPOTHESIS AND PUTTING FORTH SUGGESTIONS

i. Result of Testing the Hypothesis in the pursuit of this Research:

Hypothesis of the present research: "The Mental Healthcare Act, 2017 adequately protects the rights of women with mental illness."

Hypothesis proved: Hypothesis is true subject to the fulfilment of the following conditions, namely:

- Proper implementation of the Mental Healthcare Act, 2017 in letter and spirit;
- Enforcement of the provisions of the National Mental Health Policy of India, 2014 and implementation of its ideals and goals; and
- Incorporation of the suggestions recommended hereinafter in this Chapter.

ii. Suggestions

The Mental Healthcare Act, 2017 was introduced with the aim to bring the mental healthcare laws in India in consonance with the provisions of UNCRPD and other International Mental Healthcare Standards. It is important to note that the Mental Healthcare Act, 2017 came into force very recently, that is, from 29th May, 2018[501] on which date the Mental Health Act, 1987 stood repealed. The Mental Healthcare Act, 2017 is gender neutral, at the same time not gender

---

[501] Notification No.: S.O. 2173(E), Ministry of Health and Family Welfare, Government of India (29th May, 2018)

biased. It propagates justice and equality in mental healthcare and gives the freedom to choose the treatment to be given to a person during his/her mental healthcare. Having analysed the 2017 Act read with the National Mental Health Policy of India, 2014, it is humbly submitted that the proper implementation of the 2017 Act and the 2018 Rules in letter and spirit, read with the National Mental Health Policy of India, 2014 will proficiently improve the condition and status of women in need of mental healthcare in the country.

The NCW and NIMHANS Report (2016),[502] had put forth some important suggestions pertaining to mental healthcare of women with mental illness. Positive and constructive suggestions were also made by the persons interviewed and by the respondents to the questionnaires filled during the surveys conducted by the researcher.

Reliance has been made to all these suggestions in addition to the analysis undertaken in the course of this research, for the researcher to come forth with some suggestions of her own. After having undertaken this entire research pursuit, the researcher hereby humbly submits some suggestions to further the cause of the 2017 Act, particularly from the perspective of women with mental illness in India. Herein below are the suggestions:

- The provisions of the Draft Mental Healthcare Rules, 2017 should be incorporated in the Mental Healthcare (Rights of Persons with Mental Illness) Rules, 2018 which have been notified on 29th May, 2018;[503] and the Draft Central Regulations, 2017[504] should be passed in their present form;

---

[502] Available at http://ncw.nic.in/pdfreports/addressing_concerns_of_women_admitted_to_psychiatric_institutions_in_india_an_in-depth_analysis.pdf (Last visited on May 23, 2017)

[503] Notification No.: G.S.R. 509(E), Ministry of Health and Family Welfare, Department of Health and Family Welfare, Government of India (29th May, 2018)

[504] Draft Central Regulations, 2017 made by the Central Government in exercise of the powers conferred under Section 122 of the 2017 Act on behalf of the Central Mental Health Authority subject to modification by the Central Mental Authority on its constitution. Draft Central Regulations, 2017, Available at

- Establishment of the Central Mental Health Authority, the State Mental Health Authorities and the Mental Health Review Boards under the 2017 Act at the earliest;

- Facilitating care-giver support. The 2017 Act provides for mental health services to provide for support to family with mental illness.[505]This support should include support at the financial, medical and emotional level to the care-giver of the person with mental illness;

- The 2017 Act should ensure that women with mental illness in a mental health institution should be provided with appropriate and adequate privacy, including separate sleeping facilities from men;[506]

- Increase the number of women personnel in mental healthcare in India;

- Training health-care providers at the primary healthcare level to identify mental illness in a patient who comes for treatment before them. The health-care providers should be also trained about the basics of mental healthcare for them to be able to prescribe temporary treatment and medicine in case of mental illness of a patient when access to a psychiatrist in case of an emergency is not possible. Training Anganwadi and ASHA workers to identify traits of mental illness in a person and create awareness about mental healthcare and rights of persons with mental illness in the rural pockets of the society;

- Providing digital access to psychiatrists on a regular basis in remote areas;[507]

---

https://mohfw.gov.in/sites/default/files/Final%20Draft%20Rules%20MHC%20Act%2C%202017%20%281%29.pdf (Last visited on April 27, 2018)

[505] The 2017 Act, Section 18(4)(c)

[506] See the WHO Checklist on Mental Health Legislation (Annexure 1 to the WHO Resource Book on Mental Health, Human Rights and Legislation , 2005), Available at https://ec.europa.eu/health/sites/health/files/mental_health/docs/who_resource_book_en.pdf (Last visited on April 5, 2018)

[507] See The National Health Policy, 2017, Available at http://cdsco.nic.in/writereaddata/National-Health-Policy.pdf (Last visited on April 5, 2018)

- It is should be ensured that every person with mental illness should be treated and provided with healthcare facilities at par with persons with physical illness, and medical insurance for treatment of patients with mental illness should be made available, by health insurers, in the same manner as is made available for treatment of physical illness;[508]

- Gender sensitization and regular and appropriate training, pertaining to special needs and healthcare of women with mental illness, of healthcare professionals, mental healthcare professionals, police, judiciary, educationists, government authorities, etc. Training sessions to be interactional once in every six months for the various sectors to come together and discuss their experiences and concerns;[509]

- Integration of "inter-sectoral liaisons"[510]among various sectors involved in the care, treatment, welfare and rehabilitation of women with mental illness, including health, social justice, rehabilitation, housing, law, home affairs, police, education, etc.[511]

- Sensitizing women in general of their rights in society, and to be able to accept and acknowledge their rightfulness to decision making pertaining to their life irrespective of their mental illness;

- Disseminating information in various sectors of the society about the provisions of the 2017 Act by the Authorities under the 2017 Act, thereby creating awareness pertaining to rights of persons with mental illness, and creating awareness among the general masses about the option of psychiatric advance directives.The Indian media can play a pivotal role in ensuring that the ultimate aim of equity in mental healthcare can be reached. Awareness pertaining to the 2017 Act can be brought about through the media by discussions in the mainstream news,

---

[508] *See* the 2017 Act, Section 21
[509] *Id.*
[510] NCW and NIMHANS Report (2016), Page 244
[511] *Id.*

advertisements by the Government in the primetime news television, radio channels, magazines, newsletters and newspapers;

- Visits to women with mental illness in mental health establishments by outsiders should be supervised;

- Absolute transparency in the process of determining the status of mental illness of a person;

- The Policy makers and law makers should always ask the "woman question"[512] while addressing mental healthcare issues in the country, and while making plans and improving plans relating to mental healthcare;

- Inspections in the likes of the one conducted by NCW and NIMHANS in coming out with its 2016 Report should be made a practice to be repeated once in every six years;[513]

- The provisions relating to shelter homes, supported accommodation and half-way homes in the 2018 Rules to be implemented, the same to be backed by sufficient funding by the Government of India. There should be proper monitoring of these homes and accommodations including regular inspections to avert situations of exploitation or abuse[514] and to ensure that the purpose of setting up these homes and accommodation is fulfilled

- Applying the principle of *"best interest"* of the person with mental illness and the principle of *"medical necessity"* by the person taking mental healthcare decisions for himself/herself or by anyone taking the decision on his/her behalf, keeping in mind that the *"least restrictive"* methods of treatment for mental healthcare should be incorporated;[515]

---

[512] *See* Katherine T. Barlett, *Feminist Legal Methods,* 103 (4) Harvard Law Review 829 (1990)
[513] *See* also the 2017 Act, Section 67(1)
[514] *See* Himanshi Dhawan, *What the Deoria story tells you about India's unwanted girls,* TIMES OF INDIA (August 12, 2018), Available at https://m.timesofindia.com/home/sunday-times/what-the-deoria-story-tells-you-about-indias-unwanted-girls/amp_articleshow/65369502.cms (Last visited on August 13, 2018)
[515] *See* Ravinder v. Government of NCT of Delhi and Ors., W.P. (CRL) 3317/2017

- Increasing the funding allotment towards mental healthcare in the Annual Budget of India;
- Creating Sexual Harassment Redressal Centres in all mental health establishments;
- Discouraging the practice of long-stay patients in mental hospitals and making all efforts to locate the family and residence of abandoned women with mental illness;
- Vocational and occupational training of women with mental illness. At the same time confidence boosting sessions of counselling and character building is vital to rehabilitate the women and help them in leading an independent life;[516]and
- Follow-up with rehabilitated women by the authorities and psychiatric social workers under the 2017 Act is also necessary to avert relapse of the illness.

Finally it is suggested that educating the society in general about mental healthcare, clearing the cobwebs of stigma that many sections of the society associate to mental illness is very important for the complete fulfilment of this goal. Taking refuge with faith healers for cure to mental illness should be discouraged and the importance of timely medication and mental healthcare should be discussed and highlighted. Gender sensitization across all sections of the society that is across geographical, social, gender, cultural, economic, ethnic, regional boundaries and differences is the most vital of all steps that need to be taken for a holistic solution of this issue.

---

[516] *See* also UN, Standard Rules on the Equalization of Opportunities for Persons with Disabilities (1993), Available at https://www.un.org/development/desa/disabilities/standard-rules-on-the-equalization-of-opportunities-for-persons-with-disabilities.html (Last visited on January 1, 2018)

CPSIA information can be obtained
at www.ICGtesting.com
Printed in the USA
LVHW042108310323
743153LV00020B/332